TWELVE MIGHTY ORPHANS

Jim Dent   TWELVE

THOMAS DUNNE BOOKS ❧ *St. Martin's Press*   *New York*

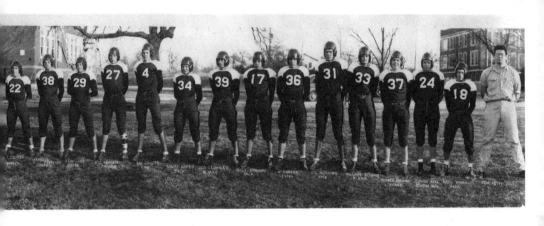

MIGHTY ORPHANS

The Inspiring True Story

of the Mighty Mites

Who Ruled Texas Football

THOMAS DUNNE BOOKS.
An imprint of St. Martin's Press.

www.thomasdunnebooks.com
www.stmartins.com

Library of Congress Cataloging-in-Publication Data

Dent, Jim.
   Twelve mighty orphans : the inspiring true story of the Mighty Mites who ruled Texas football /
Jim Dent.—1st ed.
       p. cm.
   Includes bibliographical references.
   ISBN-13: 978-0-312-30872-8
   ISBN-10: 0-312-30872-8
   1. Masonic Home and School of Texas (Fort Worth, Tex.)—Football. 2. Football—Texas.
3. High schools—Texas. I. Title.
   GV958.M37D46 2007
   796.332'62097645315—dc22

                                                 2007020527

First Edition: September 2007

10 9 8 7 6 5 4 3 2 1

This book is dedicated to those who stood by me when my life fell apart:

My mother, Leanna Dent, and sister, Janice Dent. All of my former SMU Beta Theta Pi brothers, most specifically Larry Del Papa, Joe Storhtz, Woody Berry, Jeff Skilling, John Grumbles, Carl Hohl, Del Benson, Del Deisenroth, Michael Arends, Matt Ida, Elvis Thompson, Craig Shackleton, and Ron Rhidlehuber. My great friend Jan Fikes, who helped make every visit a great one. You betcha. My sister Anna Belle and her husband John Loeb. Some great old newspaper buddies—Randy Galloway, Frank Luksa, Will Jarrett, Richard Justice, Carlton Stowers and Larry Tarleton. Friends from childhood and for life—Joe and Peggy Holladay, Richard Devine, and Doug Marcella. Hall of Famer Dan Hampton. Jill Thomason. Greg Aiello and Tito Nicholas from the happy times at Thousand Oaks. Thanks to all of the Junction Boys who were there from start to finish, especially Gene Stallings, Jack Pardee, Dennis Goehring, Marvin Tate, and Troy Summerlin. My wonderful friends from Thomas Dunne Books, Peter J. Wolverton and Joe Rinaldi, and my agent who served me well, Jim Donovan. Thank you all.

CONTENTS

TWELVE MIGHTY ORPHANS

PROLOGUE

The redbrick buildings of the old Masonic Home are boarded up and the place is now quiet. Down the hill, the dairy barn is closed, the peach orchard has withered away, and the empty practice field is the color of summer hay.

Late in the afternoon, when the native grasses sway in the wind, you can still see the shoeless orphans and a dog named Ziggy running down to Sycamore Creek. You watch a young boy in bib overalls sneak into the orchard and stuff ripe peaches into his pockets. On the football field, a tall, bespectacled coach in a dark suit and tie runs behind a player and smacks him with a paddle.

"Faster," he yells. "You've got to run faster."

Breathe deeply and you can smell the freshly picked onions and turnips stewing in the kitchen just over the hill.

Girls hit tennis balls back and forth. Others play jacks and jump rope on the nearby sidewalk. A few hide behind a tall hedge, sneaking looks at the boys grunting and knocking each other down. They giggle and point out potential boyfriends and live for the day when they will finally be allowed to touch.

Then it happens. A football is purposefully kicked deeply into the peach orchard and, seconds later, a tennis ball flies over the tall fence. No one sees the football player bend to retrieve his ball just as the young girl in the white tennis dress reaches for hers. No one sees the forbidden kiss.

YEARS LATER, THEY packed up memories from the old museum that housed more than a hundred years of photographs. Gone are the pictures of the first graduating class of 1902, the great football teams, the debate squads, the choirs, the milk slimes, a beloved dog, a duck, a rigid dean, and a legendary coach.

But on a cool autumn day, standing on the hillside east of Fort Worth, you can still see the famous 1930s Mighty Mites, a football team of undersized orphans so captivating that they grabbed the attention of an entire state and much of America for the entire decade. No one will ever forget the courageous little band of underdogs with nothing to lose, the skinny but fearless kids who brought hope to all in the cruelest years of the Depression.

Chapter 1

BOOTLEGGER'S SON

From the front porch of the farmhouse near Kirkland, Maggie Ann Brown spotted the barefoot boy running from over a quarter mile away. His feet lifted small clouds of dust and his face showed the strain of his effort. Maggie Ann could not remember seeing her four-year-old run that fast.

Little Hardy Brown's arms and legs were like miniature pistons. As he moved closer, Maggie Ann could see that he was mouthing words she could not hear. There was no telling how far he had come, or what he had seen, for the boy was a rambler and might wander the farmland all day, or fish the local creek until the rust-colored sun melted into the horizon.

Out in far West Texas, just south of the Panhandle, the land is covered in cotton and wheat and the grain elevators rise up like Greek temples. So flat are the plains that a silo some ten miles away seems to be sitting on your neighbor's property. In the early summer, when the north wind gives up and the sun's furnace kicks on, the ground starts to fracture and turkey buzzards take a rest. That July afternoon of 1928 was a scorcher, and Maggie Ann knew it was not advisable for any child to be working that hard. "Slow down, Hardy!" she yelled. "You're going to bust a gut."

The boy darted through the front yard and his right foot kicked aside a tricycle. There was an assortment of children's toys strewn across the bare ground, along with a tire iron and a rusted tractor engine.

It was a typical shotgun farmhouse with a long, narrow hallway down the middle. "Shotgun" because, if you fired a shotgun from the front door, the shot would travel down the hall and straight out the backdoor. The place once belonged to a farmer, but a few years earlier he had gotten other ideas. The economy of Childress County was now booming, thanks to an abundance of cotton and wheat. Folks, in spite of Prohibition, were ready to party. So Hardy Brown Sr. decided to lay down his plow and crank up the whiskey still.

Stills, in fact.

So much potato whiskey was cooked up on the Brown's ten acres that a twenty-four-hour guard was hired to keep the thirsty neighbors at bay. The sheriff of Childress County looked the other way as he pocketed his share, and the operation ran as smoothly as the old cotton gin out on the main highway.

Hardy Brown Sr. was a tall, dark-skinned man with thick sideburns that made his face look menacing. They said he had a lot of Comanche in his blood. The warring Comanches had ruled West Texas until the U.S. Army crushed them in the Red River War of 1874. Brown was thick with muscle and could lift a truck off the ground by laying on his back and leg-pressing it, and he did not mind letting people know that he would kick their dog asses if they decided to cross him.

This bootlegger was actually two people. There was also the happy family man who played with his kids and took them fishing. He had grown especially fond of Hardy Jr., the baby in the family, who feared nothing and was always into something.

Besides being the good father, Brown was also a fornicator and a fighter and a wild bull rider. Saturday nights in Childress, hundreds of people gathered to watch the men fistfight for fun on the town square. The local dairy owner would challenge the hardware salesman and they would duke it out until one fighter determined the other had the advantage. In the end, the two men would shake hands and go back to being friends and neighbors.

Few people wanted to tangle with Hardy Brown. Unlike the others, he did not view the event as "sport." The man had killer blood in him. He could throw a pile-driving right hand that would send you to the hospital, or worse. The toughest hombres in the county had stopped accepting his challenges on Saturday night. So, he would simply wade into the crowd and start swinging.

It was little wonder that his rivals hated him. Whiskey money had transformed the laid-back cotton farmer into the biggest bootlegger between Fort Worth and Amarillo. He loved the fact that he ruled the world of outlaw whiskey. The once quiet county was now swarming with angry family clans. At the height of Prohibition, and just ahead of the Great Depression, the business of bootlegging had erupted like a West Texas gusher. The clans battled each other every day for money, turf, and moonshine. Highway 287 was a Texas version of Thunder Road. Whiskey stills around Kirkland were as prevalent as red dirt, the product as precious as a kiss from a Wichita Falls debutante.

Naturally, the hard-charging, stone-fisted Hardy Brown became the most despised man in the county. Driving Highway 287 between Childress and Kirkland one afternoon, he realized that a green Packard was trying to run him off the road. Never one to dodge a confrontation, he steered to the side as two men jumped out of their car. Brown did not reach for a gun or a knife or even a billy club from the backseat. He pulled out a singletree.

A singletree was like a long baseball bat with a hook on the end. The device was primarily used to hitch two plow mules together for the purpose of keeping them side-by-side. The first attacker did not see the blow coming. Brown swung the long club and watched the hook sink into the man's skull. The second man tried to flee, but Brown pursued him, hacking away skin and clothing until he pleaded for mercy. He was left to suffer in a pool of blood.

As he drove away that day, Brown knew that a bounty would soon be on his head; men would come calling with killing on their minds.

A few days later, while walking along a country road with his four-year-old son, Hardy Sr. did not see the Gossett brothers step off the front porch and sneak up behind him with sawed-off shotguns. The twin blasts catapulted the unarmed man more than ten feet as a chunk of ribs and most of his spine were blown away. Little Hardy took off running and did not stop until he reached the family's farmhouse some two miles away. Maggie Brown, now standing on the front porch, felt almost paralyzed when she saw the fear in her son's eyes.

"Mama, they killed Daddy!"

"Where?"

"Up the road?"

"Who killed Daddy?"

"Them Gossett men."

"How did they kill him?"

"Shot him in the back. Both of them."

Maggie Ann was now in a panic. She dashed into her bedroom and inexplicably started pulling on stockings. She quickly put on a cotton dress and a pair of leather shoes and stashed some belongings in a cloth sack. Upon reaching the front door, she turned to her four children.

"Mama will be back just as soon as she can," she said. "I promise."

Maggie Ann took off running down the dirt road the opposite direction that Hardy had come. Every few steps one of her dress shoes flew off, and she finally tucked it under her arm and kept going. Her stockings split and now her exposed right foot was plastered with dust.

"Where is Mama going?" little Hardy said.

"She's going to the train station," his older sister Katherine said. "She's getting out of this place."

"Why?"

"She's scared of them Gossett men."

IN THE DAYS ahead, the four Brown kids lived in constant fear of the Gossett brothers. Jeff, Rebe, Katherine, and Hardy slept together in the same bed every night with the covers pulled over their heads.

Mona, the oldest sibling in the family, who had married a few years earlier, tried to bring some comfort to the family. She returned to the house where she had grown up and was accompanied by her husband, Spurgeon Clark, who had been a business partner of Hardy Sr. Mona had some news.

"Fortunately, our daddy was a Master Mason in the local lodge and his dues were paid up. That qualifies all four of you to go to the Masonic Home down in Fort Worth. It's an orphanage, you know. But I hear that it's a pretty good place. Most of all, you will be safe there."

Katherine began to cry. "I don't want to go," she said. "My friends are here. And we've got three cats and two dogs, and who's going to take care of them."

"I will," Mona said. "You've got more important things to worry about, like getting an education. You will get some learning at the Home."

Jeff cleared his throat. "When is Mama coming back?"

"From the way she ran out of here, never. I don't think we'll ever see her again in Childress County."

"Doesn't she love us anymore?" Katherine said.

"I haven't talked to her and I don't know where she is. But I'm sure she still loves you."

Hardy Brown Sr.'s body was deposited into a pine box three days later and he was buried in an unmarked grave.

Not long after the funeral, a picture on the front page of the *Fort Worth Star-Telegram* showed hundreds of trucks and cars parked about the town square of Kirkland. The caption read, "Cotton Money Comes to Town." A little farther down the page, a headline blared, FARMER SLAIN NEAR CHILDRESS.

The whole county was buzzing.

The Gossett brothers were arrested in a timely manner and then released on bond. George H. Gossett was the first to be tried in Childress County, and the result was a hung jury. Some said you could not find a single citizen in Childress County brave enough to convict a Gossett.

George H. Gossett's next trial was moved to Donley in Clarendon County, and a change of venue sent his brother, Howard Gossett, to nearby Memphis, Texas. Both trials were to set to begin the next month.

When George H. Gossett's trial ended in a hung jury, Spurgeon Clark decided to take matters into his own hands. More than just an in-law, he had also been a close friend and a loyal partner of Hardy

Brown's. The two had been inseparable at times, and some folks thought they were brothers.

One day, Clark drove to the Brown farmhouse and picked up little Hardy.

"Where are we going?" the boy said.

"To take care of some business."

Late that afternoon, a man wielding a double-barreled shotgun kicked down the front door of the Gossett farmhouse. A four-year-old boy was by his side. The Gossett brothers tried to escape and Spurgeon Clark blew them away. Moments later, Spurgeon and Hardy stood over the men to make sure they were dead. Spurgeon wanted the young child to know that justice had been served—Texas style.

"Those were your daddy's killers."

"I know."

It was a story that both Jeff and Hardy Brown would tell for years. Naturally, it was a chapter in their lives that would haunt them forever.

The next Wednesday, the Southern Pacific train pulled into the station in Childress. The four Brown children stepped off the platform into a new world. They knew they would never see their daddy again.

They were not sure about their mother.

AFTER A LONG and arduous train ride to Fort Worth, four kids with sad and dirty faces stood outside the fence of the orphanage and watched kids playing in the bright sunshine.

Footballs sailed high against a hard blue sky.

Hardy Brown looked at his brother, Jeff, and said, "I ain't never seen anything like it."

Eight-year-old Jeff Brown watched the chaos on the playground. "They played baseball at my elementary school. But I've never seen a ball shaped like that one."

As the gate swung open, Hardy Brown took off running and there was nothing the Brown kids could do to stop him. He ran straight toward a football and kicked it for more than twenty yards. Whereupon he was smacked in the mouth with a hard right uppercut. In no time,

Jeff Brown had the assailant on the ground, rapping his head with hard knuckles as the boy yelled, "Get off of me, new kid. New kids aren't supposed to be fighting."

"How'd you know I was a new kid?" Jeff said.

"Because you got shoes on. We don't wear shoes around here till October."

Jeff shucked his scarred leather shoes to reveal dirty, sockless feet.

"Now let's fight," he said.

"I don't want to fight you."

"Why not?"

"Because you look mean."

"In that case, keep your dirty hands off my kid brother."

Little Hardy puttered down the field and retrieved the football. Tucking it under his arm, he took off in the other direction. No one said a word.

Jeff Brown thumbed his chest. "We'll do whatever we feel like doing around here for as long as we feel like doing it."

Like his brother, Hardy Brown wore scarred leather shoes and overalls. There was virtually no hair on his head and the sides of his head looked like a peeled onion. Jeff Brown had yet to grow into his big ears, and his hard, angular face would have given the appearance of a boy much older, if not for the splotch of red freckles. Katherine Brown's hair was dark and curly and her skin was darker than the others. She was a year younger than Rebe, who had just turned thirteen and did not seem to comprehend much of anything. One of his eyes had been badly damaged in a fight and made a sharp right turn. His mouth was slightly agape and every few seconds he gulped the air with a loud snort.

For the last thirty seconds, a tall man in his twenties had been half-trotting for more than a hundred yards to reach the Brown kids. He was barrel-chested, with thick hands.

"That kid," he said, pointing at Rebe. "That kid looks retarded. What the hell happened to that boy's eye?"

"Went through a meat grinder," Jeff said. "Now, mister, you leave my brother alone."

"Son, you apparently don't know who I am. I am the dean of the little boys. You'll be answering to me for many years. You refer to me as Mr. Wynn."

"Well, Mr. Wynn, it's nice to meet you," Jeff said. "But you leave ol' Rebe here be."

With one hand, Big Frank Wynn grabbed Jeff Brown's hair, and with the other pulled a rubber hose from his back pocket. He spun the boy around and whacked him on the butt.

"One, two, three, four, five," he counted. "How many more do you want, boy?"

Orphans crowded around to watch. They waited for the tears to bubble up in the new kid's eyes. But nothing changed in his expression and, instead of crying, Jeff Brown burst into laughter. Wynn spun the boy around again and whipped him five more times.

Nothing seemed to faze him. The boy was still laughing and soaking up the attention from his fellow orphans when the dean kicked him in the backside and yelled, "Get your butt up that hill to the dormitory. And you can forget about your supper tonight."

Chapter 2

THE LONG WAY HOME

A lean, bespectacled man wearing a dark suit and tie strolled through the front gate in the late summer. His eyes canvassed the place as he removed a gray fedora and wiped his brow with a handkerchief.

Set on a hillside east of Fort Worth was a weedy pasture with a water tower, a dairy, railroad tracks, a small creek, a corn patch, a power plant, a smokestack, and several nondescript buildings. The smell of cow dung was enough to choke a mule.

Rusty Russell knew that life inside the orphanage held little promise. He had accepted the job as a science teacher and football coach, even though his field was math. More confusing were the events that led to his arrival in Fort Worth. A close friend had taken the position, changed his mind, and then asked Rusty to bail him out. For reasons that Russell could not fully explain, he chose to walk away from a decent position at Temple High School, more than a hundred miles to the south, where he had compiled a 20–3 record and coached his team to the state semifinals in 1925.

As Russell paused to take a long look around the place, thoughts flooded his mind. He let go of a deep sigh. People were saying disparaging things about him. He had to be crazy, they said. One of Texas's hottest young coaching properties had, by his own choice, just crash-landed on the other side of the Moon. Even his wife, Juanita, six months pregnant with their first child, did not know what to make of him. She had seen better days. She had grown up on a sprawling ranch in West Texas, enjoying some of the privileges that came with the money earned by her father, L. M. Cravens, a highly successful cotton buyer. Now, two years into their marriage, she could not figure how they were going to manage on thirty dollars a week.

Russell could only chuckle to himself as he pulled the hat snug on his head. His troubles were not all about money. They went much deeper than that. He had taken a job that provided little chance for success. No way the little underdog orphans could ever produce a winning team. Russell was the first football coach ever hired by the Masonic Home. Some wondered if he would be the last.

Standing on the east side of Fort Worth beneath a broiling sun, the man saw things that he did not like, and others he did not readily comprehend. Folks from the city said that the Masonic Home was a cold asylum situated on a distant hill, where the kids slept on hard cots, ate cold porridge, and worked their fingers to the bone. Russell had heard it all. Supposedly, the misbehaving orphans were beaten with straps and paddles. The real miscreants were kicked through the back gate and told never to return.

Just then, a shoeless orphan sauntered over the hill en route to the dairy barn. Russell walked toward him.

"Young man," he said. "Can you tell me where the football practice field is?"

"Right over there, mister," he said, pointing to the southern edge of the property.

It was a dry parcel of land covered in gravel, rocks, and prickly pear—otherwise known as cactus. It might have sufficed as a parking lot, but just barely. Even the sheep and goats had turned up their noses.

Russell tried to clear his throat. "Young man, can you tell me where they keep the footballs and all of that other stuff?"

"I know that we've got a few shoulder pads and a few helmets," the boy said. "But we haven't had a football around here in awhile. The last football we had got so beat up that it finally just gave out."

"Thank you, son," Russell said, his voice cracking. "I do hope you'll consider coming out for the football team this year."

"No thanks," the kid said, walking off at a brisk pace.

Russell felt quite alone. He was now a solitary figure set against a wide Texas sky, standing upon two hundred acres of rolling prairie that looked like something from a B Western. You could practically see Wichita from there.

Russell knew that a sane man would be kicking himself. God knows that everybody else was. Family and friends wanted to know why he would quit a bona fide high school football power to work at a Podunk orphanage. It just did not make sense. No wonder they were laughing out loud back in Temple. The Masonic Home? It sounded like a mental hospital.

Back in Temple, when Russell was winning a lot of games, people were actually calling him the next Paul Tyson. Tyson had recently led Waco High to five straight state championship games. The Tigers had lost but two games during that span, while scoring more than a hundred points nine times.

So successful was Tyson with an offensive scheme called the "spinner series" that he had attracted the attention of famous men like Knute Rockne of Notre Dame and Pop Warner of Stanford. Both would steal the idea, introduce it into their system, and pretend it was their own.

Yes, Russell dearly wanted to be the next Paul Tyson. The only problem at the moment was that he was standing in the middle of a lonesome cow pasture somewhere between nowhere and good-bye.

Yeah, you know the joke about Rusty Russell: They say the grass is always greener on the other side. Well, ol' Rusty finally found a football field that's got no grass.

So why had Russell chosen to make the leap? Because gut instinct had told him that there was magic inside this godforsaken place. The orphanage just needed somebody to warm it up: the kids needed someone to believe in. Russell knew that football could jump-start a life. Football had been his ticket off the farm. Football would eventually help the orphans navigate these tough times. That is, if he could get his hands on a football.

Russell shook his head. *What a battle this will be.*

At first, no one would have pegged Rusty Russell as a visionary.

The glasses lent a faintly comical effect, and his lean face made him seem hungry. He smiled and looked you in the eye, but he did not embody greatness. No one was ready to compare him to Knute Rockne. He was well-read, with a penchant for writing long letters and an appetite for education. Few people really knew him, because Russell rarely talked much about himself. The best example was his war record.

A college student in 1917, he was among the first from Texas to enlist for the Big War. The U.S. Army promptly shipped him to France and it was not long before he found himself working as a medic at the bloody battle of St. Mihiel on the Western Front of France.

The battle that began on September 12, 1918, would be one of the most significant and hard-fought battles of the war, one that followed five days of hard rain that brought great hardship to both sides. American forces under the command of General John J. Pershing faced several German armies that were defending hundreds of long-standing trenches. It was the first time that American-led forces used a strategy from three frontline commanders. One of those was Colonel George S. Patton, who would roll the dice by unleashing unsupported tank platoons in a cavalry-style attack outside the small village of Jonville. Acting aggressively, young Patton managed to drive the Germans back six miles to the outskirts of town. Patton, who would become one of the most colorful leaders in the history of the United States military, would learn a great deal from the battle at St. Mihiel. Two decades later, during World War II, he would use this battle plan against the Germans in the Ardennes Forest.

Day by day at St. Mihiel, the war of attrition was taking its toll on the Western armies. The weather report stated, "Visibility: Heavy driving wind and rain during parts of the day and night. Roads: Very muddy." Furthermore, the infantry was having great difficulty with the German machine-gun nests.

On September 15, 1918, Russell, a private in the Medical Detachment of the 358th Infantry Regiment, was on the front line, battling to save a man's life, when a canister of mustard gas landed a few feet away. In no time, soldiers were dying all around him in the most horrible manner. Blinded by the blast, he continued to crawl about the blood-soaked ground and to attend to the wounded. Not until they placed him on a stretcher and carried him away did the young medic cease to render aid. (There would be seven thousand casualties in six days of fighting.) He was transported to a Paris hospital, where doctors informed him he would never see again. His lungs had been singed and there were no assurances he would survive the night.

His health slowly improved, but not his eyesight. What beguiled him was the stack of unread mail on his bedside table. Virtually no English was spoken at the French hospital. His happiest day came when an English nurse, whom he referred to as his "guardian angel," learned of his predicament and volunteered to read his letters. She delivered the words he had been dying to hear, words from his mother, who began each letter, "My dear boy, I do miss you so."

Russell remained in the hospital for more than six months, and when it was time to be transported back to the states, his eyesight was returning. Without thick lenses, though, he would never see anything beyond fog and deep shadows.

Crossing the Atlantic gave the young soldier plenty of time to think. He knew that his father, a third-generation farmer, would never accept this longing desire to coach. But, more than anything, he wanted to work with young people. Coaches in his past had taught him values that he would carry the rest of his life, and he wanted to pass those lessons along to others. There was an allure to the physical demands of football. He knew that by combining a healthy work ethic with a well-designed strategy he could build a team that everyone would be proud of.

That first day back in the States, doctors tried to convince him to completely give up football. His near-blindness would never allow him to negotiate a football field, much less catch a speeding, oblong ball. But he was determined to play his senior season at Howard Payne College in Brownwood, Texas. The lanky end, in spite of being the only player on the field wearing glasses, surprised them all. He was selected to the all-conference team.

Remarkably, Russell also made the all-conference basketball team as a forward and was named the best all-round athlete at Howard Payne in 1922.

This was not a man you could stop, or even slow down. His appearance was misleading. Some were tricked into believing that he was just a gangly, freckle-faced country boy who would spend the rest of his life plowing the raw fields of far West Texas. Russell was born on December 4, 1895, to Dorothy and P. C. Russell. One reason the boy seemed so boring was that he had grown up dirt-poor outside the desolate little town of Fredonia, where education ran a distant third to the spring planting and fall harvest. School could wait—the cotton could not. Russell barely had time for school, so football seemed completely out of the question. But an ambitious high school coach saw something in the boy that could not be denied. He was fast enough to catch a jackrabbit in the open prairie.

Day after day, the coach had preached to Russell the need for speed; it was the most important element in the overall scheme of football, he said. Teams with the biggest players did not always win. Often it was the swift who managed to rise above all of the others.

Yet another lesson was drilled into the boy's head, and this one came from the thirteenth chapter of the Book of Numbers. According to the story, when the children of Israel first came to the Jordan River, Moses sent twelve spies to check out the land. They reported that Canaan was a land flowing with milk and honey, but that it was inhabited by giants. They reported, "And there we saw the giants, the sons of Anak, which come of the giants: And we were in our own sight as grasshoppers, and so we were in their sight."

The best Russell could tell, he would soon be coaching a team of grasshoppers at the Masonic Home. He had no idea where to start.

SOME SAID THE little orphans would never succeed because they did not know if a football was blown up or stuffed. That was not entirely true. Some had never seen a football. For years, the kids had been playing with two socks stuffed together.

Russell had decided to reveal the problem to Juanita, and she had come up with a pretty good idea. Her Clabber Girl Baking Powder cans were metal, shaped like a missile, and could be thrown in a spiral. This kind of imagination meant that the team's early practices came off as well as could be expected.

The official nickname of the Masonic Home football team was the "Masons," a moniker that would fade into the background years later, when sportswriter Pop Boone renamed them the "Mighty Mites." In 1927, it did not matter what they were called.

That first season on the job, no one really cared if Russell won or lost. There were larger, more pressing issues—like keeping the kids from climbing the fence and making sure the girls did not get pregnant.

"I want you to focus on being a teacher," principal Thomas Fletcher had told Russell his first day on the job. "We've got a lot of bad kids here that need a lot of attention. Football comes second."

Fletcher, in his dark suit and starched white shirt, was as rigid as the Masonic Home was strict. Teachers were expected to follow procedure and ask for nothing. The hand-me-down uniforms would have to do, as would the six leather helmets. No equipment was on order, and given the absence of an athletic budget, it was apparent that the orphans would always be a ragtag bunch.

Russell had asked the principal, "Mr. Fletcher, do we have any money at all for the football team?"

"Our football budget," he said, "is the change you are carrying around in your pants pocket."

On the day he arrived, Russell sat down to study the team picture from the previous year, hoping it might reveal some useful history. He first noticed the absence of a coach. The uniforms were threadbare, with no numbers. With the exception of one boy, the players were short and skinny. Some seemed quite frail. But Russell could not take his eyes off one full-grown man/teenager in the middle of the photograph. With his blond hair, wide shoulders, thick neck, and six-foot-six frame, he looked like a giant next to the other kids. He was someone Russell could build a team around.

The boy's name was Bob Hall. He was one of the best high school tackles in Texas, and, thanks to hard work and perseverance, had already developed into a world-class shot-putter. He had saved what little money he could earn around the Home until the day he spotted the ad for the Charles Atlas weights in a sports magazine. He sent off fourteen dollars and received a barbell and several plates that went *clang* every afternoon when he worked out on the side porch of the dormitory.

There was no track-and-field coach at the Home and no shot put ring. So Hall drew a circle on the sidewalk with a piece of chalk and taught himself to throw the shot barefooted into a pasture littered with cow manure. Amazingly, he had honed his skills while keeping his feet relatively clean. More important, he had managed to win the Texas championship with a throw of almost sixty feet. But there was little hope he could raise the cash for a trip to the national track-and-field meet. No hope at all, until the maintenance workers at the Home took up a collection of pennies that covered his train fare to Chicago.

Hall, when he arrived in Chicago, felt his heart pounding. His eyes focused on the fortresslike buildings abutting the shoreline of Lake Michigan. He was captivated by the large, dark sedans that moved about the wide city streets. Hall was really just an over-grown country boy from the Rio Grande Valley. The sight of a town like Chicago was beyond comprehension. He could just imagine Al Capone lurking in the shadows.

But he would not be intimidated by the world-class athletes he competed against on the campus of the University of Chicago. His first throw set a national record of sixty feet and three inches. Folks back at the Home cheered wildly when they heard he had won the national shot put championship. A cake and Kool-Aid party was planned as they anxiously awaited his return.

But Hall did not make his scheduled train, nor did he show up on the next one. As it turned out, a coach from a rich private school in Dallas had spotted the physical specimen in Chicago and made a sales pitch the kid could not refuse. He would pay for Hall's train fare back to Dallas, not Fort Worth, enroll him in the prep school, and guarantee him an athletic scholarship to college. Hall and the coach left together on the next train and the big tackle was never heard from again.

No wonder the first few days of football practice at the Home seemed depressing. First, Russell had to deal with his disappointment of losing a player like Hall. Then he faced the reality of coaching players that barely knew how to strap on shoulder pads. There had been no regimen or even a schedule in the previous years, and the football team had just knocked around the neighborhood, picking up games where they could. The players knew nothing about the fundamentals of the game—even blocking and tackling. This would be their first official season as a Class-B entry in the Texas Interscholastic League, and Russell was not sure they would win a single game.

He told Juanita, "You know, we've got the scrawniest bunch of kids playing football that I've ever seen. But they're a tough bunch of rascals. I don't think I've ever seen a bunch of kids with more fight in them."

Russell spent much of his time during those early days breaking up fights, while Dr. E. P. Hall, the orphanage physician, had his hands full bandaging the wounded. Russell did not know if he had been hired to coach the football or the boxing team.

Football—at least at first—was not life or death. Russell knew that his players were going to need much nurturing. That is why he did not crack the whip at first.

His first team had a friendly, skinny, awkward boy with little or no football talent—and he never stopped talking. A taskmaster would have beat him with a paddle or made him run laps until sundown. But not Russell; he actually stopped practice and let Abner McCall talk.

"Go right ahead and tell us what is on your mind," the coach would say.

"Okay, everybody," Abner would begin. "It just seems to me that the United States of America is going to hell in a handbasket. We've got women wearing those flapper skirts and smoking cigarettes. We've got the filthy rich spending more money than God. And everybody is getting drunk every night of the week. They call it the roaring twenties. I say it's the whoring twenties."

Everybody laughed, even the coach.

"I say that it's high time we clean up after the party. Or we are all going to end up in the poorhouse."

All the boys laughed and Russell smiled.

"Abner, I expect one day that you'll be a senator."

"No sir, Mr. Russell. Someday I plan to be president of the United States."

"I CAN'T AFFORD to buy any more suits," he told Juanita after one week on the job.

"Why not?" she said. "You like to dress."

"Because we're going to have to spend that money on gas for the old truck."

The old truck was a belching, smoke-billowing blue Dodge with a long, flat bed, that was used previously at the Home to haul hay and pigs. Now it was going to carry football players. While other high school teams were shuttled by a bus provided by the school district, the Home would travel in the broken-down rig with Russell at the wheel.

"I took the old Dodge out for a spin around the neighborhood," he said to Juanita. "And I sucked up so much smoke that I thought I was going to pass out."

Russell named it Old Blue.

At the Home, it seemed that everything was either broken or held together by chewing gum or chicken wire. Each day presented more obstacles. Everywhere he turned came new reminders that football was just another orphan that needed a lot of attention. Rusty and Juanita were now living in a cramped makeshift apartment on the backside of the dining hall that, at least, was rent free. A man making thirty dollars a week could use a break.

Times were so tough that Russell wondered if the folks back at Temple had been right when they said that his brain had not come back from the war intact.

In truth, a man with Russell's IQ and work ethic should have been doing better. The Texas economy in the late twenties was like a prairie fire with a gusting wind behind it. The cattle business and the oil explosion were turning average Joes into overnight tycoons. Russell, if he had chosen to walk away from his lifelong passion, could have made a fortune simply by knocking on the right door in downtown Fort Worth.

On the morning of that first day of fall practice, Russell stood on the hill outside his little apartment and gazed upon a harsh patch of land that they said was the practice field. Minutes later, Doc Hall sauntered up the hill and the two men shook hands. Hall had been working at the home since 1900—"nineteen aught aught"—and knew the lay of the land better than anyone.

"That ol' practice field down there is pretty rough," the coach said. "What'd they used to use it for?"

"To graze the goats."

"You mean to tell me they had goats that liked to eat rocks."

"That's right," the old doctor deadpanned.

Russell paused and rubbed his chin. "Doc, I grew up on a West Texas farm. I've been around sheep and goats all of my life. I know they don't need a lot of grass. But I never had one that liked to eat rocks."

"These are Fort Worth goats," the old doctor said. "Fort Worth goats are different."

Russell could barely stop laughing.

A half hour later, as the players gathered on the practice field, Russell counted heads and came up with twelve.

"Well, at least we'll have a team, if none of you boys get hurt."

One of the players spoke up. "Coach, last year we started out with six. Then we got a couple hurt."

Russell smiled. "So, I guess you had to call off the season."

"No sir. What happened was that Dean Remmert came up with an idea. He promised to increase the pay for the milk slimes if they'd suit for football. The next thing you knew, we had a whole team."

The milk slimes were the boys that rose every morning at four o'clock and milked the cows.

Russell's eyes studied each player. "How many of you boys are milk slimes?"

Each one raised his hand.

The coach laughed again. "Well, it looks like we got ourselves a professional football team."

Truth was that Russell could never remember a worse-looking team. The boys were still shoeless and would be until the end of September. The orphans did not wear shoes from April 1 until October 1. Some of the boys wore gray jerseys, others white. Everything had a hole in it. Only half of the team had leather helmets, and none of those matched. And they looked pretty funny throwing passes with Clabber Girl Baking Powder cans.

The coach was so determined to dress up the football program that, in spite of temperatures in the midnineties, he showed up for that first day of practice attired in a coat and tie. The players could not believe what they were seeing. He never even loosened his tie. While the players sweated and grunted, Russell seemed quite cool in his natty dress. It seemed humorous when he took off running down the field in his pressed suit. He swatted at players with a long paddle, encouraging them to run faster. Make no mistake: Russell was not some harsh disciplinarian with a sadistic streak. The paddle was used for the purpose of motivating his players. *Really* motivating them.

MUCH COULD BE learned about the little orphans in the first game of the '27 season against Mineral Wells High School. Mineral Wells was a small town west of Fort Worth with a lust for football and a consistently winning team. Russell cranked Old Blue, and as the truck belched, he realized there was no one to wave good-bye or to wish the team good luck. No fans from the Home would be making the trip. Neither the *Fort Worth Press* nor the *Star-Telegram* even mentioned that the Masons would be making history that night by playing their first official game in the Texas Interscholastic League.

Old Blue took off through the front gate, and Russell tried to figure in his head exactly how much money he had in his pocket. He wondered if the truck had enough gas for the return trip. Then, just before hitting the highway, he turned and peered through the back window at the players sprawled on the bed of the truck. He had insisted that sideboards be installed, so that none of the Masons would tumble over the side and into the path of an oncoming car. Russell counted exactly twelve players and smiled.

"I just hope that we don't get anybody hurt," he said to Doc Hall, who was riding shotgun.

"If we do, I'll patch them up," the old doctor said.

It was a long, bumpy ride to Mineral Wells. Russell tried to imagine what was going through the boys' minds as they passed the farms and the ranches. It had been years since most of them had ever set foot outside of the fence. A fifty-mile trip into West Texas was like entering a new world. For years, the kids had been locked inside the orphanage like inmates at a prison.

Old Blue arrived at the stadium an hour before kickoff, and Russell sidled up to the Mineral Wells head coach. "I was just wondering if you could do me a favor," he said. "If my boys happen to win the game—and I doubt they will—could we possibly take the game ball home with us?"

"Why, sure," the coach said. "My team's got plenty of footballs."

Then Russell proceeded to inform his players they would be playing for a brand-new football. "Win the game and you take it home," he said. So charged up were the little orphans that they jumped and hollered and shook their fists as they ran onto the field, and this confused the Mineral Wells fans to no end.

Russell had a bunch of boys who knew virtually nothing about the game. But in recent weeks they had been drilled into a cohesive unit. Mineral Wells was not prepared for the kind of wide-open passing game they would face. Russell knew his midgets could not run the ball against the bigger, stronger boys, so he designed an offense based on the single wing. His wingback was used as a floater and might line up at any spot on the field. He was the key receiver in this newfangled system.

Like a bunch of field mice, the Masons ran around and through the bigger Mineral Wells players. And when the scoreboard read 34–14 at the end of the game, the orphans had a ball.

Now all they needed was some gas to get back to Fort Worth.

THAT THE MASONIC home would win eight games and lose two in Russell's first season was astonishing. Granted, the competition was at the low end of the scale in Class B, and they faced none of the big-city schools from Fort Worth or Dallas.

At the end of the season, the orphans were invited to play an exhibition game in Sherman. With an enrollment of more than six hundred students, Sherman High was a North Texas football power about to embark upon the Class-A playoffs. The Bearcats needed a warm-up game. Indeed, Russell had been lured into an impossible situation with cold, hard cash. The orphans would make $250 for driving ninety miles to Sherman and acting like sacrificial lambs.

Not surprising, the scoreboard at the end of the game read Sherman 97, Masonic Home 13. The orphans were beat up and Russell was kicking himself.

Thomas Fletcher let the coach have it.

"We have limited resources here and our boys are small," the principal said. "You should have known better."

The coach was embarrassed. But in time, he knew he could justify his strategy.

At an all-school assembly two weeks later, Russell presented his twelve players with letter jackets that had been paid for by the Sherman fund. No one in the crowd could believe it. There had never been anything at the orphanage to compare it to. Football players were soon strutting around campus in brand-new jackets with "M" sewn on the front. They became overnight heroes. Every orphan looked up to them. Among the little boys sitting up front at the all-school assembly were Hardy and Jeff Brown, along with their friends Dewitt Coulter and C. D. Sealy. Their eyes were as big as saucers.

It was only a matter of time before all of the orphans would dream of the day when they would pull on a leather helmet. With Russell around, they would not have to wait long. The coach had already designed a blueprint for the entire orphanage. The boys would start playing football at age six. He organized teams for fifty-pounders, seventy-five-pounders, ninety-five-pounders, and those at one hundred and fifteen pounds and above. Even the scrawniest kids in the orphanage would have a chance to show their stuff. Practices would start immediately.

The Sherman money also allowed Russell to purchase plenty of footballs, and he managed to get his hands on some more leather helmets. He bought T-shirts and taught the boys how to add numbers to the fabric with the magic of spray paint. Some of the money was socked away in a gasoline fund for the old Dodge.

Old Blue would forever belch black smoke.

But the football program was no longer running on empty.

Chapter 3

A DICKENS PLACE

In the late twenties, the Masonic Home as a whole was still suffering from growing pains. Many of the problems dated to 1899, when the first building was completed and the gates were swung open.

The place had actually opened to a great celebration. Masons traveled from all over Texas to view the two-hundred-acre property situated on a hill in eastern Fort Worth. The *Mail Telegram* reported that most of the downtown hotels were filled with Masons. The Texas and Pacific Railroad transported the visitors on the five-mile trip to the Home to view the cornerstone-laying ceremony.

On October 6, 1899, when the first fifty students were admitted, only the "executive" building was open. But the Masonic Home would go on a building spree in the coming years, and the Masons were proud of the sprawling campus. What they would soon discover, though, was a seemingly endless headache, as the soil beneath the new buildings was tainted with caliche, an impure native nitrate with a crusted calcium carbonate. Caliche is found in dry regions like Fort Worth, where there is a constant cycle of drought.

Caliche was literally causing the Masonic Home to fall down. Constructed in 1909, the massive superintendent's residence started to lean within a year and was torn down before it fell down. One of the dormitories lasted but three years. But by 1920, contractors had learned to overcome the soft ground as four dormitories for boys and girls went up and stayed up. The dining hall was finished in 1924.

One problem with this build-it-then-knock-it-down scheme was the haphazard pattern of the layout. Fortunately, the Masons had some money to throw at the project. Each member was contributing fifty cents per year, and that added up to $200,000. That kind of money went a long way in the Roaring Twenties.

The early years at the Home, though, inspired mostly chaos and unhappiness. The original blueprint was for a vocational school that would teach the kids how to make a living. The boys spent most of their day doing farmwork, while others toiled in the print shop. Girls, in addition to shorthand were taught typing, bookkeeping, cooking, sewing, and general housekeeping. The core curriculum did not include basic reading, arithmetic, or science. So, the early graduates of the Home entered the world lacking.

Changes came gradually. In 1912, Dr. S. B. Bedinger, the superintendent of schools, convinced the Grand Lodge to make the Home its own independent school district. Slowly, the orphanage made the transition from a vocational institution to one of intellectual pursuits.

Early athletic teams were track-and-field for the boys and tennis for the girls. The ill-equipped football team competed at a club level and played pickup games around the neighborhood. Old Blue was added into the mix in 1915 to provide transportation for the sports teams.

Naturally, the Grand Lodge of Free Masons in Texas was proud of what was being accomplished. Kids with little hope and nowhere to turn were at least getting an education. Any child between the ages of five and thirteen was eligible for acceptance if their father had died while in good standing with the Freemasons. They could live at the Home until graduation. About half the kids had lost both parents. Widows were also taken care off by both the Masonic Lodge and the Eastern Star, at a separate home in nearby Arlington.

Masons in the twenties were four hundred thousand strong in a state populated by six million people. No other organization could boast of that kind of clout, either politically or in the private sector. Every city council and county commission in the state was populated with Masons. The state legislature in Austin could not keep track.

The early Masons had a colorful history, with a membership that included Stephen F. Austin, Sam Houston, William Barrett Travis, James Bowie, Davy Crockett, and James Fannin.

General Santa Anna was a Mason in good standing when he was

captured on April 21, 1936, at the Battle of San Jacinto. Santa Anna was being transported to his meeting with General Sam Houston when he flashed several secret Masonic hand signs. He even gave Houston the Masonic grip. No one was sure if his Masonic affiliation saved his life. But it obviously did not hurt.

Building the Masonic Home was a heroic deed, but the place got off to a rough start, thanks to a lack of compassion by the early administrators. Rules were harshly strict and punishment frequently swift and painful. Anyone with a notion to run away was quickly deterred by the tall chain-link fences with barbed wire across the top. A wrought iron gate was locked around the clock. The orphanage in the early years was anything but fun. It was a grim place where misbehaving kids were lashed with straps and locked up in closets.

The Home left welts on their butts and knots on their heads. The orphans would come to develop keen survival skills. Many of the boys were rousted from the beds at four in the morning to milk the cows. Because of a shortage of bathtubs, several had to trek almost a mile, even on cold, dark mornings, down to Sycamore Creek for a bath.

William Henry Remmert was both cold-eyed and quick with the paddle, and he was known to beat the boys' backsides and send them to bed without supper. Nothing got past the dean, and they said his radar worked even when he was sleeping. Hearing the boys sneaking back into the dorm after curfew, he would charge up the stairs in hot pursuit. By the time he reached the bunk area, the lights would be out and the boys silent beneath their covers. But Remmert had his ways. He would walk from bunk to bunk, placing an index finger on each boys' carotid artery, checking for accelerated pulse rates, and in a matter of seconds, the guilty were getting whacked.

Tempers mounted. A day did not pass when there was not a fight in the dormitory, or at the schoolhouse, or down at the dairy. The boys were roundly punished, but the fighting continued. Remmert doled out tear-wrenching licks with a paddle large enough to propel a good-size boat. Frank Wynn, dean of the little boys, thrashed his kids with a piece of garden hose—the *whop, whop, whop* could be heard across the campus.

Just entering the orphanage for the first time could be a traumatic experience. Most of the kids had recently lost one or both parents and were given little time to adjust to the institutional environment. Those who could not cut it were quickly back on the streets. Remmert, who arrived in the early twenties, did not mind packing an orphan's bags and putting him on the other side of the fence.

Every day, orphans were being shuttled in from all parts of the state, some traveling hundreds of miles. Little Leon Pickett had watched his father, a county sheriff, gunned down in broad daylight on the family's front porch by a known criminal. In a matter of days, Leon would be shipped, along with his brother, Perry, to a place he had never heard of.

Young Dewitt Coulter had shivered in fear on learning of his father's death from tuberculosis. "That first night at the orphanage, well, I don't have one word that fits it," he once wrote. "They put me in Dorm One, my brother Ray in Dorm Two, and my older sisters L.E. and Ima, God only knows where. I thought I would never see them again. When Mrs. Thannosh got ready to turn out the lights that first night, brokenhearted Dewitt cried."

The socially accepted vision of an orphanage was one of a cold, uncaring, menacing institution where children were to be pitied if not feared. When the Home opened its doors in 1899, the children were referred to not as orphans but as inmates. Most outsiders imagined an unloving Dickensian commune where the kids swept chimneys by day and picked pockets by night.

The Home was split evenly between boys and girls, and the mingling of the sexes was strictly taboo. Teachers and administrators laid down the law. If the orphans were caught even touching or passing notes, they would be instantly expelled.

If you did not toe the line at the Home, you had better have train fare.

Children in the Depression thirties were often told by their parents, "If you don't behave, I'll send you to the orphanage." The words haunted them like visions of the Wicked Witch of the West.

Kids who rode their bikes past the Masonic Home dreaded the

thought of ever passing through those walls and into the great un-
known. As the shadows grew longer late in the day, the redbrick buildings resembled Gothic fortresses.

Orphans in the 1900s were stigmatized as a strange breed. They
were viewed as misfits with physical deformities and little on the
brain. They were outcasts; it did not matter that they had done nothing wrong. Kids without parents were simply second-class citizens.

One of the most celebrated social experiments in the history of the
United States occurred from the mid-1800s until 1929, and it did
nothing to improve the image of the downtrodden orphan. Unwanted
children from northeastern cities were herded onto trains traveling
west. At depots along the way, they were parceled out like mailbags to
prospective takers. The children were lined up on the platform for all
to see and feel. They were poked and prodded to ascertain their value
as workers on farms or factories. In most cases, they were just another
piece of meat. They were checked for the structure of their muscle
and their teeth. The strong were usually chosen right away and normally forced into hard labor. Conversely, the young, the sickly, and
the weak normally did not make the cut.

A heavily populated orphan train from New York made its final
stop in Fort Worth, where it turned around and headed back East.
Fort Worth was the last chance for the kids not chosen along the way.
Fortunately, what they found in Fort Worth was a guardian angel. He
was I. Z. T. Morris, a kindly Methodist missionary. He gathered up
the outcasts and made sure they found homes with local families, or
at the Texas Children's Home and Aid Society.

It was little wonder that Fort Worth became known as one of the
friendliest places to downtrodden children in the hardest years of the
Depression.

Chapter 4

FROM THE DARKNESS
TO THE LIGHT

What Rusty Russell cherished about the Home was twenty-four-hour access to everyone and everything. Virtually every minute of his day was spent nurturing. That had not been the case at his previous coaching stops, where his players went home to their own families at the end of the day.

Juanita Russell was accustomed to seeing her husband rise from the bed in the middle of the night and to sit for hours at a table, drawing up plays and formations. That is why the Masons were an imaginative and well-drilled football team, and why the early seasons in Class B had gone so smoothly.

Most football experts were shocked when the little team finished the 1927 season with an 8–2 record. But it turned out to be no fluke. From 1927 through 1931, the orphans compiled a 39-11-4 record. What really captured the public's imagination was their gritty, relentless style of play. This bunch of scrawny kids played a brand of football that Texans had never seen.

Sitting on the edge of their seats every Friday night at La Grave Field were the elementary school orphans: Hardy Brown, Jeff Brown, Dewitt Coulter, Ray Coulter, C. D. Sealy, Floyd Lewis, and several others waiting for the day they could suit up with the high school team.

On Friday nights you could also count on seeing Amon G. Carter, the publisher of the *Star-Telegram,* and "Pappy" Waggoner, the richest man in the state. There were also plenty of pretty girls. Females at the Home sewed their own clothes and they showed up at the games dressed to the nines. The boys knew they were not supposed to touch. But at least they were going home with them at the end of the night.

The Drum-and-Bugle Corps, a band of middle-aged Shriners, never missed a game. Some said they were an exercise in futility. But the Shriners in their red Fez hats believed it was their God-given right to arrive a little tipsy and belt out some bad music.

Everyone had an opinion as to how the skinny kids had become so prodigious. Most of the credit went to Russell. No team received more attention from its coach. The first team meeting of the day was held right after breakfast. After classes, practice would begin at 2:30 and not end before five. The players had their own training table in the dining hall and Russell made sure there was plenty of red meat and potatoes to go around. Another meeting—normally a chalk talk—was held right after dinner before the boys retired to the dormitory for schoolwork.

Not until Russell arrived in 1927 did anyone ever take sports seriously. Life at the Home changed the day that Russell walked through the front gate. An emphasis was placed on excelling and winning. There had been few prideful accomplishments at the orphanage. Russell changed attitudes. It was not long before the Mighty Mites were the biggest thing on campus. And for the first time since the gates swung open in 1899, the kids were having fun.

Most important, Russell was a likable man that seemed to care for everyone and everything inside the Home. He threw himself into his work both on the educational and athletic level. After leading his orphans to victory on Friday night, he spent the better part of his Saturdays coaching the little boys down at Sycamore Park.

Russell knew that football would eventually bring self respect to the boys, and that winning breathed life into battered souls. But he also knew that football was a diversion, a way to forget dead mothers and fathers. A boy who learned team values rarely felt orphaned.

Men like Doc Hall and William Henry Remmert were instantly drawn to Russell, as they recognized his drive to build character.

Rusty Russell was the master of the subtle push. He rarely raised his voice and employed the paddle only to make a boy run faster. This man was not a firebrand. He was straight off the pages of a Dashiell

Hammett novel, a real-life Nick Charles in his dark suits and steam-pressed fedora.

As it turned out, Russell was one of the most imaginative and most organized football coaches in the state. Day by day, he was starting to remind people of Paul Tyson. Opposing coaches never knew what to expect when they faced a Russell-coached team.

Almost every team in the state at the time ran the single-wing formation on offense and the six-man line on defense. But Russell shattered that mold every time the Masons stepped on the field.

In the single-wing, all four backs were normally tightly bunched. It was rare when the tight ends were flexed, even a yard or two down the line of scrimmage. This was a compact formation that was tailored to the running game.

But in the Russell system, the backs and ends were always flexed. At times, his players were spread out from sideline to sideline. This caused great consternation among defensive coaches. They simply could not cover the little orphans that were like water bugs darting through the secondary.

The dogma of the day in football was that games were won in the trenches. But with 140-pound guards and tackles, Russell had to come up with other ideas.

"Divide and conquer," he told his players. "That is the only way we're going to be able to win."

On defense, Russell refused to go with the standard six-man line. The Mites often shifted from a three-man to a five-man line, and might even on occasion try a one-man line.

The Mighty Mites were winning, and winning big, because Russell could outthink everyone. Coaches across the field glared at him with hate-filled eyes. Football at the time was a power game that relied on size, strength, and brute force. No other coach in the state could approach Russell's passing ingenuity. No coach could stop it.

In an age when coaches were generally leather-necked taskmasters, Russell was more laid-back than a cotton farmer. Unlike most of the other coaches, he did not have a nineteen-inch neck. His wife liked to pull up a lawn chair in the afternoon and watch the practices while their baby daughter, Betty, played in the grass. The strongest invective they ever heard him use was "gol-darn."

This, however, did not mean that Russell was not fiercely driven to win. In the press he said, "It's not if you win or lose, but how you play the game." But he told his players, "I don't want to see anybody smiling around this locker room after a loss."

In spite of his quiet countenance, Russell coached a very motivated football team. They showed up every Friday night with fire in their eyes.

"We have to always be ready to win in the fourth quarter," he said. "We will *always* be the strongest team in the fourth quarter."

Russell and the Mighty Mites enjoyed an early success that was unmatched. But it also came with a measure of frustration. Thousands attended the games, but it seemed the Masons were toiling in relative obscurity. The *Fort Worth Press* and *Star-Telegram* barely covered their games. Class-B teams were considered second-class citizens that did not even play for a state championship. The best you could hope for in the minor leagues was to ascend to the regional championship game, and even then the sporting press normally ignored you. Meanwhile, the big schools like Central and Polytechnic always landed on the front page.

What the sportswriters failed to recognize was that the Masonic Home was rapidly outgrowing the competition. By 1930, very few of the small country schools could stay on the field with Russell's team. This occurred in spite of the fact that the orphans were badly outweighed. Truly, the grasshoppers were getting the best of the giants.

For the 1930 season, Russell managed to add two big-league schools to the schedule. The Home managed to tie Fort Worth North Side 6–6 and Central 7–7. The only loss of the season was to a junior college team by the score of 6–0.

In ten games that season, the Masonic Home outscored its opponents by the aggregate of 216–37. Still, they were going nowhere fast and were still regarded to be among the bottom-feeders of Texas high school football.

Few people knew that Russell was working on a plan that would attract a lot of attention to the Masonic Home and shake up the structure of high school football in Texas. When the Masons finished the 1931 season with an 11-0-1 record, and won the Class B regional championship by the score of sixty to zip over Clarendon, he decided to spring it on the public.

Russell wanted to play with the big boys. No, the Masonic Home did not come close to qualifying for the Class-A level. They had about one-tenth the enrollment of most of the Fort Worth schools. The dictatorial Texas Interscholastic League would never approve of his little scheme.

But Russell knew about a backdoor. There was a little-known provision that would allow the local district to accept teams that did not meet the enrollment requirement of five hundred students. Russell had already canvassed the six coaches of District 7A and knew he had the votes. The door was open for a bold, sweeping move into Class A—the major leagues of high school football.

In the spring of 1932, District 7A of Fort Worth welcomed the orphans. This was major news across the state, as it meant the district was defying the powerful TIL. It meant a new day was dawning in Texas high school football. Some people would accept it with a smile, others with two clenched fists. It was the most controversial move anyone could remember. Many teams around the state had tried and failed to be admitted into the elite competition. Russell, however, knew how to politick, and he knew how to get things done.

He could not wait to break the news to his players.

"You came to the orphanage with nothing," he said. "And I want you to leave with something. That's why we will be playing in Class A next season."

The cheering could be heard all the way down to Sycamore Creek.

Chapter 5

HOPE

The sounds of the Shriners Drum-and-Bugle Corps blared from a hill on the east side of Fort Worth and it was enough to make dogs howl and orphans cover their ears.

Men dressed in red fez hats and yellow, billowing pants had come to entertain the crowd that huddled against the blue norther that blew in from the Panhandle and swept across the hillside, where the aimless congregation of buildings stood. Third-graders Dewitt Coulter and Hardy Brown, bundled in overalls, sweaters, and stocking caps, watched every move of the high school boys boarding the bus for the state championship game.

Four years had passed since little Hardy's arrival at the Masonic Home, and the wide, toothy smile suggested that he had adjusted well. Teachers at the orphanage thought he was the happiest kid around.

"Golly, Dewitt, I want to be just like them football players when I grow up," Hardy said.

That morning, the Masonic Home Mighty Mites were set to hit the highway to Corsicana for the biggest game in the history of Texas high school football, and no one could believe it. Not the hundred or so wide-eyed boys and girls waiting to see them off. Not the sporting press finally reveling in their improbable rise. Not the fans that trooped from town to town to see them play.

The whole state was talking about how Russell, in just his first Class-A season, had coached the Mighty Mites all the way to the state championship game. He had beaten the odds that were something like a million to one. Remarkably, the Mites would not lose a single game in 1932, and stood on the brink of becoming the biggest story in the annals of Texas football. Thousands upon thousands from all over the state were headed to Corsicana to witness the game.

As the last player filed onto the bus, Hardy Brown skipped along the redbrick road and pressed his nose against one of the side windows, peering inside at the boys wearing letter jackets, faded jeans, and neckties. Then he placed both hands against the cold glass, his warm fingers leaving tiny imprints.

"Look, Dewitt," he said. "You can see my fingers right there on the window. That won't come off. It's almost like I'm going with them."

Dewitt giggled. Then he walked up to the bus and did the same thing.

For Dewitt and Hardy, who would enjoy a friendship of more than sixty years, the moment would be frozen in time. Old men drinking beer on a warm summer afternoon several decades later would recall December 26, 1932, as the greatest day of their lives. More than anything else, it would inspire them to become great football players. They would remember how the moment aroused their passion for the game. For, in truth, the 1932 championship game down in Corsicana was just the beginning of a long and wonderful ride that would take the boys farther and higher than they ever imagined.

This is how the journey began.

ON THE DAY after Christmas, a dark sky blanketed Fort Worth. Cow pens stood empty in the stockyards. Oil prices in the midst of the Great Depression swung lower than Herbert Hoover's approval rating, and Fanny Brice's "Second Hand Rose" held forth as the most familiar sound on the radio, just ahead of static.

Up in the Texas Panhandle, vicious winds peeled the topsoil off the plains and prairies, creating a waking nightmare called the Dust Bowl.

Texans had once viewed it all with a cynical disbelief. Three years earlier, on the day the stock market crashed, they had shrugged, laughed and popped open another Pearl beer. A filthy-rich Fort Worth

oilman named Fred Foster, dining one night at the fashionable Westbrook Hotel, lit a cigar with a thousand-dollar bill and, like the others,
scoffed at the notion that the almighty Texas economy would ever col-
lapse. For this was a place with a big sky and bigger dreams, a place
where Jesse Chisholm had driven his herd into town in the spring of
1867, inspiring hundreds of range bosses to follow. In Fort Worth,
men rolled up their sleeves and went to work while the women carried
six-shooters and did most of the bootlegging.

The *Fort Worth Press* captured this gunslinger attitude back in October 1929:

> There was money for everybody, the farmers who owned the land,
> the drillers, the financiers, the lease holders, the geologists, and even
> the crooks who sold the false stock.

Fort Worth had burgeoned into one of America's great success stories after the Big War. Gushers spewed in hamlets like Gunsight, Ne-
cessity, and Eastland in West Texas, as most of the money flowed
straight into the streets of Fort Worth, where the Worth Hotel rose up
as a twenty-seven-story monument to the almighty dollar. On any
given day, a fortune seeker could purchase an oil lease at the hotel's
front door and, before crossing the lobby, sell it for a profit.

The cattle business, the packing houses, the railroads, and the oil
industry combined to create boundless wealth. Five thousand people
a month were moving in by the midtwenties. Niles City, located just
outside the city limits, was annexed into Fort Worth in 1921. Why
not? Of the 651 citizens, seven were millionaires.

Money seemed to fall out of the sky. William Randolph Hearst
turned his eyes to Texas in 1925, purchasing the morning newspaper
known as the *Fort Worth Record*. Hearst announced to everyone that
he might just buy up the whole town. But local entrepreneur Amon G.
Carter, determined to keep outsiders at bay, wrested the *Record* away
from Hearst and merged it with his own paper, the *Fort Worth Star-
Telegram*.

Fort Worthians loved to dance and sing, and why not? In the twenties reasons abounded to celebrate. A local dancer by the name of Ginger Rogers won a Charleston contest at the Majestic Theatre. Prosperity was spelled "b-o-o-t-l-e-g-g-i-n-g." Just like the gangsters in Chicago and New York, the whiskey runners in Fort Worth took full advantage of Prohibition. The oil dollars were like an endless river, and some of the most fashionable women in town cavorted in flapper skirts and were courted by men with bad intentions.

By the midtwenties the race was on in Fort Worth to see who could build the highest building. The Waggoner Building went up with a copper-trimmed canopy, brass-plated door handles, cherrywood paneling, and Italian white marble on the walls. Few cities beyond the East Coast could brag of a more sprawling skyline. The cattle business had driven this growth since 1876, when the railroad linked Cowtown to Chicago. Cows were herded off the train by the thousands each day, sold to the highest bidder, and chopped up for boots and steaks. A quarter-million head passed through Fort Worth every year. Only Chicago could brag of more cow dung.

This streak of prosperity might have continued ad infinitum if not for the domino effect of the stock market crash, followed by the Great Depression that closed down the banks and sacked the job market. Fort Worthians swore they would never panic, but of course they did. And no one was fooled by an advertisement taken out in the *Star-Telegram* and paid for by several civic leaders that read, "The signers of this document believe that the Depression has spent itself; that good times are on the way and that 1931 will see a marked recovery in practically all lines of business."

Proof to the contrary could be found on every street in late 1932. The economy had turned on a dime—in the wrong direction. Men who once sped through town in new Cadillacs now survived on handouts: *Just a nickel to buy a cup of coffee.* As cattle prices plummeted, soup lines multiplied. City Hall had to lock its doors during the daytime to keep the homeless from camping out in the hallways. "Brother, Can You Spare a Dime?" was moving up the charts.

And on the morning of December 26, in one of the worst years of the Great Depression, the streets of Fort Worth stood virtually empty.

From a penthouse atop the Fort Worth Club, Amon Carter pulled back the drapes and peered out at a baffling sight. He saw some of the tallest structures west of the Mississippi River. His eyes settled on the Flat Iron Building, a twin to the architectural marvel in New York. At the center of the city stood three world class hotels—the Blackstone, the Westbrook, and the Worth. To the south loomed the spanking new, twenty-story Texas and Pacific Railway Station, shaped like a giant jukebox with floor-to-ceiling chandeliers in the foyer. In years past, trains would have rumbled in and out of the station with the sync and rhythm of Harry James's big brass band. Now the rails were silent.

All that moved along the streets of Fort Worth that day was blowing trash. Carter, a beefy man with a wide, friendly face and a prominent nose, dumped a cigar ash into a waste can as W. T. "Pappy" Waggoner walked up. Both men were immune to the tough times by having earned considerable wealth back in the twenties.

"Well, Pappy, what time are we leaving for the big game?" Carter said.

"More important, are we going by car or train?" Waggoner replied.

"The very question I've been pondering. And here's my solution. I say we take the train. Oh, it's going to get a little crazy. But I can see snow in those clouds, and that's a pretty bad highway down to Corsicana."

The words had barely departed Carter's lips when the first flakes cascaded down. And within minutes, the world changed. Cars began to stream through the streets, horns honking. The parking lot of the Texas and Pacific was filling up. "Everybody in town's got a ticket on that train," Carter said. "and they don't give a good goddamn if two fat cats get left behind." It actually came out as "gawddam," a word used so frequently that some folks thought it was Carter's middle name.

The men grabbed their topcoats and cowboy hats and rushed toward the elevator, but in a matter of seconds Carter was back inside Suite 10G, plucking from the cabinet two fruit jars filled to the brim with a clear liquid.

"Hell, Pappy," Carter said with a belly laugh, "we almost forgot our potato soup."

NOT SINCE THE first thunderclap of the oil boom in 1917 could anyone remember such a crowd on the downtown streets. What at first appeared to be yet another listless morning in a cheerless town had turned downright boisterous. A hand from above seemed to be controlling the swirling activity. Sidewalks bustled along Lancaster Avenue, as Masonic Home fans waved orange and white banners. They had been living for this day; piggy banks lay smashed all over town.

A round-trip ticket to Corsicana cost a buck, a ticket to the game fifty cents. There would be no Pullman or dining cars or even a cash bar. But most of the travelers would be half in the bag when the 900 series locomotive, pulling fifty cars and transporting over a thousand people, rumbled into the Corsicana station.

Standing on Platform One a half hour before the train was to depart was H. H. "Pop" Boone. The man's real name was Harry Holman Boone, but few people knew that. He went by "Pop." Now he was clenching half a cigar in his teeth and holding a typewriter case in his right hand. He shook his head. "This is going to be a drunk crowd. But at least they seem like happy drunks."

The revolving door of the Texas and Pacific station was now spinning like a slot machine down in Galveston, home of the outlaw seaside casinos. Herds of people pushed through the front entrance, the footfalls on the marble floor creating a rumble only a cattle drover could love. Voices filled with excitement echoed against the vaulted marble ceilings, as spirits had been lifted by the contents of the ubiquitous fruit jars. Some called it moonshine, others white lightning. The homemade brew had a powerful kick and braced the merrymakers against the biting cold and the Depression blues.

Pop Boone laughed again as the fans pushed past. One of the revelers recognized the old sportswriter from the *Fort Worth Press*. "Hey, Pop, how you think our little orphans'll do today against those big ol' Corsicana boys?"

"Oughta be a defensive struggle," Pop said. "Corsicana gave up only a couple of touchdowns all year. But the Mites'll do okay."

In about four hours, the high school football championship of Texas would be decided down in Corsicana, a flyspeck on the Texas map, between Angus and Blooming Grove, where the cotton was always shoulder high by the Fourth of July. The matchup between Fort Worth Masonic Home and Corsicana High fired up the imagination. It was enough to lure the populace out of hiding, to loosen the grip on those wallets and coin purses. For a few hours at least, the Depression would be put on hold.

Masonic Home, the tiny orphanage on the east side of town, was the classic underdog—skinny kids with tattered jerseys, bony knees, and dirt-smudged faces. Corsicana, in turn, represented the muscled-up bully that ruled the playground. Naturally, the local bookies had made the Tigers a fourteen-point favorite.

Boone, whose column was called "Pop's Palaver," had labored overtime explaining to his readers how the little band of orphans had come so far so fast:

> In the first place, it is just short of phenomenal that a team of such power and brilliance could be culled from the smallest Class-A high school in Texas. There are only 141 students in Masonic Homes' school and only seventy-one are boys. Most of them don't weigh over a hundred pounds. When it is remembered that schools such as Waco, Abilene, Amarillo, and others have student bodies of thousands, with hundreds of boys to choose from, the wonder of this thing becomes apparent. The stamina, skill, fight and dogged determination of those twelve youngsters that make up the Masonic Home team must go down in the history of Texas high school football as the greatest singular accomplishment ever.

Some were surprised that Masonic Home could even field a team, given the shortage of boys and their overall size. The equipment was just hand-me-down stuff. Tailback Scott McCall had grown tired of sharing a helmet, so he simply stopped wearing one during the 1932 season. Back in 1927, when McCall started playing on the junior high team, no one could even locate a football to practice with.

Everything began to change that year, when H. N. "Rusty" Russell arrived at the orphanage. Harvey Nual Russell looked more like a college professor. His soft-spoken persona provided no clue that a football guru lurked within. But the Masonic Home, playing a schedule of small-town schools, had started winning right away in 1927, and had not lost but one game since 1930—that to a junior college team. Now, as Boone had written, the Masonic Home was by far the smallest school playing Class-A football.

On first blush, the jump to the big leagues looked like suicide. Class-A teams needed an enrollment of at least five hundred students, and the Masonic Home, in the high school grades, came up about three hundred and fifty short.

What happened during the 1932 season was mind-boggling. The orphans stung seven local teams by the combined score of 145 to 33. Polytechnic High, with its sprawling new campus and an enrollment of more than a thousand students, fell 18–0.

The first opponent in the playoffs was Woodrow Wilson High of Dallas, and the Wildcats, upon hearing about the ragtag orphans, laughed loud enough to be heard thirty miles away. Woodrow Wilson, with its fifteen hundred students, flaunted its status as one of the elite football schools in Texas. Some said the 1932 team was the best ever. The Wildcats boasted a plucky, strong-armed kid named Davey O'Brien, the same little quarterback who would win the Heisman Trophy at TCU in 1938. But against the grinding, hustling, scrappy, sack-happy little Mites, O'Brien completed only one of eighteen passes. The 40–7 defeat was especially embarrassing, since the game was played before twenty thousand fans at TCU Stadium.

In round two, the Mites were a ten-point underdog against the powerful Sherman Bearcats, the same team they had lost to 97–13 just five years earlier. It did not help that a blizzard had blasted Fort Worth forty-eight hours before kickoff. If the Mighty Mites could not pass, they could not win. At least that was the opinion of the sporting press.

The Bearcats would outweigh the Mites by an average of thirty-five pounds in the line.

Over the years, the remarkable mind of Rusty Russell had concocted a passing strategy like none other. It was a bold experiment. Teams of that era—whether it was high school, college, or the pros—rarely let it fly. And Russell was not ashamed to revert to smoke and mirrors.

Against Sherman, though, Russell totally dismissed the pass. The Mighty Mites were going to play some power football on the ground. Big tackle Allie White did most of the blocking, as McCall scored on an eleven-yard run in the first quarter, followed by Glen "Donkey" Roberts's thirteen-yard dash that preceded Harold McClure's two-yard, game-capping touchdown. The 20–0 victory left the doubters scratching their heads. The Mites had outgained the Bearcats in yardage 280–99.

Up next was Amarillo, a team that would win three Texas championships in the thirties.

Amarillo brought forty-seven players to Fort Worth, along with two more feet of snow from the Panhandle. TCU players volunteered to shovel snow off the field and piled it four feet high on the sideline. All that was left was a thin coating of ice.

The Golden Sandstorm outweighed the Mites by almost fifty pounds per man in the line. In the second quarter, when the sun popped through the clouds and turned the field into a mud bath, Amarillo started to wear down the smaller kids with fresh reserves. An odd sight was the white-shirted giants towering over the mud-caked Mites. Only one reserve had suited up and he would be saved in case of an injury.

Early in the game, Amarillo quarterback Woodrow Dunaway smashed into and through the center of the line for a 6–0 lead. Allie White proceeded to bull his way into the backfield and blocked the placekick with his chest. The Mighty Mite tackle was one of the toughest kids playing football anywhere. That season, during a driving rainstorm against Poly High, he had suffered a four-inch gash just above his right eye, and the blood flowed down his face. He was ordered by Doc Hall to lie down on the rain-soaked field while twelve stitches closed the hole. When the old doctor was finished, White did not even hesitate. He picked up his helmet and trotted back into the game.

Now, thanks to his block of the extra point, Amarillo still led only 6–0.

In spite of the size disadvantage, the Mighty Mites started moving the ball on the ground. McCall kept his legs churning and was gaining four, five, six yards per carry. The Golden Sandies were trying to rough up McCall after the whistle. Meanwhile, the officials were turning a deaf ear to Russell's complaints.

When the Mites' drive stalled at the thirty, Russell decided to go for it on fourth down, and Donkey Roberts saved the day by carrying two Sandies on his back all the way to the twenty.

Two plays later, with the ball at the eight-yard line, Russell reached into his bag of tricks. Halfback Reece Newsome plowed into the line and appeared to be stopped for no gain. No one knew that Newsome had slipped the ball into Roberts's stomach before going down. The kid they called Donkey, thanks to his big ears, was now dropping back to pass. He swung a flare pass to McCall, rounding the left end, and there was no one between him and goal. McCall scored with ease. More important, he hammered the extra point kick through the uprights and Masonic Home led 7–6.

Up in the press box, radio broadcaster Byron Saam told his listeners on WBAP, "That's the greatest drive I've ever seen. The Mites desperately needed eight yards and *they got it*."

Russell's worst fears were realized in the third quarter, when McCall was sucker punched as he lay at the bottom of a pile. No flags were thrown. McCall limped to the sideline, dropped to one knee, and started throwing up blood. Doc Hall wrapped his arm around McCall's waist and helped him to the dressing room. No one expected him to return.

With the Mites' best tackler out of the game, the Golden Sandies began to gain huge chunks of yardage. Amarillo was lining up with a first down at the Mites' twelve-yard line when McCall, suffering from two cracked ribs, staggered out of the locker and, against the wishes of Doc Hall, limped back onto the field.

The Sandies could not gain an inch with McCall back at line-backer. Howes lost three yards on two carries, Dunnaway was sacked for a three-yard loss and, on fourth down, McCall tore through three blockers and put Howes on his back. That is where the game ended.

McCall was carried off the field on the shoulders of his teammates and, in spite of his great pain, smiled all the way.

No one could believe that for the first time a Fort Worth school was going to the state championship game.

No one could believe it was the little orphans.

THE FORT WORTH station looked like a land rush ten minutes before the train's departure, as fans scrambled toward Platform One. Not to be deterred was the Shriners Drum-and-Bugle Corps, fresh from the orphanage, banging their drums and blowing their horns.

Pop Boone pulled deeply on his cigar and winced. "What's that song they're playing?"

"Would you call that a song?" Amon Carter said.

The band rambled off key and then marched—"stumbled' might be a better description—into the first passenger car. The cacophony prompted several passengers to flee for other parts of the train. The conductors yelled, "All aboard!" and the train lurched forward, heading southeast toward Corsicana, a small town eighty miles from Fort Worth that was hardly ready for the three-ring circus headed its way.

Stadium capacity in Corsicana was only six thousand. Workers had toiled all week through sleet and snow to add another six thousand bleacher seats. A more logical site for the game would have been TCU's twenty-thousand-seat stadium. But Russell had lost a coin flip with the Corsicana coach.

Really, it made little sense for the game to be played in Corsicana. The stadium could not possibly hold all of the Mighty Mites' followers. Russell had offered Corsicana school officials more than the normal fifty-fifty split of the gate to waive the traditional coin flip and to play the game in the larger Fort Worth venue. But they balked and hired a construction crew to expand the stadium.

At that moment, two other special trains from different parts of the state were rumbling toward Corsicana. Each was packed with Mighty Mites fans. One had departed earlier that morning from Lubbock in West Texas, and yet another from Tyler in East Texas. Fans, in spite of the tough times, would be traveling by car from all over the state. They were coming in from San Antonio and Longview and Sweetwater. Some would find their way on foot, others on horseback. Nothing could stop them from seeing their beloved Mighty Mites.

This love affair between the general populace of Texas and the little band of orphans was hard to fathom. Granted, most folks in the state were long in love with the game of football. It was as indigenous as oil wells and tumbleweed. But most football fans focused all of their energy on the local team. Living in Midland meant your heart went out to the Rebels. In Port Lavaca, the sun rose and set on the Sand Crabs. Folks in Winters lived and died with the Blizzards.

But the Mites had become like a magnet to anyone looking for something to cheer about. They were a reason to live during the Great Depression. A daily newspaper cost only three cents, and ninety percent of the folks were getting their news from the ink rags. Predictably, the sporting press had become captivated with the underdog orphans, to the point that typewriters clacked night and day with the heart-warming stories. This was especially the case in Fort Worth, where the Mighty Mites now received more coverage than the TCU Horned Frogs. The Mites, playing in a stadium that held but five thousand fans, were already outdrawing the big college team.

It seemed that everyone from El Paso to Orange, from Dalhart to Brownsville had taken a fancy to the perennial underdogs in the tattered uniforms.

That morning, *Star-Telegram* sportswriter Leroy Menzing had written:

Whether it's the Gulf Coast or in the Panhandle, you can find ardent supporters of the Mighty Mites. They are not just the boys of Fort Worth, but of the entire state, and if they should defeat Corsicana for the championship it is doubtful there will ever be a more popular champion.

In the depths of the Depression, people needed something to cling to. The Mites were the classic underdog, a team for the common man and woman. There was nothing glitzy about the little boys that toiled every Friday night against the bigger boys and came away the winner most of the time. It was the blue collar style of play that inspired the mass appeal. And it did not cost a great amount of money to see the boys play in 1932—a ticket to the game was a dime and a hamburger a nickel.

What better time for the Mighty Mites to emerge as a kind of public property—much like Texas or Texas A&M, or, on a more national level, Notre Dame or Army. The popularity of high school football in Texas had taken off like a fiery burst from a Roman candle. Texas would always be a state of romantics searching for heroes. Naturally, the rough-hewn boys playing football would soon be idolized like the cowboys of old.

This organized version of high school football had taken root in Texas only twenty years earlier. Still, it seemed that everyone wanted a piece of it. Football players had been placed on a pedestal, much like cowboys or the oil wildcatter. Texans did not need to watch B Westerns at the Saturday morning picture show to know what a cowboy looked like.

In some respects, Texas was still a raw and rowdy frontier in the 1930s, and the high school kids in shoulder pads and leather helmets furthered that tough image. Stadiums started filling up right after the end of the Big War. West Texans especially would soon go gaga over football, as the "Oil Belt," which included Ranger, Cisco, Eastland, Breckenridge, and Abilene, became an overnight obsession. Other towns on the fringe of the Oil Belt were Wichita Falls, Electra, and Burkburnett.

In the Oil Belt, the roughnecks, speculators, wildcatters, and tool-pushers had money to wager and an insatiable appetite for winning. Recruiters combed the countryside searching out the best football talent. So hungry were the little towns for a state championship that football fans went to any length to lure a top prospect into their school district. One of the most popular tricks was hiring away any father with talented football-playing sons. A roughneck making a couple of bucks a day in Mineral Wells would gladly take five bucks to pack up move his family to Breckenridge. That is, if he brought along his sons.

A famous story that still makes the rounds in West Texas involves the father of two football-playing sons in the 1920s that refused at any dollar amount to move his family into Breckenridge. The man worked as a math teacher at a country school and enjoyed the lifestyle there. When the Breckenridge money people knocked on his door, he sent them away. But Breckenridge fans were not the kind to take "no" for an answer. Furthermore, they had had a plan. They would wait for the math teacher to take his family on their annual summer driving vacation. While the family was out of town, the boosters uprooted the house and moved it into their school district. They also left this note on the door: "We moved your house. You can move it back. But you have to pay for it."

The family stayed in Breckenridge and, as the story goes, the two boys became all-state players for the Buckaroos.

To the people living outside of the state, it probably seemed inconceivable how obsessive Texans would become with high school football by 1930. Trains packed with fans rumbled about the state, as everyone wanted to see the show. Many wanted to bet on their teams.

The Texas Interscholastic League was started in 1914 with six hundred members, mainly for the purpose of regulating football. The TIL helped bring the sport to a fever pitch. By 1930, the organization had grown to six thousand members.

Until the Depression, most football fans could have cared less what it cost to follow their teams around the state. They came in automobiles, trains, and wagons, and were usually filled to the neck with outlaw whiskey. The oil patch mentality engendered a gambling spirit. Bookies worked the stands and took bets from anyone with the money to back it up.

By the start of the 1932 season, the Depression was like a black cloud hanging over Texas. But that did not stop the true believers from following the Mighty Mites to every game. And it certainly was not about to slow down the three trains loaded with fans now converging on Corsicana. People from all walks of life were coming, regardless of the financial sacrifices.

One of the vagaries of this wild rush to Corsicana was the diversity of people it attracted. Pop Boone and Amon Carter were an odd sight as they boarded the Union Pacific out of Fort Worth together. Here were two men born into different worlds, viewing life through different prisms.

Carter was both a cheerleader and a one-man Chamber of Commerce. He was the personal friend of Charles Lindbergh, Franklin D. Roosevelt, Amelia Earhart, Gary Cooper, and Will Rogers. He had helped found the *Fort Worth Star-Telegram* in 1909, and by 1923 had ascended to the publisher's office. Not a minute passed when Carter was not banging the drums on behalf of Cowtown. He had been a force behind Fort Worth's phenomenal growth, literally herding businesses to his city. He even picked a verbal fight with Dallas, which he considered a fancy, snooty, silk-stocking kind of town.

One of Carter's proudest moments was coining a phrase that had swept the city: "Fort Worth is Where the West Begins." Each day it was emblazoned across the top of page 1A of the *Star-Telegram*.

There was nothing Amon Carter would not do for his beloved Fort Worth. The man also possessed an amazing aptitude for ignoring the obvious. Thanks to the grand power of personality, he actually believed he could will away the Depression. One of his front-page editorials in early 1932 stated that the dark economic cloud consuming America was nothing more than a "ridiculous spectacle, idle gossip, unfounded rumors, and a state of hysterior [*sic*]."

Granted, the Depression arrived late in Fort Worth and did not seize the city until the end of 1931. Unlike most of America, the wide presence of oil dollars kept the Texas economy chugging along even after the stock market crash of 1929. Cowtown had been lubricated by the great Ranger oil strike, and most of the big hitters were convinced the economy was indestructible. That feeling began to fade, though, as the banks started to fail.

In January 1932, one of the city's biggest financial institutions, Texas National Bank, cratered as customers made a rush on the front door and demanded their money. Lawmen attempted to force people outside, but they refused to budge and the bank began paying out.

Two weeks later, the First National Bank, with its $24 million in assets, stood on the brink of disaster. A huge mob crashed into the lobby as thousands demanded their money. Within minutes, the streets were clogged and hundreds more were pushing their way inside. Sheriff Red Wright and a posse of deputies were dispatched. But there was no turning back the panicking masses.

That afternoon, Amon Carter was at home in bed with the flu. But when he heard about the bank run, he dressed and hurried downtown. He climbed upon a lobby table and, much like George Bailey in *It's a Wonderful Life,* began to address the depositors.

"I was sick in bed," he said. "And I just couldn't believe this thing when I first heard it. Why, this is the safest bank in the world and you'll soon find out. It is paying off every dollar just as fast as you are passing your checks, and for every dollar it is paying you, it is taking in six more. Why, right now two and a half million is coming from the Federal Reserve Bank in Dallas."

Just then a convoy of heavily-armed men swept into the lobby with huge sacks of money.

"See there!" Amon cried. "What did I tell you!"

He then convinced Pappy Waggoner to address the people.

Waggoner slowly climbed up on the same table and raised his right hand. "I hereby pledge to you every cent I own and possess in the world that you shall not lose a single dollar in this bank!"

Folks knew that Waggoner was the richest man in Texas. But that still did not stem the tide. So Carter sent out for cheese sandwiches and hot dogs and managed to convince two orchestras to haul their instruments into the bank lobby. They played "Singing in the Rain" and "Hail, Hail, the Gang's All Here." The music soothed the crowd and before long every customer that had withdrawn money was now putting it back in.

If Carter was the city's biggest booster, Pop Boone was its biggest cynic. He was not afraid to smack the big boys around in print. This is not to say that he was critical of the athletes he covered. But Pop was never one to blindly follow the company line—especially when it was being espoused by the Big Hats. He was a perfect fit for the *Fort Worth Press*, the smaller and the much feistier of two newspapers.

Pop stood by the common man while Carter's allegiance was to progress at any cost. It agitated city promoters to no end that Pop Boone often shared with his readers his views of the Great Depression. City fathers preferred to ignore the ugly beast. But the "Popper," as he called himself, was not one to overlook winos curled up on the street.

"We have panhandlers everywhere in the downtown area," he once wrote. "I don't mind giving a panhandler a two-bit piece. I never turn a guy down and I never ask him what he wants it for. I never give them more than two bits and I try to believe in my heart it will do 'em good. Sometimes a guy needs a drink worse than he needs a meal, although that seems an awful thing to say.

"I'd much rather hand a guy two-bits than have one of those low-down sneaks lift my radiator cap. Three times now my radiator cap has been swiped and they cost me two bucks apiece. Thieves can't possibly get more than twenty-five cents for them. I hope that when I come up to my car and catch one of those so-and-so, blankety-blank thieves snitching the cap off my radiator that the guy won't be very big or tough. If he is, then I'll probably get sent to the hospital."

Carter had trouble hating a fellow Fort Worthian. But Pop Boone had tested his patience. Not only did he write for the competing newspaper, he took shots at his own town.

Carter peered across the aisle at the aging writer now dreamily watching the empty farmland rush past.

"Pop, I'm surprised your rag could come up with enough dough to send you all the way to Corsicana," Carter said.

"Actually, I'm paying my own way," Boone said. "But looking at that bulge in your pocket, I was wondering, Amon. Could a rich man spare a poor man a shot of liquor?" (Boone spelled it "licker" in his column)

Carter realized his fruit jar was protruding from beneath in his topcoat. "I don't drink with the enemy," he said.

"I'm not the enemy, see," Boone said. "We're both on the same side when it comes to the Mighty Mites. Look, Amon, it's high time that you started thinking about building a new stadium for those boys. The whole town, the whole state is trying to get tickets to their games."

The Mites played most of their home games at La Grave Field, situated on the banks of the Trinity River between downtown and the stockyards. The park had been built in 1926 for the Fort Worth Cats of the Texas League and was not well suited for the game of football. No more than five thousand fans could squeeze into the place, and flocks of fans of the Mighty Mites were being turned away in droves each time they played.

As the train rumbled south, Music could be heard from one end to the other. Practically all of the fifty passenger cars had its own barbershop quartet, and most were stuck on "Sweet Adeline." A drunk walked from car to car announcing "Next Stop Ennis! Next Stop Ennis!" There would be no stopping in Arlington, or Oak Cliff, or Ennis, or anywhere else along the route. Whizzing past the small towns, the farms, the ranches, and the dairies, Pop began to compose in his head the story that would appear that very afternoon in the *Press*.

"Some people asked me if there were any drunks on the train," he wrote. "I said the real question was whether there were any sobers on the train."

Carter was now working his way from car to car, hoping to find a sucker willing to bet on Corsicana. The man loved to drink, gamble, and womanize. But mostly he loved to bet on football games. He managed to find a half-dozen bookmakers willing to give him the Mites plus ten, and it did not seem to faze him they were shading the line by four points.

It was twelve-thirty, an hour before kickoff, when the train pulled into Corsicana and slowly passed the stadium. Passengers with a good view of the stadium could not believe their eyes. All twelve thousand seats were already occupied. Fans ringed the field six and seven deep and some were trespassing onto the playing surface. There would be no room for the Fort Worth fans.

"This is a bunch of crap!" a man sitting next to Boone yelled. "The damned Corsicana fans done took everything."

The band stopped playing and the quartets stopped singing.

The Mighty Mites were on the field warming up, and Pop craned his neck to catch a glimpse of Rusty Russell. It was not what he had hoped to see. The easygoing, bespectacled coach wore a worried expression for the first time he could ever remember. Pop sensed chaos.

Something did not smell right.

Chapter 6

THE DARK HORSE

The town of Corsicana was in chaos thirty minutes before kickoff. Pop Boone surveyed the scene from the press box and unleashed a long trail of cigar smoke.

"You let a stinking little town have a game of this magnitude and look what happens," he said. "Should've played the game in Fort Worth."

Fans were pouring over the walls behind the south end zone and others had torn a hole in the chain-link fence on the west side. So many loitered on the field that the teams had little room to warm up. Boone surmised that Rusty Russell's worried look had something to do with the drunken riot about to break out.

The Mighty Mites actually had more urgent problems. Food poisoning had swept through the team the previous night, when six players started throwing up right after returning to the hotel from a local steak house. Some had vomited and suffered from severe diarrhea until the sunrise. Russell did not suspect a conspiracy. But Doc Hall did.

"Somebody put something in those boys' food," Hall said. "I just know it."

It did seem shady that the entire backfield had gotten sick, and that Scott McCall, the team's best player, was the most affected. Doc Hall had treated all of the players with paregoric, an antiperistaltic designed to head off the symptoms of diarrhea. But it was too late to save some of the boys already running to the toilet.

At seven that morning, Russell had considered contacting the Texas Interscholastic League about postponing the game. Half a dozen of his players were still lying on the floor, barely able to move, and the kickoff was but six and a half hours away. Now, though, McCall was beginning to keep fluids down and the others said they were feeling better.

"It's not like we can call back to the Home and order up a bunch of new football players," Hall said. "This is all we got—twelve orphan kids."

Doc Hall was known to speak his mind, and had been doing so around the orphanage for the last thirty-two years. Some thought he was just a crotchety old doctor. Deep down, though, there was nothing he loved more than attending to the needs of the orphans. In truth, he treated the kids as if they were his own. Somehow, he managed to juggle a profitable practice in downtown Fort Worth with his work at the Masonic Home. He fixed broken bones, removed tonsils, and settled stomachs. Everyone knew that Doc Hall spent more time with the kids than he did with his paying patients, but he had never asked the Masonic Home for a dime.

Every few weeks, principal Thomas Fletcher would ask, "Doc, when are you going to send us a bill?"

Doc's standard response: "You worry about being the principal and I'll worry about taking care of the kids."

Good to his word, the bill had never arrived.

Hall was a thin man who chain-smoked and was propelled by nervous energy. Some of the kids made fun of him (behind his back, of course) because his right eye was not aligned with his left. The right eye, in fact, was known to wander in just about every direction. Sometimes it was hard to tell if he was looking at you or around you.

More than anything in the world, Doc Hall loved football and football players. He never missed a practice or a game. Russell could always count on him to fix the injured kids and to get them back onto the field as soon as possible. He could also count on hearing plenty of opinions.

"I'm telling you, Mr. Russell," he said. "I have seen a lot of food poisoning in my in life. I know for a fact that somebody did us dirty on this one."

Russell would not be ruffled. "We can't know that for sure. And I don't want this to get out. The Corsicana coaches don't need to know that we've got a weak bunch of players."

Doc Hall had been up all night trying to get the boys ready to play a Corsicana team with forty-four healthy players. Like the coach, he was worried that the weakened Mighty Mites would not have the energy to last four quarters.

An hour before kickoff, Russell tried to focus on the game, but spent too much of his time dodging inebriated fans. Most were hustling bets with local bookmakers. The Home was getting fourteen points and men like Amon Carter and Pappy Waggoner were scooping up all of the action they could find, as were most of the Masons. Carter was as aggressive about betting as he was about life. At the racetrack, he spent most of his day at the hundred-dollar window and was known to drink and play poker in Suite 10G of the Fort Worth Club for forty-eight straight hours. Carter, unlike many of his gambling buddies, was no degenerate and won far more often than he lost.

Russell wondered if the plungers would still be flaunting the same confidence if they knew the Mites had been wearing out the hotel toilets.

The scene on the field was nothing short of bizarre, and Russell prayed the police would show up and fix the mess. But he sensed the masses were going nowhere. Some had traveled great distances and were emotionally attached to the little football team that made such big headlines. Men were mostly dressed in suits and ties. Some wore fedoras and topcoats. Women were decked out in dresses and fine jewelry that had been locked away for years. Folks, at least for this one day, were acting as if the Depression had never happened. Tomorrow they would again be scraping pennies together and praying for relief from a strangled economy.

The game was to be broadcast over KFJZ radio back in Fort Worth, right after *The Lawrence Welk Show*. The lineup following the game was *Amos 'n' Andy*, Guy Lombardo, and Groucho Marx.

In the press box, play-by-play man Byron Saam gazed down upon the madhouse and tried to make sense of it all. He told his listeners,

"They say we are going to play a football game here today. I don't know how. First, they're going to need a bulldozer to get all these people off the field. Then they're going to need a mighty big drunk tank to hold them all."

Russell searched the crowd for a single cop and found none. He wanted to walk across the field and demand that Corsicana coach Johnny Pierce do something. But there was no way he was going to make it through the crowd. Up in the press box, Pop Boone was searching the crowd with binoculars for anyone vaguely resembling a law enforcement officer.

"I ran into one cop when I came through the gate," Boone said to another sportswriter. "And he was stinking-assed drunk."

Six thousand seats had been haphazardly added to the stadium and seating capacity was now twelve thousand. Boone and the other sportswriters estimated that at least eighteen thousand, either by hook or crook, had found their way inside, and that meant that the stadium attendance record was about to be broken in triplicate. Some had climbed light poles to get a better view, others were standing atop cars and buses out in the streets, hoping to catch some of the action.

Russell studied the low gray clouds. A sudden snowstorm would be devastating. The field was already icy slick, as most of the grass had been worn away by the wear and tear of the long season. Farmland in this part of the country was black with rich minerals that produced a mother lode of cotton. It also produced loose topsoil that provided little traction. This would be yet another strike against the Mighty Mites' passing offense.

Russell could not remember the last time a pleasant thought had passed through his mind. He had dreamed of the day when he would lead the ultimate underdog into the biggest game of the year. Granted, it had taken only five years to build this program from the ground up. But now it seemed the whole world was trying to ruin it.

The last couple of weeks, Russell had found time to scout Corsicana. But now, as he stood on the field and measured the brawny Tigers up close, they looked different. He saw a bevy of large, raw-boned country boys with a fierce determination in their eyes. Some boasted thick beards and looked almost as old as Russell himself. In physical stature, they were men, compared to his boys. There really was no telling just how old these boys might be, as the Texas Interscholastic League rarely checked birth certificates, and it was fashionable around the state to keep the veterans around past graduation. The orange vertical stripes on the Tigers' jerseys enhanced their animal-like auras. On offense, they utilized a powerful running game that knocked the wind out of the opposition. Their defense was the best by far in the state, allowing only two touchdowns all season. They would outweigh the Mighty Mites in the line by forty pounds per man.

Russell noticed that his players were spending too much time sizing up the Tigers. So he rounded up the boys much earlier than he had planned and they all headed back to the dressing room for some mental refueling. He could only keep his fingers crossed that the crowd problem would be resolved by the time they returned.

Worry was carving a hole in Russell's stomach. Two days earlier, he had agreed to something that he now regretted. If the game ended in a tie, the state champion would be crowned on the basis of twenty-yard-line penetrations. This was a bad idea. There was nothing wrong with having cochampions in the case of a tie.

Now the coach was trying to envision how the game would play out. He considered all of the elements—the field, the weather, the crowd, the powerful Corsicana defense, and the dehydration of his players. His calculations further depressed him. He could actually see the game ending in a scoreless tie.

"WE WILL DO our very best to keep the crowd back. But if a ball carrier comes into contact with a fan, he is down at that point. The police chief, however, assures me that he can keep the fans behind the lines."

The voice belonged to Roy Henderson, the head of the Texas Interscholastic League, a man Russell did not trust. He knew that Henderson had disapproved of the Mites' promotion into Class A, and he sensed that the TIL would someday exploit its power and kick the Mites back down.

In the past thirty minutes, local police had somehow managed to move the restless crowd back behind the boundaries. But Russell was not sure they would stay put.

As the opening kickoff sailed into the air, eighteen thousand voices sounded like a locomotive roaring past.

Russell felt discombobulated. Fans were breathing down his back and he had been knocked around a few times. But as he surveyed his players on the field, he realized that at least some of their energy had been restored. In spite of having only twelve players, this was an outstanding team that had come together practically overnight. Leon Pickett and Allie White were two of the best linemen in the state. Scott McCall, Donkey Roberts, and Harold McClure were outstanding runners and receivers. Perry Pickett was still learning the quarterback position, and his passing would suffer on this windy day. But Russell knew that Perry was a gamer and he would find a way to move the offense.

On the first play, Picket called forty-seven sweep. Tailback Scott McCall was to carry the ball around right end—the "four" back through the "seven" hole. Center Roland Kelsay snapped the ball toward McCall, who had inexplicably taken off in the other direction. The ball sailed high into the wide open spaces and then rolled and rolled. Leon Pickett scrambled for the ball and managed to dive on it just ahead of four Corsicana players.

McCall walked slowly back to the huddle with his head down. For years he had struggled with a stuttering problem. "Ga-ga-goddamn," he said. "I f-f-forgot my own ga-ga-goddamn number."

His teammates laughed and that helped to settle a few nerves. It did nothing, however, to kick the stagnant offense into gear. In the first quarter, Pickett was 0 for 7 against the strong wind. Players consciously avoided the sideline for fear they would come into contact with a fan and be called down. Both teams were punting enough to keep birds away from the stadium.

Late in the first quarter Bailey Thorpe, all 120 pounds of him, circled under a punt at the Masonic Home twenty-yard line. Fans were starting to encroach onto the field, and a cluster of rowdies tried to encourage the little orphan to run it all the way back. But their loud voices became a distraction and he fumbled the ball and watched it roll to the fifteen-yard line, where it was recovered by Corsicana. The Tigers had their first official "penetration" of the day.

Minutes later, Thorpe fumbled again and the ball rolled inside the twenty, where Corsicana recovered another freebie. They now led 2–0 in penetrations.

The sidelines were becoming more ragged by the play. There was simply not enough room for everybody, and about half of them needed to go. Russell complained to the officials and got nowhere. By the middle of the second quarter spectators were ten yards beyond the boundary lines, and that is when the police, the referee, and Henderson convened and decided to temporarily halt play. The players removed their shoulder pads and took a seat on the field while the police barked at the crowd through megaphones: "If you don't leave the field immediately, we are going to call off the game." Fans stood their ground. Five, ten, fifteen minutes passed and nobody budged. The delay of game reached fifty minutes and the head coaches were called to the middle of the field.

"Look," Henderson said to Pierce and Russell. "We can't tell these fans to leave, because they'll start a riot. We can't stop the game, because we have a championship on the line. We are going to allow the fans to come onto the field and stand behind the offensive huddle."

"You've *got* to be kidding," Russell said.

"We have no other choice."

"Let me ask you something, Mr. Commissioner," Johnny Pierce finally spoke up. "What happens if a pass is intercepted? How is the player going to return it through the middle of that crowd?"

"We'll just have to see what happens."

The weirdest scene in the history of Texas sports had just gotten weirder.

Then it took a horrible turn for the worst.

Russell could not believe his eyes as a huge section of the west stands collapsed. Hundreds of fans were slung to the ground like ragdolls. Those in the upper rows had fallen some fifteen feet, and there were piles of people everywhere.

Russell's heart felt like it was beating out of his chest. There was no telling how many fans were down. And the coach had no idea where Juanita, Betty, and his new baby, Rusty Jr., were sitting. Russell had been so distracted before kickoff that he had forgotten to check on his family.

All eyes were now on the scene of the catastrophe. Russell studied the area for familiar faces and saw plenty. Several orphans were tangled in the mess and it was not difficult to read the fear on their faces. Police and regular citizens rushed toward the fallen victims and began to unpile them.

There came a voice from behind the Masonic Home bench. "Rusteeee." It was Juanita. She and the kids had been sitting a few rows up on the east side and were safe. For the first time since the stands fell, the coach was able to breathe.

Across the field, rescuers were still digging. What they found brought a great sense of relief to everyone. There were no broken bones and only a few scattered injuries. Some had suffered abrasions and others sprained ankles. One man had to be taken to the hospital with a separated shoulder, but quite miraculously, most of the fans seemed okay.

"If nobody's really hurt, that's amazing," Russell said to himself.

Russell could not believe what happened next. The referee walked over to the Masonic Home sideline said, "Okay, fellas, let's play ball."

"What!" Russell protested. "Can't we at least wait for those people to get up off the ground?"

"We got a game to finish," Roscoe Minton yelled. "Now get your boys back on the field."

Henderson, asserting his power, strode quickly toward Russell. "Get your boys ready or we'll drop a penalty flag on you."

Russell wondered if they would be in the same rush if the Mighty Mites were ahead by two penetrations.

The coach was still confident that the Mighty Mites could win. They had displayed their normal grit and hustle. But he would learn that the fifty-five-minute delay, followed by the collapsing of the stands, had taken the starch out of his sick players. They became sluggish, losing two fumbles, and by halftime Corsicana had a three–zip lead in penetrations.

Even the most casual observer realized that neither team was likely to score in the second half. Both offenses were in a rut.

"The Mites have lost their piss and vinegar," Pop Boone said in the press box. "Every time the ball goes on the ground, the Corsicana boys get it."

No one in the stands or the press box could comprehend what had gone wrong with the Mighty Mites. Four interceptions and two fumbles had destroyed any momentum they could muster. They were not the same feisty kids. The game was now in the fourth quarter and time was running out.

"They're getting tired," Boone announced to everyone in the press box. "It's been a long season and they only got twelve boys."

Late in the game, with the game still tied 0–0 and Corsicana holding a 3–1 lead in penetrations, Scott McCall threw up a desperation pass. The ball sailed high into the gathering darkness and was intercepted and returned to the Home fifteen. Corsicana now led 4–1 in penetrations, but it hardly mattered with only seconds left to play. The Tigers hammered the ball into the line and the Mites tried to steal it away.

McCall approached the referee. "What if I steal the ball and take off running? I can't get through that ga-goddamn crowd."

"Just do-do the best you-you can," Roscoe Minton said.

The clock ticking down, Corsicana was one yard from the end zone. McCall shouted at his teammates, "We are not going to let them score! We are not going to let them score!"

In one last act of defiance, McCall, White, and Leon Pickett teamed to stop running back Don Kessinger twice, just inches from the goal. As the game ended, Minton scooped up the ball and pulled the trigger on the final gun. Hundreds of fans took off running in all directions, and it could be said that Minton finally found a way to disperse the crowd.

Russell, as he pushed through the masses en route to the dressing room, could not understand why so many people were slapping him on the back. Then he remembered the wagers. The Masonic Home bettors had taken anywhere from ten to fourteen points.

In the dressing room, the coach never mentioned the food poisoning to the gang of reporters. The next day in the *Star-Telegram*, Minton was quoted as saying, "Corsicana had more fire and fight than Masonic Home. The Mighty Mites looked tired and I guess the long schedule got to them."

Russell could have played the role of the victim. He could have told everyone that his team had been thrown a curveball at the last minute. He could have pointed to a possible conspiracy with the food poisoning. No doubt, his team had been badly handicapped by the diarrhea that robbed them of energy. Russell could have corrected the critics who said that his team ran out of gas at the most crucial point in the season. He had several chances to inform the press about the weakened condition of his players. But the good soldier never uttered a word.

Why?

For one, it was not his style. He had been taught long ago never to whimper or moan or to blame someone else for his troubles. Life is tough, so accept the consequences. With the good also comes the bad, and vice versa. What buoyed his spirit was knowing there was outstanding talent on the way up—boys like Hardy Brown, Jeff Brown, Dewitt Coulter, and C. D. Sealy. The best days were still ahead. His first five years at the Home had brought radical change. There would be other trips to the big game. Now it was time to refocus and get back to work.

"Someday we will win a championship," he told the Mighty Mites.

They believed him.

Chapter 7

LITTLE RASCALS

Old Blue trucked the fourth-grade orphans into the tree-lined Sycamore Park, where the boys from Riverside were waiting.

"Orphans! Orphans! Look at the dumb *orphans.*"

The little footballers were now fighting mad. Before the truck could sputter to a halt, ten-year-old Hardy Brown leaped from the back and confronted the first heckler.

"Who're you calling an orphan?" he said.

"You."

"Not any more." Hardy connected with a left-right combo that sent the boy flying. Teeth were loosened and blood dripped from his nostrils. He would not be playing much football that day.

Hardy sneaked a peek at Mr. Russell, who looked the other way. Russell had set the brake, stepped out of the cab, and was now nonchalantly arranging the whistle around his neck.

Just twelve hours earlier, Russell had coached the varsity team to victory at La Grave Field. After the game, he caught a few winks, rose from bed at dawn, drank some coffee, and fired up Old Blue for the trip down to Sycamore Park. Now he was trying to pretend that he had not seen Hardy Brown smack the Riverside kid in the face.

C. D. Sealy, the little team's quarterback, grabbed Hardy by the arm. He was practically out of breath.

"Mr. Russell saw it. And he didn't do a danged thing."

The code of the Masonic Home was that orphans could call each other "orphans." But nobody on the outside would ever get away with it. Most of the kids around the local neighborhoods were starting to learn.

Nobody crossed little Hardy Brown.

After six years at the Home, Hardy was not much different than the other boys in size or overall athletic ability. But everyone could see that a fire was burning inside the boy. He did nothing at half speed. Football had become second nature to Hardy, and he loved to mix it up with the others. Russell had not once instructed him on how to block or tackle, because he was a natural at both and loved the contact.

The game of football can be a rush of adrenaline for those who are not afraid to hit or be hit. In truth, football is anti-intuitive. You were not born to strap on shoulder pads and to smack somebody in the teeth. Football is not for everybody. Football is something you must learn either through instruction or by watching others. Studying the bigger boys as they beat the hell out of each really fired Hardy up.

What his friends saw in Hardy were actually two personalities. As a football player, he was a scrapper and a fighter. But around the Home—going to class, working in the dairy, attending Sunday worship service—he was a quiet, polite boy, always saying "yes sir" and "no ma'am" and minding the teachers. He was practically a straight-A student. The little girls adored him because of his smile and good looks, and they always kept an eye on him.

C. D. Sealy had once said, "Hardy Brown, you're going to be a lady-killer one day."

Hardy frowned. "You're crazy. I'm never going to kill any ladies."

Because it was late September 1934, the diminutive orphans were still barefoot. Their football uniforms were no different from their everyday wear—overalls badly worn at the knees and a dirty T-shirt. Most did not even possess a leather helmet. The Riverside football team owned more gear than a war platoon: shoulder pads, hip pads, thigh pads, knee pads, leather football shoes with cleats, and brand-new helmets that matched.

Orphan Mike Simmons once wrote of these Saturday morning games, "One of my Baptisms in football was playing right guard, with Freckles Holman playing the other. We played in coveralls and barefooted. All of the boys played football, from fifty pounds and up, even Corky Nelson, whose leg had been removed from just below the knee. He wore a wooden leg, and that was one of our better weapons against the Peacock Brothers of Poly High, or North Side's Firehall Steers, which were our toughest competition at Sycamore Park each Saturday morning."

As the teams warmed up, the referee approached Russell. "Coach, congratulations on winning your high school game last night. I really think you got a shot at that state championship this year."

Russell nodded and smiled. It had been two years since the high school team had reached the state championship game against Corsicana.

The referee went on. "I sure enjoy watching your high school team. But I can't wait for this game to start. You got a bunch of savvy little boys here."

Russell knew that of course, otherwise he would not have matched his seventy-five-pounders against the hundred-and-five-pounders from Riverside. He was putting third and fourth graders up against junior high boys.

What Russell saw on this fine autumn morning was a bunch of orphans endowed with football moxie. Little Hardy Brown, with his fearlessness and full-speed aggressiveness, was at the head of the class. No one could singlehandedly bring him down. On defense, he was the hardest hitter for a ten-year-old that Russell had ever seen.

The brothers Ray and Dewitt Coulter had arrived at the Home five years earlier as a couple of cowering kids who were homesick night and day. Then they started to grow. Plenty of leg was sticking out of their overalls.

"I hope nothing happens to the Coulters," Rusty had said to Juanita. "They'll be the first big players we've ever had on the high school team."

C. D. Sealy was a feisty kid who had a decent arm for a little quarterback and ran the football with the same fire as Hardy. C.D. was called "Wheatie." A cereal-eating contest had been held in the dining hall one morning, and C.D. had knocked down eight bowls of a new brand called "Wheaties." Regardless of how much he ate, "Wheatie" still looked like a broom handle with feet.

Just about all of the boys that came to the orphanage were tagged with a nickname. There was a Dinky, Pinky, Donkey, Red, Soap, Chigger, Chicken, Moko, Choc, Floppy, Tinfoil, Beer Belly, Fish Ear, Curly, Baldy, Freckles, Pee Wee, Trash Can, Possum, and Buck.

Leonard "Snoggs" Roach got his nickname because he was snaggletoothed. The boys were still learning to spell. More apropos might have been the use of his last name. He was about the size of a roach. Snoggs, even on his best days, weighed no more than sixty pounds. That did not stop Russell from putting him in the starting lineup each Saturday morning at Sycamore Park. The boy was a gritty, low-flying fireball that hit below the knees and turned kids upside down.

Clyde "Teague" Roberts was from the town of Teague, Texas. Floyd "Brownie" Lewis got his nickname from his large brown eyes.

No one knew much about Cecil "Crazy" Moseley, because he rarely talked. Teachers were baffled that he muted himself even when he knew the answer to their questions. That was about 99 percent of the time. A paddling in front of the entire class had never changed his mind.

One of his teachers, Mrs. Billingsley, caught the kids in the act of passing notes one day and yelled, "Give me that, Cecil." Instead of handing it over, Crazy stuffed it into his mouth and swallowed. His fellow orphans loved it, but Mrs. Billingsley was left with no choice. She pulled out the paddle again.

Crazy's brother, Miller Moseley, was the brightest student in the entire school and an outstanding end on the junior high team. At least Miller opened his mouth from time to time.

"Crazy" had been Cecil's handle for so long that few kids could remember his Christian name. This so incensed his sister, Dorothy, that one day she wagged her finger at the perpetrators. "If y'all don't stop calling him 'Crazy,' he's going to think he *is*."

Crazy did not seem to mind. He just laughed.

One of the rites of passage at the Home was crossing Black Bridge at Sycamore Creek with a freight train bearing down on you. This was part of the fun-and-games of summer weekends, when the creek called out to the boys as the sirens once lured Odysseus. The boys would wait until the train rounded the bend and then dive into the deep, clear water. One day, everyone jumped but Crazy. He took off running, and with his arms wildly pumping, he looked like he was trying to outrun the train.

"Jump, Crazy, jump!" they yelled.

When the train passed, the other boys quickly climbed back onto the bridge and looked for Crazy. They looked everywhere. They prayed. A minute passed, then another. There was not a ripple on the water. There was no sign of Crazy.

"Crazy's dead," Wheatie finally said. "That train ran him over."

They waited and prayed. Then, from the other side of the bridge, a head suddenly popped out of the water. Crazy had made a last-second leap and managed to hold his breath underwater for more than two minutes.

"Crazy, you're really crazy," Wheatie shouted down at him.

Crazy laughed, but not a single word came out of his mouth.

SATURDAY MORNINGS WITH the little boys had become as gratifying to Russell as the games under the Friday night lights of La Grave Field. It seemed that the orphans, in spite of their size, were born to play football.

Today, Russell knew he could sit back, relax, and enjoy the show. The boys would not need much coaching—for sure no motivating. The Riverside players had taken care of that when they called them "orphans."

In spite of the huge weight disadvantage, Russell knew his boys were a lot tougher than the Riverside kids. God knew, he had been breaking up fights around the orphanage since the day he walked into the place in 1927. Still, one of his players had yet to catch on to the tough-guy image. His name was Dewitt Coulter and he was by far the biggest player among the diminutive orphans. Dewitt, even after five years at the Home, still suffered from homesickness. The orphans often picked on him.

A couple of minutes before kickoff, Russell noticed Dewitt propping up something on the bench. He walked over and noticed that Dewitt had a teddy bear.

"What is that, Dewitt?" Russell said.

"His name is Pudge," Dewitt said. "I brought him because he wants to watch the game."

"I'll keep an eye on him," Russell said. "I'm sure he'll enjoy watching you boys play."

Russell chuckled to himself. Sometimes he overlooked the fact they were really just kids—ten-year-old boys, in fact. Yes, they were the most resilient cusses he had ever seen in his life. Some were meaner than snakes. But deep down, they were just a bunch of shoeless little orphans.

Russell felt sorry for little Dewitt as he trotted onto the field to start the game. The boys were giving him an earful.

"Why'd you bring that teddy bear to the game?" C. D. Sealy asked. "You ain't nothing but a big mama's boy."

Dewitt looked as if he could cry. "I don't have a mama anymore," he said.

Riverside was now teeing up the ball to start the game, and Hardy Brown could not wait to get his hands on it. He returned the kickoff ninety yards for a touchdown. Then Sealey connected with tight end Ray Coulter over the middle for a sixty-six-yard score. "Snoggs" Roach scooped up a fumble and returned it for a touchdown, and even Crazy got into the act, returning a tipped pass for a touchdown.

The Riverside boys tried to step on the orphans' bare feet, but the Mighty Mites were too quick. The Riversiders rammed their shoulder pads into Snoggs's gut, but he just laughed. Snoggs did not even wear a helmet.

The score was 61–0 midway through the third quarter, when the Riverside coach asked Russell to call off the dogs. Hardy and the boys packed their meager belongings and took off.

Old Blue sputtered toward home.

And no one dared to call them orphans.

Chapter 8

TILL THE DEATH

Life inside the football team rarely got off track, because Rusty Russell stayed true to the regimen. Russell was probably the most organized man the orphans would ever meet, and there was no questioning his value as a role model.

On the other hand, life around the orphanage was known to become as calamitous as the scurrying of rats under the henhouse. With so many orphans concocting so many schemes to get in and out of trouble, the two deans—Frank Wynn and William Henry Remmert—always had their hands full. It seemed they were always breaking up fights, or catching kids trying to sneak through the fence, or busting them with stolen grape juice. Not a single day passed when Remmert or Wynn did not dole out licks.

The orphans had learned to give Big Frank Wynn a wide berth. Big Frank, the dean of the little boys, could clear out a room by walking into it. He stood six foot three and weighed 260 pounds. His water started boiling at thirty-three degrees.

Wynn was in charge of the boys of ages five through thirteen. When an orphan reached his thirteenth birthday, he came under the purview of William Henry Remmert.

Wynn was waxing and polishing his black Ford one afternoon as the sun was setting over Fort Worth. Hardy Brown decided to play a little prank. Big Frank was working a rag over one of his rear hubcaps, so Hardy placed his head between the sun and the tire and managed to block out the light. The hubcap was now in the shadow created by Hardy's head. Big Frank turned around and glared at the boy. Hardy should have heeded the warning and bolted. But his little gag seemed innocent enough. Big Frank finally threw down the rag and stormed across the driveway. He snatched up Hardy, turned him upside down, and held him by his ankles. Then he shook the boy until every bone in his body rattled, and then dropped him squarely on his head.

As Hardy lay moaning on the ground, the boys thought he was dying. But he got up and staggered back to the dormitory. On reaching the front steps, he turned and set his menacing eyes on the big man. "When I grow up," he said, "I'm going to kill Mr. Wynn."

He was not the first orphan or the last to feel that way.

No one else at the Home, not even William Henry Remmert, meted out the same harsh brand of punishment. It seemed that Big Frank owned a sadistic streak. He did not want to punish, he wished to maim. Boys had been beaten for years by a rubber hose that left purple welts and deep bruises from their ankles to the middle of their backs.

At age eight, John Mayo weighed no more than seventy pounds soaking wet. He was one of the most imaginative, fun-loving, and clever kids in the Home. He never seemed to stop laughing. Normally he hung out with the older boys because they found his jokes and pranks hilarious. Mayo feared nothing, and this really endeared him to the big kids.

"There is not a room in this orphanage I can't break into," he told them. He was not bragging. The boys had seen him in action enough to know he could jimmy any lock.

John Mayo lived in dormitory Five, situated on the third floor of the little boys' building. Crazy, Teague, Wheatie, Brownie, Snoggs, and Hardy were on the same floor in dorm Six. The building was separated into eight different dormitories, ranging from the five-year-olds on the first floor to the twelve-year-olds on the fourth. You celebrated your thirteenth birthday by moving into the big boys' dorm.

Most of the boys were quick to break the rules. Many sneaked out of the orphanage at night to carouse the neighborhood. Mayo liked to walk the streets of the Poly neighborhood with his older buddies. One night, they were stopped and interrogated by the Fort Worth cops.

"Where do you boys live?"

"Oh, sir, right here in the Poly area," Wheatie said.

"Give me your addresses."

The older boys had their fake addresses already memorized. They casually reeled them off and the cops were starting to believe them. Then John Mayo blurted, "I live right in the middle of Sycamore Creek."

"What's your name, boy?"

"Red Soap."

The cop flashed his light in the boy's eyes. "Okay, let me get this straight. You want me to believe that your name is Red Soap. And you're telling me that you live in the middle of Sycamore Creek with the snakes and the fishes."

"That's correct, sir."

"Well, then it looks like we're going to have to call Mr. Wynn."

Wheatie knew he needed to think fast. "Look, officer, little John here's my brother and he's not real bright. Slightly retarded, really. He lives with me. And I was wondering if you please wouldn't call Mr. Wynn."

"Go home," the cop said. "I don't care where you live. Just don't let me see you out on these streets again tonight."

The boys took off running. When they got back to the Home, Wheatie grabbed his little buddy by the collar. "Where in the hell did you come up with Red Soap?"

"I don't know. I couldn't come up with anything else. All you guys took the good names."

Wheatie had never thought about that.

MOST OF THE kids were let out on Saturday mornings to catch a movie that cost a dime at the nearby Poly Theatre. John Mayo went to see *The Mark of Zorro,* starring Douglas Fairbanks, and it stuck in his mind. The masked man actually had two identities, Señor Zorro and Don Diego. Señor Zorro wielded a mean sword and was the champion of the oppressed people in Spanish California. Zorro left his mark—"Z"—on people, places, and things. That afternoon, upon returning to the orphanage, Mayo left his mark all over the dorm walls—"AZP."

"What the hell does that mean?" Wheatie asked.

"It's my new name. 'Arizona Pete.'"

"I still don't get it," Wheatie said.

Neither did the rest of the boys.

The boy seemed hurt. "Red Soap was no good. What's wrong with Arizona Pete?"

The boys shook their heads. Arizona Pete it was.

Two days later, they were standing on the front porch of the little boy's dormitory when somebody yelled, "Here comes Big Frank!" They all ran for their lives except Arizona Pete.

Big Frank strode up the steps and hovered over Pete. "What the hell you looking at?"

"You."

"Oh, so you want to get smart. Bend over."

Arizona Pete did not shed a tear as the rubber hose connected ten times.

At seven-thirty the next morning, Big Frank rang the bell on the front porch that meant the boys had twenty seconds to line up on the side-walk for roll call. Most were already in place. Hustling around the corner of the dormitory, the last to arrive was Arizona Pete.

"I made it in under twenty seconds, Mr. Wynn," the boy said.

"Doesn't matter. You were last. Bend over."

Big Frank whacked him twenty-five times, then said, "I hear you been writing your initials all over them walls."

"Not me, sir."

"Bend over."

Arizona Pete got ten more.

As the boys prepared for bed that night, Big Frank strolled into the bunk area with the hose dangling from his right hand. His eyes were wide, his chest rising and falling.

"Hardy Brown," he yelled. "Round up four or five orphans and come get him."

"Come get who, sir?"

"Mayo. He's lying on my office floor and he can't get up."

The boys looked at each other and did not say a word. Together they slowly walked down to the dean's office, where Arizona Pete was sprawled on the linoleum floor.

"What'd you do, Pete?" Hardy said.

"He said I had a piece of candy in my pocket."

"How many times did he swat you."

"At least a hundred. I can't get up."

"Can you roll over?"

"Hell no. My butt's on fire."

They picked him up and carried him back into the bunk area. A pall fell over the room as they carefully laid him down on his bunk.

Arizona Pete needed the help of three boys to rise from his bunk the next morning. But he was the first in line for roll call.

Day after day, the boys warned Pete about staying out of trouble.

"I ain't doing nothing," he said. "He's beating me for no reason— no reason at all! I didn't have candy in my pocket. I had a piece of gum."

Wynn was required under Home rules to have a witness present before closing the door and administering a whipping. Lately, he had been calling upon one of the dorm mothers, Mrs. Summers.

"I'd like to get my hands on that fat Mrs. Summers," Arizona Pete said.

"Now hold on, boy," Wheatie said.

"You don't know the story. She comes in the office, and while he's whipping the tar out of me she yells, 'Hit him harder! Hit him harder!' "

Two nights later, as the boys were preparing for bed, Wynn again strolled into the dormitory with a wide smile. The hose was dangling from his hand.

"Hardy, round up the boys and come get him," he said. "He's on my office floor."

The boys walked in as Mrs. Summers nonchalantly strolled out. This time, Arizona Pete was in the fetal position. His body quivered from the pain.

"Get him out of my sight," Wynn yelled.

The boys quickly scooped up Pete, who screamed, "Shit!"

"Lay him down on the floor," Wynn barked. Then he whipped him ten more times.

Pete was shaking from head to toe when they carried him away. Instead of walking up the steps, the boys proceeded down the staircase to the front porch, where they gently laid Arizona Pete on the cool floor. They had worked out a plan and it was time to discuss it.

"He's bleeding from the butt," Hardy said.

Hardy's eyes studied each of the boy's faces. These were his best friends—Wheatie, Teague, Crazy, Brownie, and Snoggs.

"We've got to do something," Hardy said. "I say we take him straight to Mr. Fletcher. Let Mr. Fletcher see what he's doing to Arizona Pete."

Wheatie spoke up. "I've got a better idea. Let's take him to Mr. Russell. Mr. Russell will put his foot down on this."

Hardy shook his head. "Mr. Fletcher is the principal, and he's the one who hires and fires. We need to take him to Mr. Fletcher. We need Big Frank fired."

All of the boys nodded in agreement.

The five little soldiers carried the wounded comrade down the sidewalk toward Mr. Fletcher's residence. Arizona Pete, in spite of his great pain, did not make a sound. Arriving at the front door, Wheatie raised his hand to knock on the door.

"Hold it, guys," Pete said. "This is a bad idea."

"Why?" Brownie said.

"What happens if Mr. Fletcher doesn't see it our way? What if he doesn't throw that bastard out tonight? First thing in the morning, he'll whip *your* butts until *you* bleed."

There was a long silence. Then they quietly carried Arizona Pete back to his bunk.

ACCORDING TO THE Sunday afternoon schedule, Frank Wynn was to escort about thirty older boys from Dorm Eight down to the Trinity River for a day of recreation and swimming.

Neither Wynn nor the boys were particularly fond of the arrangement.

But at precisely three o'clock, they marched down to Inspiration Point, just north of River Oaks, and the orphans started diving into the water. Wynn followed the boys without ever noticing that a hard rain had raised the Trinity over its banks. The river was churning. The water was even dirtier than usual and you could not see your hands three inches below the surface.

Whirlpools had developed along the shore. In a matter of seconds, some of the boys were in trouble and yelling for help. They were being pulled down by the strong undercurrent. Fortunately, Leo Tiburgen, the strongest swimmer of all, had yet to jump into the water. He surveyed the scene and dived in. One by one, he started rescuing the struggling swimmers. Then, with everyone back on the shore, the boys suddenly realized that Wynn was missing.

The orphans stood on the bank and studied the water for any sign of the dean. Suddenly his head broke through the surface and he seemed to be smiling. Then, he vanished again beneath caramel river.

"He's all right," one of the boys said. "He's just jacking around."

No one jumped in to save him.

Seconds later, Wynn's head popped out of the water and he again he seemed to be smiling. Some of the boys were now pointing and laughing. They started trying to guess where he would surface again.

A minute passed, then another, and another. The boys were now standing anxiously at the edge of the water. They realized it was no joke. The man was in trouble. But nobody was willing to jump into the river to attempt a rescue. One boy did run toward town to find a telephone. But the others stayed put on the water's edge, not ready to help the big man in this deathly crisis.

The Fort Worth police arrived in about ten minutes, as did an ambulance. The bloated body of Frank Wynn floated to the surface about a half hour later. His face was blue, his wide-open eyes filled with white mucous. One of the officers attempted mouth-to-mouth resuscitation, but quickly gave up.

The ambulance slowly carried him away.

*　　*　　*

WHEN THE SWIMMERS returned without Wynn, word spread through the orphanage like wildfire.

Wheatie Sealey grabbed Leo Tiburgen by the arm and breathlessly said, "Is he dead?"

"He's really, really dead."

"How do you know?"

"I saw the ambulance take him away."

"How dead did he look?"

"Deader than a doornail."

Children's voices rose up.

"The bastard is dead!"

"Good riddance!"

"He deserved what he got!"

"God is on our side after all!"

Two days later, they buried Frank Wynn at a cemetery not far from the Home.

Chapter 9

DUCK LUCK

Astranger waddled into the orphanage on a day when the Mighty Mites were feeling blue. Being the curious type, and a little hungry, he webbed his way into the middle of the practice field and began to quack.

"That duck is older than me," Doc Hall said. "And fatter than a pig."

This duck was going nowhere fast. He even walked like an old duck.

The boys gathered around and studied him from beak to webbed feet. It was a white, long-necked domestic duck known as a common. And, like Doc Hall had observed, quite heavy.

"Can you pet a duck?" tackle Paul Smith asked.

"If you don't mind losing a couple of fingers," the old doctor said.

"Maybe this duck will lay us some eggs."

"Son, his egg-laying days is over."

The duck arrived on a day when the kids needed a pleasant distraction. They were down in the dumps after losing the opening game of the 1934 season to the Wichita Falls Coyotes by the score of 9–6. It was but their third loss since 1929 and, in truth, the Mighty Mites had nothing to be ashamed of. The Coyotes were one of the best football teams in Texas year in and year out, and had been ranked number two in the preseason polls. But that did not seem to ease their pain. The orphanage was in a state of depression and the Saturday morning trip to the Poly Theatre to see the moving pictures had to be called off.

The kids now waited for the Monday afternoon practice to begin. In the meantime, they walked circles around their new friend.

"I think this duck is lucky," quarterback Perry Pickett said. "What do you think, Doc Hall?"

"It's hard to tell about ducks. I do know one thing about this one. He eats a lot of june bugs."

"I've got a name for this duck," Smith said. "They call us the Mighty Mites. We'll call him the Mighty Duck." Laughter like that had not been heard around the Home for days.

The players started lining up for calisthenics when they saw Rusty Russell approaching the practice field. But the coach, known for his strict practice schedule, did something that surprised all. He walked over and took a long look at the duck.

"Where did this duck come from?" he said.

"It's the Mighty Duck," Smith responded. "He just waddled in. We think he's lucky. Can we keep him, Mr. Russell?"

Russell smiled the knowing smile. Then, as he often did, he said nothing.

The whistle blew and the boys started doing side-straddle hops. They expected the duck to split, but he just stood there and watched.

As the scrimmage began a few minutes later, footballs flew and the orphans slammed into each other like bumper cars at the state fair. But the duck never moved. He flapped his wings and tried to fly off. But old age and a belly filled with june bugs had subverted any hopes of a quick getaway.

FRIDAY EVENING, AS the boys were boarding Old Blue for the trip to La Grave Field, Russell noticed that Paul Smith was carrying something other than his helmet. His hand was wrapped around a handle connected to a large box draped in a blanket.

Russell chuckled to himself and approached the boy.

"What have we here, Paul?"

The boy's eyes were glued to the ground. "Mr. Russell, I was just thinking we could use some luck. The boys and I think that the Mighty Duck is lucky. Mr. Russell, we *need* a win."

The past few days, Mighty Duck had taken to the orphanage like a duck to water. He had attended each practice that week, and when the boys retired to the dormitory at night, he floated about the pond and waited for them to get up. Then he followed them around all day. No wonder he had become tethered to the place. The boys were catching june bugs and feeding him morning, noon, and night.

"Where'd you get the cage?" Russell asked.

"They carry chickens to the slaughterhouse with it. The chicken man said we could borrow it."

"What are we going to do with the Mighty Duck when we get to the stadium?"

"I thought he'd sit on the bench and watch the game."

Russell rubbed his chin. He stepped back to consider all of the factors.

"Who's going to clean up the poop?"

"I will," the boy said.

"We'll take the duck with us this time," Russell said. "But if we don't win . . ."

"We will, Mr. Russell. We will."

Maybe the duck was lucky. The Mites defeated the North Texas Agriculture College that night by the score of 19–6. The Mighty Duck quacked loud enough to be heard above the squawk of the drum-and-bugle corps. He quacked in gratification each time one of the boys tapped the cage. Then he rode with the boys on the bed of Old Blue and quacked all the way back to the orphanage.

The next week, in front of yet another packed house, the Mites defeated Fort Worth Stripling 28–6. North Side fell the following Friday night 13–6. The Mites then waxed Weatherford 60–zip. His Duckness sat on the bench for each game. The boys had agreed that he could stick around until they lost a game.

The toughest game of the 1934 season was next against the Poly Parrots. The newspapers were hyping it as some kind of heavyweight title rematch, because in the last two seasons the Mites had defeated the Parrots by the combined score of 41–0. The schools were separated by no more than a mile, and the folks of the Polytechnic area, a hardworking, blue-collar neighborhood, were tired of hearing about the glory of the little orphans. Some were a little miffed that their daughters preferred the orphan boys over the ones from their own school.

The fans were not the only ones with hard feelings. Word on the street was that Poly coach, Luther Scarborough, regretted ever voting the Mites into the district. In turn, some of the fans regretted that Scarborough had ever been hired. Some wondered if he could coach foam to rise.

Regardless, Scarborough was plotting to rid the neighborhood of his greatest nemesis. He was planning a campaign to oust the Mighty Mites when the District 7A coaches met again in the spring to vote on their status. If it were up to Scarborough, the Home would soon be on its way back down to Class B.

The Mites and the Parrots fought like a couple of angry birds from the opening kickoff. Poly took a 6–0 lead. Then Pickett moved the offense sixty yards with seven straight completions. He dived into the end zone for the tying score, but the extra point fluttered right off the post. The teams were so even that it seemed appropriate that the game would end in a 6–6 tie.

"We didn't lose," Paul Smith told his teammates after the game. "So that means that Mighty Duck stays."

Mineral Wells fell the following week 19–0, setting up a rematch with Poly for the district championship. The Mighty Mites and the Mighty Duck were ready.

IT WAS SCHEDULED for a Saturday afternoon at La Grave Field, and fans started lining up outside the gates before the sunrise. The streets of Fort Worth were jammed with cars throughout the morning, and a police escort was required to get Old Blue through the gridlock. Rusty Russell was at the wheel as old Blue smoked its way to the stadium—twelve players and one quacking duck in the back.

Points came grudgingly in one of the most physical battles that anyone could ever remember. Players from both sides were limping off the field, and Russell wished he had more than twelve players to suit up. Thankfully for the Mites, the game was being controlled in the line by Masonic Home center Bob White, along with tackles Allie White and Paul Smith.

Scoreless in the fourth quarter, the game now hinged on penetrations. At least it seemed that way. So the Mighty Mites tried to imagine that the twenty-yard line was actually the goal line. Perry Pickett completed a thirty-yarder to James Thrash that moved the ball to the Poly nineteen. The Mites led 2–1 in penetrations and managed to maintain that edge until the clock ticked down.

Some believed it was the luck of the duck. But the sporting press in Fort Worth was convinced that it was more a matter of talent. Many were writing that the Mighty Mites were on their way back to the state championship game, and reasons abounded to support those opinions. The wide-open Russell passing offense, with Pickett completing passes all over the field, had taken Texas football by storm. The past three seasons, Pickett had grown up with the intricate system that was so far ahead of its time that opposing coaches worked night and day hoping to defense it.

In the first round of the postseason, the Mites tore through highly respected Dallas Tech 32–0. The next week, unbeaten Highland Park never crossed midfield, and Masonic Home captured the regional finals 13–0.

All that stood between the Mites and yet another trip to the state finals was Amarillo. Typically, the Golden Sandstorm, in their bright gold uniforms, was a harrowing sight to behold. The Sandies would wear down the orphans on a snow-covered field, where the temperature rose only to eleven degrees, and as the late afternoon light slipped away, Sandies kicker Virgil Pettigrew kicked a wobbly fifteen-yard field goal that seemed to quack as it wobbled over the crossbar. Amarillo won 3–0.

Frustration gnawed at the lining of Russell's stomach. Two shots at the state title had slipped through his fingers. Perhaps his greatest disappointment was that no one believed the Mighty Mites could do it in the first place.

It was a long, painful seven-hour bus ride from Amarillo back to

Fort Worth. The players rarely spoke as the bus traversed the slim, winding roads. But the trip was not made in total silence. The Mighty Duck quacked all the way.

Back at the orphanage, the boys filed quietly off the bus. One of the orphans toted the Mighty Duck down the steps. Most nights they would have turned him loose, fed him some june bugs, and watched him waddle off toward the pond. But not this time. The boys and their duck were headed straight toward the kitchen situated behind the dining hall.

"Where are they taking that duck?" Russell asked Doc Hall.

"We lost. He's going to the broiler. He's for dinner."

Russell shook his head.

"He ducked in," the old doctor said. "But he won't be waddling out."

Chapter 10

MILK SLIMES

It seemed that every day Hardy Brown was answering questions concerning the death of his father. The other kids would not let it go, and Hardy did not know what to tell them.

Wheatie Sealey was now on a mission.

"How'd your daddy die?" he asked his buddy.

"My daddy got shot. That's all I know."

"What happened to your mama?"

"Who knows?"

"Ever hear from her?"

"Nah."

Wheatie's curiosity was piqued. The story circulating about the Home was that Hardy's mother had murdered his father, gunned him down in broad daylight. Yes, it made sense. Why else had the Brown kids never heard from their mother? Why were they left behind at the Home during the two-week summer vacation while most of the others visited aunts and uncles and went fishing and camping?

Wheatie dreaded taking it up with Jeff Brown, who was four years older than he and tougher than a side of Angus. But he needed answers.

"All I know is that I miss my daddy very much and that I think about him every day," Jeff said.

Wheatie was surprised to see tears filling Jeff's eyes.

"I'm sorry, Jeff. I guess I ask too many questions sometimes."

Wheatie was about to walk away when Jeff said, "Hardy will tell you all about it someday. He knows more than he's letting on."

Wheatie shook his head.

"Hardy is my best friend," he said. "I should leave him alone about it."

MILK SLIMES.

They were proud to be *milk slimes*.

At the Home, your thirteenth birthday was the day of demarcation, the day you moved into the big boys' building, became eligible for the milking team, and came under the tutelage of William Henry Remmert, the strapping, six-foot-six former cop who wielded a paddle like Babe Ruth swung his forty-two-ounce bat.

Wheatie, Brownie, Crazy, Teague, Snoggs, Dewitt, and Hardy moved into the big boys' dorm within weeks of each other. And they would never forget that first morning when they walked into the milking barn and saw Jeff Brown with a turnip in one hand and an onion in the other. Between bites, he squeezed a cow tit and squirted the milk into his mouth.

Jeff Brown, age sixteen, was the perfect role model for the Home. He was a manly boy. On the football field, he loosened teeth and sent opposing players to the hospital. His macho attitude was the reason he was chosen as the leader of the milk slimes. It was an unwritten rule that the rough-tough football boys would work in the dairy, where they would pass along to the youngsters the honor code of the Home. You stepped over the threshold into manhood on the day you walked into the milking barn. There was little adult supervision around the milking barn, so the boys were basically left to set their own rules.

"Come on over here, boys," Jeff said. He was sitting on a stool with the stub of an unlit cigar sticking from his teeth. "Let me show you how to get a handle on ol' Bessie here." He grabbed two of the cow tits and began squirting milk into a pail.

"It's not hard, really," he said. "Just make sure your hands are warm and that you treat the old cows gently. It's just like being with a woman. That's what I've always said."

Wheatie cleared his throat. "Have you ever been with a woman, Jeff?"

"Of course. Haven't you?"

Jeff was not bragging. The girls on the inside were off-limits. But the girls on the outside were getting friendlier by the day.

Jeff stood up and pointed toward the fence. "The girls out there know their stuff. You'll find out soon enough. You'll be amazed at some of the things they'll teach *you*."

The boys smiled. School had officially begun.

"A couple other things you need to know," Jeff said. "It is an *honor* to be a milk slime. Don't ever forget that. And if anybody gives you crap, you just haul off and plug the bastard. Mr. Remmert and Mr. Russell won't do a thing about it—that is, if the kid was giving you crap about being a milk slime."

The title of milk slime was actually a misnomer. Of all the boys in the orphanage, the milk slimes were afforded the most respect. Other boys were jealous of the milk slimes and the girls thought they were cute. To be a milk slime was to be among the elite rich. Most of the time you walked around with folding money in your pocket. The pay was a half cent a gallon and it amounted to $1.75 per month. Those lucky enough to haul the milk from the dairy to the kitchen made another three bucks a month.

As a milk slime, your day began at four o'clock in the morning, when you rose from bed and sprinted three-quarters of a mile to the dairy. You were done by seven, in time to eat breakfast and to attend Mr. Russell's first football meeting of the day. You milked again for an hour in the afternoon before running full speed to the practice field. Russell allowed the milking boys to be a little late to practice and normally started the calisthenics without them. But if they were not on the field by the start of the daily scrimmage, the coach started checking his watch.

"Where are the milk slimes?" he would say. Then, like clockwork, they would come charging down the hill with leather helmets in hand.

RAIN HAD BEEN falling for three days in Fort Worth and the area behind the milk barn was now a quagmire. It looked like a hog-slopping pen. Jeff Brown's excitement could not be contained. Yes, the conditions were right for one of the biggest football games of the year at the Masonic Home.

The Big Milk Slimes versus the Little Milk Slimes.

In effect, it was the senior varsity football team against the junior high. Mostly, it was a chance for the older boys to push the younger boys around. Not a bully in his right mind would miss this game.

On the side of the big boys was Jeff Brown, Miller Moseley, Norman Strange, Gene Keel, Fats McHam, Don Stephens, Buford Hudgins, and Buster Roach.

For the little milk slimes it would be Hardy Brown, C. D. Sealy, Basel Smith, Snoggs Roach, Teague Roberts, Crazy Moseley, Dewitt Coulter, and Ray Coulter.

"We'll take names and whip their butts," Jeff Brown said. "I can't wait for this thing to get started."

According to the rules of the Home, this intrasquad scrimmage was never supposed to occur. The boys could fight all they wanted to down at the water tower. But football players around the Home were not supposed to play football without pads. They were too skilled at blocking and tackling, and Thomas Fletcher feared that an unsupervised game, without shoulder pads and helmets, would produce broken bones and ruptured spleens.

Rusty Russell had concurred. But at the moment it did not stop him from finding a place where he could watch every minute of the action from a hilltop in the distance. He tried to get far enough away so that the boys could not see his smile.

In the world of Texas high school football, Russell was known as a gentleman coach. His suits and fedora were pressed, and he looked like something straight out of a Hart, Schaffner & Marx catalogue. His boys played a sophisticated brand of football that was far ahead of its time. His playbook was thicker than the Fort Worth phone book.

But Russell did not always show all of his cards. Deep inside, he loved hard-nosed, hard-hitting football, and he rarely reined in his boys, even when the other team started bleeding. The Mighty Mites were known to use the leg whip, a move that could break bones. They punched and gouged and threw the cross-body block with the force of a log rolling down a fast mountain stream.

Russell wanted his key players to be tough, and he knew that they could learn that toughness on the practice field as well as at the dairy barn. It was a culture that would introduce them to manhood. Granted, the milk slimes might have been doing some uncivilized things around the cows. But the coach was willing to turn a blind eye every now and then.

No one knew the milk slime culture better than Jeff Brown. He was so tough that the boys walked around him like a swamp. That season, Brown had introduced a blocking technique to the Mighty Mites that was the talk of Texas high school football. Russell, through the years, had taught the boys to block low around the knees. But Brown had sized up the situation and come to the conclusion that blocking up high was better. He tried to envision how he would block a fence post. Hit it low and the fence post might not budge. But hit it high and the fence post would topple over.

Brown called his new blocking technique the Humper. He would crouch low, straighten his back, spring forward, and throw his right shoulder into the face of the opponent. It was almost like throwing a punch, only you did it with your shoulder and not your fist. The preferred result was a broken nose, or perhaps, a few loosened teeth. A commentary on just how tough high school football was at the time was that the TIL still considered the Humper a legal block.

Game time for the milk slimes had finally arrived. Rain was blowing horizontally and lightning crackled high in the Texas sky when the big milk slimes kicked off to the little milk slimes.

Everyone expected Jeff Brown to throw the first Humper of the day, but, instead, the honors went to his little brother. Hardy Brown threw his right shoulder into Fats McHam's chin and knocked him for a loop.

Jeff seemed outraged. "What the hell do you think you are doing, little brother?"

"Acting just like my big brother," Hardy said.

At age thirteen, Hardy was going through a growing spurt. He was pushing five foot nine and his chest was filling out. While most of the other players on the junior high team still had their baby fat, muscles were popping out all over Hardy. His man strength was coming on at an early age. There was no question as to who was the leader of the junior high team. He did not have to raise his voice to get other boys' attention. Russell knew that Hardy was already ready for the high school team, but he would have to wait a couple of seasons to become eligible.

Some of the older boys were trash-talking the little orphans like Snoggs Roach and Basel Smith. Hardy started pointing at the older boys and yelling, "Why don't you pick on me?" To which there was no response. There was not a high school boy, not even Jeff Brown, ready to take a walk down to the water tower and duke it out with young Hardy. They had watched him play in the midget games for years down at Sycamore Creek and knew he was not a boy to be messed with.

Remarkably, the little boys were holding their own in the early going against the high school team. Hardy scored the first touchdown of the day, following a block by Crazy Moseley, and with mud flying everywhere, he ran forty yards for the score. The little orphans jumped up and down and slapped him on the top of the head.

The high school boys were getting frustrated. They could not move the ball against the hustling little defense and were forced to punt. Two plays later, C. D. Sealy reared back and threw a thirty-yard touchdown pass to Ray Coulter and the little Mites suddenly had a two-touchdown lead.

Now the high school boys were really pissed. They huddled. "I don't care what you have to do," Jeff Brown said. "Bloody 'em up and break their legs. But we can't lose this football game."

High on his hilltop, Rusty Russell was getting worried. He certainly could not break up the game with the little Mites leading by two touchdowns. But he was concerned about the health of his high school team. They were getting roughed up. Russell could not afford any injuries, not with the 1936 season just around the corner.

Russell felt better when the big milk slimes finally drove down the field with Gene Keel throwing a touchdown pass to Miller Moseley.

The older boys forced a punt and were determined to tie the game. Jeff Brown, normally a guard, moved to fullback and started powering his way down the field. The only little orphan that could stop him was his own brother. They were butting heads like a couple of bighorn rams in the hills of North Africa.

As the rain pounded down, Jeff managed to slip-slide into the end zone to tie the score. Russell now had his excuse. The last vestiges of daylight were fading and the boys were ankle-deep in mud. He sauntered down the hill and pulled the whistle out of his pocket.

"You boys know you shouldn't be out here in this storm," he yelled. "You could catch your death of cold. Get inside and take a shower. Then get your behinds to the dining hall."

Nobody complained. The high school boys wanted nothing more to do with Hardy Brown.

THE TOUGHEST PART of being a little milk slime was surviving Jeff Brown's initiation, one that included a hell week like no other.

For Wheatie, Snoggs, Crazy, Teague, Brownie, and Hardy, it all began one night in the dormitory, when Jeff strolled into the room and told the boys to sit down side-by-side on one of the beds. He was holding a twelve-inch hunting knife in one hand and a whet stone in the other. He stood before the boys, sliding the shiny blade across the hard black stone.

"Listen up," he said. "This is the first rite of passage into milk slimedom. We don't need anybody around here who's going to be squeamish. You've got to be tough to work in the dairy. So here's the deal. I cut a chunk out of your ear, you bleed a little, and that's that. I get blood and you can go. Who wants to go first?"

Crazy Moseley raised his hand.

Jeff sat down next to Crazy. "My, you have big ears," he said.

Jeff pinched Crazy's right lobe and carved out a quarter-inch chunk. Blood oozed down his neck and onto the front of his shirt.

"You're through," Jeff said. "Now, that didn't hurt, did it?"

Crazy smiled.

"You're going to make a great milk slime," Jeff said. "Who's next?"

Jeff started hacking on Snoggs's left ear, but nothing came out.

"I ain't much of a bleeder," Snoggs said. "This might take a little while."

Snoggs finally bled and was sent on his way.

Brownie and Wheatie were quick to bleed and that left only Hardy.

"Come here, my kid brother," Jeff said.

In one quick motion, Hardy plucked the knife from Jeff's grip and opened a half-inch gash in his right lobe. He smiled from ear to ear as blood flowed down the front of his shirt. Given the joy on his face, they knew that it would not be long before Hardy would replace Jeff as the master of pain.

THE NEXT NIGHT, a long cord was hung from the transom above the door. A stool was placed in the doorway.

"Tonight I'm going to hang you guys," Jeff said. "Just like those cowboy shows on Saturday morning. Who wants to go first?"

Crazy raised his hand.

Unlike the hangings in the old west, this nylon cord would stretch. The little milk slime would swing for a couple of seconds before his feet finally touched the floor. Everyone would laugh and then Jeff would hang the next boy.

Jeff tied Crazy's hands behind him and wrapped the cord around his neck. Then he kicked away the stool. Crazy started to sway. He swayed and swayed. Then he swayed some more. His eyes started to bug out. His body began to shake. He started making choking sounds. His feet could not reach the floor. As the boys gasped, and Crazy begged for air, Jeff lifted him up by the seat of his pants while Hardy unwrapped the rope from his neck. They prayed they were not too late.

Crazy's body was limp as they laid him on the floor.

"What are we going to do?" Brownie said.

"Haul him into the shower and run some cold water on him," Jeff said. "Bring him out of it. He'll wake up with a little cold water on his face."

The boys thought about alerting Mr. Remmert, but decided to follow Jeff's instructions. Four of them carried Crazy into the shower and laid him down on the cold concrete floor. Soon, with the water cascading over his head, Crazy began to cough.

"Are you okay, Crazy?" Wheatie asked.

Crazy laughed. They knew he would be fine.

The boys were relieved that they had not called Mr. Remmert. The new milk slimes would have been spending the next four weekends cleaning the dining hall instead of watching the moving pictures.

They were also glad that Jeff Brown had called off hell week.

For a few days, anyway.

WHAT BONDED THE orphans more than football or fighting or swimming in Sycamore Creek was death.

All had felt its dark presence. Each life had been changed by it. Death had brought them there.

Parents had died in every imaginable way. Every member of Jeffrey White's family perished in a house fire while he was at school. There had been tragic car accidents, hunting mishaps, and train wrecks. Murders accounted for a large share.

Bob Hall's father, a country physician down in the Rio Grande Valley, made a house visit one afternoon and was paid for sewing up a child's gashed forehead with fresh shrimp caught in the nearby Gulf of Mexico. The shrimp were so delectable that the doctor started peeling and eating as he drove the farm-to-market road toward Brownsville. Within minutes, he collapsed into the steering wheel and began gasping for breath.

Seven-year-old Bob Hall was strong enough to pull his dad into the passenger's side of the car. The kid jumped behind the wheel and took off for the nearest hospital. He drove sixty miles an hour, but could not save his father, who died from salmonella.

C. D. Sealy's father, a pumper on an oil rig, came home hot and tired one summer afternoon and poured an entire pitcher of iced tea over his head. Seconds later, he fell dead on the floor. He was twenty-eight.

The Moseley family was the picture of health and happiness as they picnicked one afternoon in the countryside outside of Dundee, Texas. The three kids—Miller, Cecil, and Dorothy—were busy chasing june bugs as Mildred Lucille and John Harrison "Harry" Moseley relaxed on a blanket. It was a hot day in North Texas and they were running out of water to drink. So Harry, in spite of protests from his wife, scooped some water out of a nearby pond and drank it.

Two weeks later, he died of typhoid.

Being orphaned was enough to bear. But that was just the beginning of the long and arduous journey. Being shipped to a distant orphanage brought on more trauma. In most cases, there was no waiting around and little time to digest the death of one or both parents. Most had never heard of the Masonic Home and were ill-prepared for the adjustment.

Doug Lord's journey was different.

Jesse Allan Lord had taken his nine-year-old son to buy shoes one Saturday afternoon at Thom McAn's on Elm Street in downtown Dallas. Father and son were drawn to the sound of a radio in the back of the store and the voice of a football play-by-play announcer.

"Who's playing?" the elder Lord asked.

"Highland Park and the Masonic Home," the store manager said.

"Well," Lord said. "The Masonic Home is my favorite team."

Lord, a devoted thirty-third-degree Mason, never missed a Tuesday night lodge meeting. He followed the Home's footballers the same way an ex-student at Texas A&M worshipped the Aggies.

"We beat Highland Park every time we play them and we're going to win today," he said. "And by the way, Doug, you're going to be playing for the Home someday."

The boy's jaw almost hit the floor. "The Masonic Home is for orphans," he said.

"That's right, son."

The boy knew that his dad did not crack jokes. Jesse Allan Lord was a straightforward man who meant what he said and said what he meant. He labored long hours each day at Fulton Bag and Cotton Company on the edge of downtown Dallas and brought home an honest paycheck.

Doug could never forget the first day he had visited his dad at work. Lord was the head pressman for a company that mainly produced flour and feed sacks. He was responsible for operating three large presses that spat out the bags in various colors. The son did not recognize his father when he first saw him. The elder Lord was covered from head to toe in red, blue, and green ink.

In the Depression thirties, when safety regulations barely existed, no one paid much attention to the heavy amounts of lead in ink. It was the lead that got into Lord's arteries and started the deterioration of his kidneys. Penicillin was not yet available for public use, and kidney dialysis was nothing more than an idea. Lord knew that his kidneys were shot and he was about to die a slow death.

A few days after the trip to the shoe store, father and son sat down for a serious talk.

"I am not long for this world," the elder Lord said. "I am sorry, son. I wish it could have been different. But you have to make me one promise."

"What is that?"

"That you will go to the Masonic Home."

"I promise."

Doug would always remember his dad as a large, warm-hearted man with brute strength that he rarely abused. Except for the time a drunken driver slammed into the side of the family car and took off.

Jesse Allan Lord jumped out of his car and pursued the other man's auto on foot up Forest Avenue for several blocks until he caught him. He pulled the man out of his car and beat him to a pulp, then waited for the police to arrive.

Watching his dad suffer and die was the hardest six months of the young boy's life. Lord was moved into St. Paul's Hospital, and the doctors offered little hope and no pain medication. His body was racked with agony and they finally had to bind him to the bed with leather straps.

Doug visited his dad every night. On one trip, he told the nurse, "You know my dad is about the strongest man alive. He's going to break one of those leather straps."

The nurse laughed.

Minutes later, in a fit of great pain, one of the straps flew apart.

Nine days after watching his father die, Doug packed his bags for the Masonic Home.

"You don't have to go," his mother, Martha, said.

"I promised Dad I would go. I'm going."

Off he went.

The first few days at the orphanage away from his mother and other relatives and close friends made Doug terribly homesick. On the third day, he walked into one of the bathroom stalls and had a huge cry. After awhile, he dried his eyes and walked out.

"I will never do that again," he promised himself.

Doug knew instinctively that you just did not talk about death around the orphanage. Kids avoided it like spinach. It was part of the unspoken code. Death was to be left behind at the front gate. (One exception was the gossip surrounding the murder of Hardy Brown Sr.)

Doug Lord was five foot eight and 120 pounds with jet-black hair when he arrived at the Home. Not exactly a rail of a boy, but not a muscleman, either. "Chicken" Roberts nicknamed him "Fat" Lord.

"I am not fat," the boy said.

"You will be someday," Chicken replied.

The first few weeks at the orphanage were always the toughest because the old hands were protective of the pecking order. Early on, they did not call you by your name. You were simply "new kid."

Leon Pickett remembered being frustrated at being called "new kid."

"My name is Leon goddamn Pickett," he said.

So the kids started calling him "Leon 'goddamn' Pickett."

Doug Lord could not stand "new kid." It was not long before he was angling for a fight. He challenged Kelly White, a boy his age. That is when Hugh Musselwhite, an older boy, stepped in. "Hey, new kid, why don't you fight somebody like me?"

Lord was unaware that Musselwhite played on the varsity football team. That kind of status automatically meant you were one of the toughest kids inside the fence.

The orphans trooped in huge numbers down to the water tower to witness the greatest mismatch ever. Young Lord had not yet raised his hands when Musselwhite began to whale on his head. The fight was over in the first ten seconds.

Chicken Roberts escorted Lord to the back door of the dining hall. He knew better than to take him to the infirmary, where the nurses would report such foul play to William Henry Remmert.

Earl Bodiford, the head cook, was an angel of mercy in such times. He fetched a bag of ice and placed it over the boy's face to slow the swelling.

"You're a new kid, aren't you," Bodiford said.

"Yeah, I guess that's going around."

Bodiford sat with the boy and studied him. "You're just like the rest," he finally said.

"What do you mean?"

"You kids fight for one reason and one reason alone."

"What's that?"

"Because you're mad you lost your daddy."

Lord felt like crying. Deep inside, he knew the other orphans might understand. But crying was never allowed at the Home.

This was all about becoming a man.

Chapter 11

MARBLE EYE

It made sense that with all of the fighting around the Home the orphans would soon turn to boxing. Prizefighting was America's number-one spectator sport, from the cramped, smoky neighborhood saloons to the gigantic outdoor arenas in New York. Baseball stood a distant second. Saturday mornings at the moving pictures brought newsreels of Jack Dempsey, Max Baer, Joe Louis, and Primo Carnera.

The favorite around the Home was James J. Braddock, known as "Cinderella Man." How could the orphans not love an underdog? Most of them celebrated for days in 1935, when Braddock, just a year off the government rolls, pulled the biggest upset in the history of boxing by defeating Max Baer for the world heavyweight championship.

Boxing stirred the blood just like football. The boys had listened to the championship fights on the radio and paid rapt attention as Mr. Remmert recounted stories of America's most popular athletes. They could barely believe that a hundred thousand people had crowded into Yankee Stadium to see Max Baer fight Joe Louis in a nontitle bout. The big fighters outshone presidents.

To the surprise of everyone, Dempsey had showed up at the Home in 1932 to sign autographs and visit with the kids. The orphans followed him around campus like hungry puppies. Dempsey was photographed holding Betty Russell, the four-year-old daughter of Rusty Russell. A picture of the great champion was prominently displayed in the big boys' dormitory.

Doug Lord had come to worship the iconic fighters. Boxing had been on his mind since scoring a knockout at the neighborhood golf course about three days earlier. The fifteen-year-old Lord had caused quite a ruckus that Saturday afternoon while working as a caddie at the Glen Garden Country Club. He had been goaded into a fight by a fellow bagman five years his senior. No one was more surprised than Lord when he unleashed a wild haymaker that knocked the much larger boy sprawling on his back.

The caddie master quickly telephoned Mr. Remmert, who came tearing down to Glen Garden with paddle in hand.

"But Mr. Remmert," Lord said. "He called me an orphan."

"Well, Lord," Remmert replied. "You *are* an orphan."

Lord was one of the smallest kids on the football team. But he was a born ringleader. The boys followed him everywhere. With Lord as the point man, they were not afraid to sneak out at night for the purpose of chasing the neighborhood girls and hopefully snagging a kiss. So, it did not take him long to convince four of his buddies to make the trek to Will Rogers Coliseum, where the Golden Gloves were to be held, and to enter matches. None of the boys had ever worn boxing gloves, but they all loved to fight.

They had no idea just what they were getting into. First, they had to fill out pre-fight applications. The aspiring pugilists were going to need release signatures from their parents.

"What are we going to do now, Lord?" said big Ray Musselwhite, the younger brother of Hugh. "We don't have any parents."

"Follow me," Lord told the boys. "I have a plan."

They walked a few blocks to a candy stand and borrowed an ink pen from the salesman. Lord started forging signatures. None of the boxing officials suspected chicanery, because the boys seemed well-mannered and, with the exception of Ray Musselwhite, were quite small.

As their applications were being approved, one of the Golden Gloves officials gathered the orphans around him.

"Each of you will need a pair of tennis shoes to fight," he said. "And, of course, you will all need a mouthpiece."

The boys looked at Lord, hoping he had more answers. As it

turned out, these were the cold, hard facts: Between them, the orphans possessed but one pair of tennis shoes. None had ever seen a mouth-piece.

The boys were leaving the coliseum when yet another light went off in Lord's brain. He reached down and plucked a filthy, slimy, spit-covered mouthpiece off the dirty floor.

"We'll just wash it off," he said.

No one said a word.

Nothing could have prepared Lord for what lay ahead. He would be the first orphan to step into the ring in the opening round of the Golden Gloves. His opponent was a man almost ten years his senior who boasted four years of service in the United States Navy. The sell-out crowd roared when the well-known local serviceman was intro-duced, then fell silent when Lord's name came through the speakers. Lord sat frozen as the powerful fighter climbed into the ring. Then he heard the stirring words of encouragement.

"Go get 'im, Lord," one of the boys whispered. "You can *do* it."

Indeed, it surprised everyone that the plucky Lord managed to hang on for the full three rounds, backpedaling and swinging wildly. The Navy man grew frustrated that he could not knock down the kid. Lord was still standing at the final bell. But he still lost a unanimous decision.

As the orphan fighter stumbled back through the ropes and out of the ring, he was shocked to see a familiar face sitting in the front row—the face of William Henry Remmert.

"M-Mr. Remmert," Lord said. "I didn't know you were going to be here. I—"

"Don't worry, Lord," he said. "I'm proud of the way you handled yourself."

Remmert, in fact, was impressed that the boys were showing such gumption. He was amazed at how organized they were. The shoes and mouthpiece were passed from orphan to orphan between bouts. No one even bothered to wipe off the mouthpiece.

The Mighty Mites fared well, considering their lack of experience. What no one predicted was that big, clumsy Ray Musselwhite would be a natural inside the ring. He fought as if his life depended on it. He threw a left-right combination that devastated opponents.

Musselwhite, at age fourteen, stood six feet tall and was an oddity around the Home. His thick shoulders and muscled arms made him stand out among the orphans. Rusty Russell often wondered why most of the kids who grew up at the Home really did not grow at all. Why were they so different from the boys on the outside? God knows they were fed well; Russell had made sure they ate steak at least three times a week.

The coach had been thinking a lot lately about his undersized kids. Was it possible that the trauma of being orphaned could possibly stunt one's growth? No, Russell thought. There was nothing scientific that suggested that emotions could be tied to one's physical stature. But it certainly seemed more than a coincidence that most of the boys walking around the orphanage were below average size. Some were downright runty. That is why he gave thanks for boys like Musselwhite, who had a bright future with the Mighty Mites. He could also say grace over Hardy Brown, along with Ray and Dewitt Coulter.

The Golden Gloves would span five nights, and it was clear from the start that Musselwhite was sticking around. Night after night, fight after fight, he continued to gather steam as the bigger, stronger, more experienced fighters fell like bowling pins. No one in the crowd of more than five thousand fans would have ever suspected that Musselwhite had never boxed, much less that he was sharing shoes and a mouthpiece with four other orphans.

Golden Gloves officials were surprised that Musselwhite reached the finals of his weight classification while fighting with only one eye open.

He was approached by the referee just before the finals. The man had many questions.

"Son, I was just wondering why you keep one eye shut when you fight," he said. "It just doesn't make any sense to me."

"Well, sir," Musselwhite said. "I only got one eye."

"What! Son, you shouldn't be out there fighting with one eye. Why in the hell didn't our doctors catch that?"

Musselwhite, at Lord's behest, had worn the glass eye during the prefight examination. Then he had stuck it in his pocket when it was time to fight. This was not an unusual practice for Musselwhite. The glass eye was used mostly for playing marbles.

The past ten years, Musselwhite gone had through a large supply of glass eyes. The boys liked to gamble at marbles and losing meant he had turned the globe over to the winner. This caused great consternation among the Home's medical staff.

"Do you have any idea what one of these glass eyes costs?" the orphanage eye doctor once said. "Lose one more, son, and you'll be a one-eyed boy the rest of your life."

Musselwhite was on his fifth or sixth eye, and he had honestly lost count.

Now he had some explaining to do to the referee. The man looked deeply into his good eye. "Son, if you plan to fight tonight, you'll have to stick that marble in your eye socket."

"But, sir—"

"Don't backtalk me, boy," the referee said. "I'll have you thrown out of the Golden Gloves."

Musselwhite knew what would happen when the bell sounded for the start of the first round. His opponent landed a straight right to the orphan's chin and out popped the eyeball. It bounced on the canvas and began to roll . . . and roll. The other kid stared in disbelief at the fake eye that seemed so real. He actually believed that he had dislodged the boy's eye—the retina, cornea, lens, pupil, and iris—and that poor Ray Musselwhite was now half blind. As his opponent looked down and watched the eyeball roll and roll, Musselwhite really had no choice. He swung wildly and hit the boy squarely in the jaw. He fell like a sack of potatoes. The referee quickly counted him out and Ray Musselwhite was crowned the champion of the Golden Gloves.

Five thousand fans were on their feet, cheering their lungs out.

Ray Musselwhite reached down, picked up the eye, and stuck it back into the socket.

The cheering died in midthroat.

Chapter 12

ZIGGY

"Fairbanks!"

William Henry Remmert was in the habit of changing the boys' names, and now he was summoning Doug Lord. Lord brought to mind the actor Douglas Fairbanks, the athletic and acrobatic Hollywood star who played mostly swashbuckling characters, including Zorro.

About the only thing that the orphan and the actor actually shared was the first name. There was no physical resemblance.

"Fairbanks!"

Lord came running.

"What can I do for you, Mr. Remmert?"

"Fairbanks, your dog pooped under one of the bunks last night. Again! One more time and he's back out on the streets."

Ziggy was a brown, muscled-up bulldog that was the toughest creature in the neighborhood. His most distinctive marking was a squiggly white line across his forehead. When the orphans looked at Ziggy, they did not see a brown mutt with a crooked marking. They saw an orange-and-white beast that matched the school colors. They saw an "M" on his forehead that, of course, stood for Masonic Home.

Some of the boys believed Ziggy had been sent from heaven.

"Why else would God send us an orange-and-white dog?" Teague Roberts had said to Mr. Remmert.

"That dog is not orange and he's not white," the dean deadpanned. "That dog is browner than the poop he leaves on the dormitory floor."

Animals normally did not last long around the orphanage. Most were either run off by Remmert or quietly disposed of. School admin-istrators did not particularly dislike cats or dogs. But they knew the animal population could quickly multiply if left unchecked. Ziggy managed to stick around because he scared off every stray animal that wandered onto the property. This pleased Remmert and he allowed Ziggy to sleep in the big boys' dorm on cold nights.

About the only trouble that Ziggy ever caused was chasing a female dog into a storm sewer below the street adjacent to the orphanage. Ziggy was attempting to mount the lady when the two got stuck inside the narrow passageway. The dogs howled for help and a city crew finally had to dig up the street to free them.

Ziggy was really just one of the boys. He hung around the practice field during the afternoon workouts. He followed the boys to the milk-ing barn and the schoolhouse and the dining hall. He loved the trips down to Sycamore Creek and was usually the first into the water. He gladly played the role of daredevil dog when the boys stood on the railroad bridge with a train bearing down on them.

Ziggy flaunted his doghood one afternoon when he spotted a trained pit bull swaggering onto his turf. He attacked the bigger, stronger dog and tore into his hide with the force of an angry lion. The pit bull took off running for the hills and never came back.

Most important, Ziggy was smart. The boys knew he would never poop on the dormitory floor. That was why Lord was trying to ex-plain the situation when Remmert cut him off.

"I don't want to hear about it. Your dog has got to stop crapping in the house."

Lord wanted to tell Mr. Remmert that the real culprit was his own dog, Missy Lou, a long-haired mutt that did not know the difference between "sic 'em" and "sit." Instead, Lord swallowed the words and retreated to the bunk area, where, at that very moment, he found Missy Lou squatting beneath his own bed. He grabbed the dog and stuck her nose in the excrement. Missy Lou took off squealing in the direction of her master and leaped squarely onto Remmert's lap. The dean's pressed white shirt was now covered with dog doodoo.

"Fairbanks!"

"Mr. Remmert, I guess we know who's been doing her business on the clean floor."

"I don't want to hear about it, Fairbanks. I want you to teach Missy Lou to never do it in the dormitory."

"Yessir."

Lord knew Missy was too stupid to learn anything. But that did not stop Mr. Remmert from loving the dog like the child he never had. In spite of his ill temper, Remmert mollycoddled the little dog. He baby-talked her. The boys suspected that Missy Lou slept at night between Remmert and his hefty wife, as they could not imagine the couple ever attempting sex.

It was an early Sunday morning when Lord and his crew took off for Sycamore Creek with Ziggy trotting behind them. They were halfway across the pasture when the boys realized that Missy Lou was about twenty yards behind the pack. They tried to shoo the dog back to the dorm, but she was determined to follow.

"That's the dumbest dog I ever saw," Lord said.

As they approached the creek, Ziggy shot off in pursuit of a pair of rabbits and the boys could see him bounding over the tall grass. The chase covered more than a hundred yards, but Ziggy returned with a cottontail in his mouth. The boys planned to skin and cook the tasty morsel right after a dip in the creek.

First they had to cross Black Bridge before the next train. They were about halfway across when they heard the lonesome whistle of the Santa Fe locomotive. There was no reason to run, as Sycamore Creek was right below them. They were certain that Ziggy would follow them as they dove into the cool water.

Ziggy jumped. Missy Lou did not.

Lord was in a panic when he realized that the little dog could not be located. The boys rapidly scaled the wooden stanchion, hoping for a miracle. But Missy Lou was nowhere to be found. They followed the railroad tracks for more than a hundred feet until they found her. Missy Lou had been caught up in the train's cowcatcher and dragged to the end of the bridge, where her body tumbled into the tall weeds. She was dead.

The boys stood around her with heads bowed.

"What are we going to do?" Ray Musselwhite said.

"We ought to just bury her," said Chicken Roberts. "There's no way we can tell Mr. Remmert. No way."

Lord picked up the dog and held her in his arms.

"That wouldn't be right to Mr. Remmert," he said. "He loved this little dog."

The boys began the long journey back to the big boys' dorm. Lord carried Missy Lou like a baby all the way and stood on the sidewalk while Chicken summoned Mr. Remmert.

The six-foot-six man wearing a dark suit and cowboy boots walked slowly down the steps. His face was ashen.

"What happened, Fairbanks?" he said.

"We were on the Black Bridge. The train was coming and we thought everybody had jumped. Ziggy always jumps. We just thought Missy Lou would be right behind us."

"Couldn't you have saved her?"

"No sir," Lord said as he bowed his head. "I am real sorry."

Tears began to roll down the big man's cheeks. His entire body was shaking. He took the little dog from Lord and began to walk down the long sidewalk. They had no idea where he was going.

They just hoped they would never see him cry again.

Chapter 13

DAY OF THE PAUPER

The train chattered east from Los Angeles in the fall of 1938, carrying America's most popular underdog toward his day of reckoning. At practically every rail stop, Seabiscuit was led by his handlers down the gangplank and into the bright sunlight, as adoring fans scrambled to catch a glimpse. They gathered to see the tiny racehorse with the sad little tail and stumpy legs that would not straighten all the way.

If there was ever a racehorse that belonged in an orphanage, it was the mud-colored Seabiscuit. He had won only five of his first thirty-five starts while floundering in the lowest claiming ranks. His original owner, along with countless trainers, had turned their backs on him. In 1936, an obscure and apparently foolish man named Charles Howard bought him for a bargain-basement price and turned him over to a trainer and jockey who had frequented the winner's circle about as often as a three-legged mule.

What the trio found beneath Seabiscuit's hostility and fear was a workmanlike competitor with guile and tactical speed. It was practically the same discovery that Rusty Russell had made at the Masonic Home back in 1927. Like the Mighty Mites, Seabiscuit had nothing to lose, and, upon finding his stride, never stopped running, or winning, for that matter. He was the champion of the working man and woman during the Great Depression.

At the moment, Seabiscuit was headed cross-country for the match race of the century against the unbeatable War Admiral. The event, thanks mostly to the "rich horse versus the poor horse" angle, was to become the most talked about thoroughbred race anyone could remember. Seabiscuit hailed from the other side of the tracks. In contrast, War Admiral boasted the 1937 Triple Crown, along with eleven straight victories. Breezing to wins at the Kentucky Derby, the Preakness, and the Belmont Stakes, the stunning chestnut colt had gained status as the greatest racehorse of all time.

Seabiscuit versus War Admiral was being hyped by the press as a contest of two competing worlds. In the camp of War Admiral was the eastern banking establishment, with jewels, jingle, and all the bells and whistles. Backing Seabiscuit were the scrapping have-nots that trumpeted the cause of the dark horse. So compelling was the matchup that President Franklin D. Roosevelt insisted on staying apprised of even the tiniest development leading to the November 1 race. This was especially curious, since the marauding Germans were at the moment plotting to take over the world.

Columnist Dave Boone wrote in the *San Francisco Chronicle:*

> People who never saw a horse race in their lives are taking sides. If the issue were deferred another week, there would be another Civil War between the War Admiral Americans and the Seabiscuit Americans.

On a glorious sunny afternoon at Pimlico Race Course, when men peeled off their topcoats and women revealed bare shoulders, fifty thousand fans watched from the grandstand and another ten thousand stood in the infield. The track had been built to handle about a third of that number. Grantland Rice wrote that the crowd was "keyed to the highest tension I have ever seen in sport" when the two horses stepped onto the racetrack at precisely four o'clock.

At a time when TV sets were just snow-filled little boxes, forty million Americans, including F.D.R., listened to the race call over the radio. What they heard was the magnificent, crackling voice of Clem McCarthy describing how Seabiscuit had grabbed an early lead and how the horses were now neck-and-neck as they roared into the final turn.

Rusty Russell, some fifteen hundred miles away, was glued to his radio. Like so many others, he had been swept up by the emotion of the story. In the final sixteenth of a mile—as Seabiscuit pulled away to win by four lengths—Russell's wife, Juanita, watched her husband's eyes sparkle like sunlit water.

It was a stunning upset. Ninety-five percent of the everyday press had picked War Admiral to win. Seconds after Seabiscuit crossed the finish line, ten thousand men, women, and children jumped the rail and started chasing after America's grandest male. Now America was turning its eyes to the Mighty Mites.

FORTY-TWO DAYS later, on a cold December morning, Russell cranked up Old Blue and heard the rusty engine sputter and moan. According to habit, he turned and peered through the back window to make sure that all twelve players were on board and sitting down.

"We've got twelve," he told Doc Hall, riding shotgun. "That's all we need."

Doc Hall cleared his throat as his wandering right eye sought out the coach.

"This is a big day for the Mighty Mites," he said. "I sure hope those big ol' boys from Dallas don't chew us up."

Hands on the wheel, eyes straight ahead, Russell set his sights once more on that elusive dream that he had been chasing for the past six years—the Texas high school championship. Twice in his coaching life he had driven the same highway, only to hit a roadblock; a tie against Corsicana in 1932 cost the Mighty Mites the trophy, and, two years later, they were defeated 3–0 in the state semifinals by Amarillo High.

Today, in the quarterfinals in Dallas, the Mites would face a Highland Park team so powerful that the writers had practically handed over the crown to the Scots. Pop Boone had offered this opinion in the *Fort Worth Press:*

> Outweighed something like twenty-five pounds to the man, decided underdogs according to most of the bookmakers, coach Rusty Russell's gallant little band will tackle the huge Highland Park Scots at Ownby Stadium. Kickoff will be at 2:30, with thousands of the

Mighty Mites' supporters following the Masons down the pike. Highland Park coach Redman Hume, never a modest footballer, is convinced his team can do 'whatever it wants to do,' against the Mites, and he is confident in the physical superiority of his lads. The odds against the Mighty Mites are almost overwhelming.

Russell laughed when he read the story. He knew his team was runty and weak. So what? No other team in the state could count as many playoff wins as the Mighty Mites the last half dozen years. Amarillo had won three state titles (1934–36), but the Masonic Home in the postseason was 1–1 against the Golden Sandstorm.

All Russell had to do was to look in the rearview mirror to know just how the public felt about his little team. Cars filled with orange-clad fans stretched for miles behind Old Blue. They had started lining up outside of the orphanage at dawn that morning to make sure they were part of the parade. Fans had become so obsessed with the Mighty Mites that some never wanted to let them out of their sight.

Since 1932, Masonic Home crowds had been turning out in mind-boggling numbers. Friday night at La Grave Field was like a carnival, as thousands pushed through the gates and the fire marshal turned a blind eye. No one could blame him. Gate receipts built highways and fed the poor. Everybody benefited.

Well, not everybody. The Home's football program was still no better off financially than it had been in 1927. What money that had been earned by the Mighty Mites had mostly been spent on hiring more teachers and constructing new buildings. Russell's salary the last eleven years had risen from thirty bucks a week to fifty. At the moment, he had fifty cents in his pocket and was not sure if Old Blue had enough gas to carry the orphans back to Fort Worth.

What saddened Russell was the sight of his players still wearing the same old threadbare uniforms. Furthermore, he knew Old Blue was ready to drop a transmission any minute. He knew the Highland Park Scots would be transported by chartered bus if the game were played in Fort Worth. There would be heat on that bus. Russell peered through the back window again to see his players huddled beneath old blankets, teeth chattering.

The Masonic Home was only about twenty years behind the schools that really played big-time Texas football. Unlike the other head coaches around the state, Russell was a one-man band. He did not have a single assistant coach. If not for the presence of Doc Hall the last eleven years, it would have gotten pretty lonely on the sideline.

Conversely, Redman Hume enjoyed a staff of five assistants that coordinated the offense, defense, and kicking teams. On nights when the Scots did not play a game, Hume dispatched his men in all directions to scout other teams. Russell had duly noted that a Highland Park coach had attended every Mighty Mites game that season. Why was Hume so obsessed with the tiny band of orphans? Because in the first game of the regular season just three months earlier, the Home had defeated the Scots by the score of 14–13.

The difference between's Russell's workload and that of the Highland Park coach was almost comical. Russell's workday started not long after sunup, when he met with the team. Then he taught science classes all day and conducted practice for two hours in the afternoon. He normally held a chalk talk with the boys right after dinner. He was responsible for making sure that the uniforms were washed and that the numbers were spray-painted onto the jerseys. Late at night, if there was a ruckus in the dorm, he was normally called out to administer punishment.

On top of that, he had been promoted two years earlier to the position of principal of the entire school system. The man was lucky if he could find time to sleep.

Most of all, Russell loved to nurture his boys and to prepare them for life after the orphanage. Russell often wrote long letters to his players. His words were not so much about blocking and tackling as they were about living the right way.

To Miller Moseley he wrote, "You might just be the toughest football player in the state. But what is most impressive about you is your drive in the classroom. Teachers at the Masonic Home have never seen a brighter student. I doubt you will find a better math student anywhere than Miller Moseley. You have a bright future, young man. Everyone is pulling for you."

A few months later, Moseley would earn an academic scholarship to Texas Christian University.

After Russell's arrival, the entire climate at the Home changed. Those who had never set foot into an orphanage might have been taken aback by the peaceful and the pastoral nature of the place. Kids walked about campus with wide smiles. They did not seem bothered by the fact that they had no shoes for six months out of the year.

Kids were coming to the realization that being a Home kid was cool. They might have longed for a mother's kiss and a father's embrace. But there was a camaraderie among boys and girls that was unmatched at other schools. The kids worked together, ate together, slept together, laughed and cried together, milked cows, played tennis, played football, and suffered together when William Henry Remmert pulled out his paddle.

The reason that the Mighty Mites ascended so rapidly was that Russell never stopped working. Every evening after practice, he was on the road scouting upcoming opponents. This, of course, placed a huge burden on Juanita and the two kids—Betty, ten, and Rusty Jr., seven. To get acquainted with his daughter, he had started taking Betty on the scouting trips.

Traveling money was about as sparse as palm trees in downtown Fort Worth, and most of it came straight out of the coach's pocket. This had put a crimp on his wardrobe. Russell had not bought a new suit in more than three years, but remained the best-dressed coach on any sideline in Texas. Besides, how many men wore a dark suit, fedora, and a tie knotted all the way up while driving a smoke-belching flatbed truck with tires as bald as Jack Benny?

On the seat next to Russell was the secret to his magic. It was a thick binder with more than seven hundred plays. Most teams of the era used no more than a dozen. Russell was willing to forgo sleep virtually every night of the football season so he could sit beside a small lamp in his bedroom and draw up plays. It was not unusual for Juanita to wake up at two, three, or four in the morning to find her husband hunched over a bedside table, his damaged eyes a couple of inches above the paper.

Halfway to Dallas, Old Blue passed through Grand Prairie and Doc Hall chuckled at an image dancing inside his mind.

"I guess we're going be throwing the ball over the lot today. That ought to drive those rich bastards crazy."

Russell laughed.

"They already think I'm nuts," he said. "The Dallas papers are calling me the 'mob bomber.' "

"I don't know if that's such a bad thing," the old doctor said. "Maybe they're just a'scared of you."

The coach shook his head. "I doubt it. But they've never seen a coach sending five boys out on pass plays. Shoot, I was doing that all the way back to the 1927 season. God knows I've tried a jillion things."

"Hold on," Doc said. "This ain't exactly been a bed of roses."

"Truth is, about ninety percent of the stuff I tried wasn't any good. But we took the ten percent and made it good."

Doc cleared his throat and slapped the dashboard.

"Mr. Russell, have you ever thought about coming up with a name for this offense? After all, you brought the baby into the world."

"I've thought about it. But I really don't know."

Doc thumped a cigar ash through the side window.

"To me, it defies explanation," he said. "And I doubt that anybody'll ever come up with a name."

Little did Russell know that in the decades ahead coaches all over America would copy his blueprint and call it the "spread offense." By the nineties, it would become one of the most popular formations in all levels of football. All Russell knew at the moment was that his detractors believed he was from another planet. In truth, he couldn't have cared less what they thought. What mattered the most at the moment was that the Mites held a 3-0 record since 1932 against the rich and powerful Highland Park Scots, and that nobody could take that away from them.

Russell's record against Highland Park had inspired a *Dallas Morning News* columnist to suggest that the well-heeled suburbanites pool their money and hire away the mad scientist.

Pop Boone had once asked him if he would consider taking the job at Highland Park.

"No sir," he told the writer. "I enjoy the role of the dark horse just fine."

Indeed, they would be the dark horse today. All of the experts were picking the Scots to win. And, of course, no one could avoid the comparisons to Seabiscuit versus War Admiral. The orphans were the tiny horse with the short legs and all the beauty of a mesquite patch. Conversely, Highland Park would be decked out in brand-new black uniforms with gold trim and gold helmets. Not a thread would be torn, not a sock unraveled, not a speck of paint missing from their helmets. They were truly the War Admiral of the high school football set.

Nowhere in Texas could you find a wealthier suburban city than Highland Park, located five miles from downtown Dallas and built on monster oil revenues going back to 1917. Highland Park had initially sought annexation by Dallas. But when hundreds of monied people around Dallas began buying up land and building mansions along Turtle Creek and Preston Road, Highland Park turned around and told the big city to shove it.

Highland Park was the very reason that Amon G. Carter hated Dallas. In Carter's fertile mind, Dallas was a place where all men dressed in white tie and tails and women were fashionably gowned and bediamonded. On business trips to Dallas, the Cowtowner carried a sack lunch and refused to set foot inside restaurants or hotels. He would not be caught dead in Neiman Marcus.

Not an orphan alive would have felt welcome in Highland Park, or at SMU's Ownby Stadium, for that matter. Ownby Stadium was a new, redbricked fortress in the midst of a private university so lush and wealthy that coeds drove Cadillac convertibles with 353-cubic-inch V-8 engines. If Highland Park and SMU were an expensive Paris fragrance, the orphans were the aroma of the Fort Worth Stockyards.

Here was the great irony. Anyone traveling east on Highway 80 between Fort Worth and Dallas that frosty morning never would have suspected that the Mighty Mites were feeling like a truckload of cow manure. Horns were honking and the drum-and-bugle corps was playing. It seemed that half of Fort Worth was on its way to Dallas. Russell had to stay alert just to make sure that nobody plowed into Old Blue. Ahead of the football team was yet another long flatbed truck with musicians decked out in red fez hats and yellow billowing pants. They were playing "Happy Days are Here Again." Or at least it sounded like it.

"That music makes my ears hurt," Doc Hall said.

Russell just smiled.

For the last half hour, Doc Hall had been so lost in conversation that he failed to notice a mail sack on the floorboard of the truck. Now he was curious about it.

"Those are the telegrams we got just this week," the coach said. "I'm going to read some of them to my guys before the game starts."

"Mind if I take a look?"

What Doc Hall found were more than a hundred telegrams. Well-wishers from New York and Wyoming and Los Angeles and South Dakota and Oklahoma and Detroit and from towns all over Texas had been burning up the wires all week.

"How in the world do all these people know about the Mighty Mites?" Doc said. "I mean, we've never had a game in New York that I know of."

Russell shook his head. "We've been in newspapers all over the country. A guy from Detroit sent me one with our team picture the other day. They say that our story has been going out on the AP wire on a daily basis."

The Associated Press was indeed turning the Mighty Mites into cult heroes. National cult heroes. Sportswriter Harold Ratliff, who operated from the Dallas AP office, had become enamored of the orphan footballers. He covered most of their big games and his reports were not restricted to the Texas papers. In fact, dozens upon dozens of stories had made the national wire since the 1932 championship game against Corsicana. A sample of this writing:

> The Masonic Home Mighty Mites remain the number-one football attraction in all of Texas—the team most widely known. If they win, their coach, H. N. Russell, is flooded with telegrams and telephone calls from all over the country. If they lose, it's the same. It has often been said that the Mighty Mites have a twelfth man—the combined pep squads from all the teams in Fort Worth—but also a thirteenth man: sentiment. They're even cheered by the followers of a team that takes a beating from them.

An America looking for heroes believed in the Mighty Mites. It was the same obsession the nation held for Seabiscuit. People would go to any lengths to shed the Depression blues, and the best way to forget adversity was to believe in the underdog—an underdog with the heart of a champion. Many of these Mighty Mites believers lived as far away as Los Angeles and New York. Russell knew this from the sack of telegrams he received every day.

As Old Blue crept down Mockingbird Lane and turned onto the SMU campus, Russell could not believe the traffic jam ahead. He could see almost no empty parking spaces. In the distance, fans were already filling the upper rows of Ownby Stadium. More than forty thousand fans of both schools would somehow squeeze into the place.

Russell was waved into a side gate of the stadium and directed to park next to the west grandstand. As his players jumped off the back of the truck they were greeted with a noise that had become all too familiar.

"Orphans! Orphans! Look at the stupid little orphans!" The Highland Park fans were letting them have it.

Russell had seen it all before. Most important, he knew his boys would really be ready to play.

Chapter 14

LET IT FLY

As the last scrim of high clouds faded into a blue sky, Rusty Russell looked into the stands to see that every seat was occupied, including the make-dos in the aisles. Fans stood shoulder-to-shoulder around the south end zone and they were starting to shove their way onto the sidelines. Russell did not care if the crazies came over to the Mighty Mite side of the field. Only he, Doc Hall, and one substitute would be taking up space. But there were fifty Highland Park Scots and six coaches camped out on the other side, and chaos was in the making.

Football stadiums in the thirties did not mirror the grim conditions of the Depression. Fans wore their finest clothing to the big games and some of the women showed off expensive jewels. Most men wore a pressed gabardine suit and a fedora; practically every female on the Highland Park side donned something fashionably French from Neiman Marcus.

In 1907, Herbert Marcus Sr. and A. L. Neiman had opened Neiman Marcus at Main and Ervay in downtown Dallas. They had left Atlanta to open a world-class department store in Texas, in spite of an offer to invest in a new, sugary soda pop that would become known as Coca-Cola. But Neiman and Marcus never looked back. The Highland Park crowd had already turned their business into a huge success.

Russell had never set foot in Ownby Stadium, but he knew all the stories. The place had been erected in 1926, thanks to a huge contribution by a rich alumnus named Jordon Ownby. Its completion sparked a firestorm of protest among the academicians, because after more than a decade of existence, SMU still did not have a library.

SMU, it seemed, was in greater need of all-Americans than Rhodes Scholars. Ownby Stadium would witness some of the most electrifying games in the history of the Southwest Conference, and Russell had read about Bobby Wilson, the "Corsicana Comet," who had single-handedly carried the Mustangs to the 1935 Rose Bowl. Others who tore up the grass at Ownby Stadium were TCU's "Slinging" Sammy Baugh, the "Sweetwater Six-Shooter," Texas A&M's Jarrin' John Kimbrough, "the Haskell Hurricane," and Texas Jack Crain, "the Nocona Nugget." Just a few weeks earlier, little Davey O'Brien, the 1938 Heisman Trophy winner, known as the "Napoleon General," had played his final regular season game at Ownby Stadium. Ironically, the Mighty Mites had shut down O'Brien and his team during a 1932 high school playoff game by the score of 40–7.

Now, as Russell gathered his boys around him, he turned in time to see a black Ford roar through the fence on the south end of the stadium and four men jump out.

"Guess that's how things are done in Dallas," Doc Hall said. "Place is sold out, so you just tear down the fence."

Before the words were out of his mouth, more than a hundred fans rushed through the huge hole.

The Mighty Mites hardly seemed fazed by the ruckus. This was mostly a senior team comprising some of the Home's greatest players ever. Little Gene Keel could sling the football with any quarterback in Texas, and guard Jeff Brown was one of the toughest players anywhere. Nothing could match ends Miller Moseley and Norman Strange. Moseley stood five foot eight and slashed between defenders as if his feet were strapped to roller skates. Years later, he would be named to the Texas High School All-Decade Team.

Minutes before kickoff, Russell wrapped his arm around Keel. In his soft West Texas drawl, he said, "This is the biggest team we've ever played. We're not even going to worry about running the football. Throw the short one and we'll move it up and down the field."

It was true that the Mites were physically overmatched. Buster Roach weighed in at 128, guard Jack Bates at 126, and Moseley at 124. The Highland Park tackles tipped the scales at over two hundred pounds, and halfback Dick Dwelle, at 185, was bigger than any Mighty Mite on the field.

To start the game, Keel misfired on two of his first three passes, then punted out of bounds at the Highland Park thirteen. On the Scots' first play, Dwelle roared around the left end like the Cotton Belt Line bound for St. Louis. He broke through the arms of Strange and Brown and rapidly pulled away from the smaller boys, going eighty-seven yards to the end zone. The newspapers reported that the Highland Park fans rooted wildly and then sat back smugly, believing the game had already been won.

The Scots were brimming with confidence a few minutes later, when Dwelle passed into the left flat and Hubert Jordon weaved his way forty-three yards through defenders for a touchdown. Keel had the last shot at the three-yard line, but was leveled by three blockers.

Both teams would have trouble kicking extra points, and Dwelle's second straight miss made the score 12–0. That is where it stood at halftime.

In the third quarter, Keel began picking apart Highland Park in rat-a-tat fashion. He completed quick shots to Moseley, Roach, and fullback Buford Hudgins. After six straight completions, Keel spotted Moseley breaking free in the middle of the end zone on a hook pattern. He fired a low bullet into his gut. Jeff Brown's extra point kick flew wide of the right upright and the Mites trailed 12–6.

One of the Home's most visible and loyal fans was a man named Charley "Two Guns" McCoy. He never missed a game, and everyone knew he was there. When the Mites scored, "Two Guns" liked to jump the railing and do handsprings across the field. His cowboy hat never fell off.

This time, the Dallas cops chased him back into the stands and told him to stay there. But Masonic Home fans knew the law officers were merely wasting their breath.

Maddening to the Highland Park crowd was that both tackles were knocked out of the game with injuries, and that Dwelle was hammered unconscious when he tackled fullback Don Stephens at the Highland Park twenty-three. The Mighty Mites were stinging the Scots with ankle-high tackles, and Brown had finished off the big tackles by clubbing them with the fearsome forearm move known as the Humper.

On third down from the Highland Park twenty-three, Keel hit Roach along the sideline and the little halfback sprinted into the end zone. To the frustration of all the Masonic Home fans, Brown missed yet another extra-point kick. Now the game was tied 12–12.

But it was not unusual in this era of high school football that games be determined by twenty-yard-line penetrations. During tight games, fans were constantly apprised of this statistic, and when their teams crossed the twenty, they cheered as if a touchdown were on the books.

After Roach's touchdown, Russell pulled his team to the side.

"Gentlemen, we lead this game with three penetrations to two," he said. "If we can get one more, there's no way they can catch us."

Keel took the pep talk to heart. With receivers running short hook patterns, he completed seven straight passes, moving the Mites to the Scots' eighteen-yard line. The drive would soon stall. But without Dwelle on the field, Highland Park had no chance of reaching the end zone in the final three minutes of the game.

Remarkably, Keel had thrown forty passes and completed twenty-one, impressive statistics in an era when the off-tackle plunge was more popular than Mrs. Baird's white bread. The Scots had attempted five passes, completing two.

Up in the press box, *Fort Worth Star-Telegram* sportswriter Frank Tolbert could barely find the words.

If my hands weren't shaking so, I might write a good story on how the Masonic Home's little football-playing boys came from behind in the fourth quarter here Saturday afternoon with their undeniable passing magic and splattered Highland Park's caveman Scots all over Ownby Stadium's gridiron. The score was 12–12. The Mason lightweights won on penetrations, 4–2. But Highland Park's most powerful team in history was beaten as if the score had been 59 to 2.

Leaving the field that afternoon, the Mites were approached by several of the Masons wearing dark suits and flashing wads of cash.

The Mighty Mites, a thirteen-point underdog, had helped their followers cash some large wagers with local bookmakers.

The Masons were now handing out dollar bills to all of the players and saying, "Take your Sunday gal to the movies. Buy her something pretty."

The orphans were undefeated and headed to the state semifinals. They were also headed uptown with folding money.

Chapter 15

LOVE THY NEIGHBOR

The chartered bus from Fort Worth pulled into Lubbock six days after the celebrated upset at Highland Park. Old Blue was too worn for the grueling 250-mile journey into West Texas, so the orphans traveled in style—with seats, heat, and a roof over their heads. More than a hundred cars followed, along with a flatbed truck carrying the shivering Shriners.

The road to the state championship cut through South Plains all the way to Texas Tech Stadium, where, in twenty-four hours, the Masonic Mighty Mites and the Lubbock High Westerners would play in the state semifinals. The Mites were one step closer to Rusty Russell's dream. That morning, Harold Ratliff had filed yet another AP report that made newspapers all over America:

> The talk of Texas today was a gang of kids, who, according to all averages, should have been through with football a month ago. The Masonic Home Mighty Mites average 147 pounds to the man and stand as the "miracle team" of the Texas Interscholastic League. They're in the state semifinals and journey into far West Texas to tackle Weldon Chapman's mighty Lubbock High Westerners. Again, Masonic Home will be the underdog and the critics will sorrowfully shake their heads and say, 'Well, this is the last game for the Mighty Mites.'

At the moment, the Mites were not acting like a defeated bunch of orphans. They were laughing and slapping each other on the back as they got off the bus in Lubbock and swaggered into the locker room at Texas Tech Stadium to dress for the afternoon practice.

What they found that day at the center of the locker room were boxes stacked to the ceiling.

"Mr. Russell, you better come here and take a look," Doc Hall said. "You're not going to believe what I just found in these boxes."

Russell reached into one of the containers and pulled out an orange jersey with white numbers. The numbers were actually stenciled onto the fabric. From another box, he plucked a shiny pair of orange pants. He found black socks with orange vertical stripes. In yet another box were the helmets—orange, with a white stripe. Not a speck of paint was missing, and they actually matched.

Russell took off his glasses and rubbed his eyes.

"Where did this stuff come from?" he said to Doc Hall.

The old doctor shook his head.

"Highland Park."

Nobody breathed.

Finally, Russell said, "I've never heard of such a thing in all of my life. Who paid for all of this stuff?"

"Seems like the Highland Park folks took up a collection," Doc Hall said. "They call themselves the Highland Park Club. They wanted us to have new uniforms for the rest of the playoffs. Hell, they feel sorry for us."

Russell was still digging through boxes when he came upon shoulder pads, hip pads, thigh pads, and knee pads. Yet another box was filled with jock straps.

Fullback Don Stephens grabbed a pair of the new shoulder pads and put them on over his shirt and tie.

"I like the way this new stuff feels," he said. "I might just wear these shoulder pads all day."

Pop Boone had ridden with the team to Lubbock, and now he sauntered into the room. He flicked a cigar ash on the floor. "A rich guy from Dallas told me this stuff might be coming. It's a nice gesture. But I got to tell you something, Mr. Russell. This is going to sound a little cynical. But it looks like the Highland Park people are trying to hire you away from us. That's what the Neiman Marcus crowd is putting out."

Russell looked Boone directly in the eye.

"You tell them I'm not going anywhere. We've still got a state championship to win."

That was the cue for twelve Mighty Mites to start ripping through boxes as if it were Christmas morning. What they found were jerseys and pants that fit, along with the same numbers they had been wearing all season.

"How in the world did they know what size I wore?" little Buster Roach said. "Man, these pants fit like a glove."

The helmets, the jerseys, and the pads were practically tailored to fit the twelve Mighty Mites. It was not long before every player on the team was suited up in the new gear. That is when Russell pulled a yellow sheet of paper from his pocket.

"Gentlemen, I have something I need to read to you. This telegram came this morning and I think you'll find it pretty darn interesting. It's from Dick Dwelle. He's the Highland Park captain. You remember him. He tore us up pretty good in the first half.

"This is what he wrote to you: 'The entire Highland Park football team is behind you, win, lose, or draw. We are hoping that you beat Lubbock High. Everyone knows that the Masonic Home Mighty Mites possess the heart of a lion.' Signed Captains Dwelle, Munney, and Seay.

Jeff Brown raised his hand.

"Coach, this is pretty confusing. One minute they're calling us a bunch of stupid orphans and the next they're sending us Christmas presents. Why'd they change their mind?"

Before Russell could answer, Doc Hall blurted, "Because they're sick and tired of losing to us."

"Hold on," Russell said with a knowing smile. "Jeff, you have to remember, there are a lot of good people in this world."

Buster Roach stepped forward.

"Mr. Russell, if it's all the same to you, I don't mind wearing our crummy old uniforms against Lubbock High. We're not a charity case."

Russell took a moment to consider what the boy had said. "Buster, I understand what your saying. We've come a long way over the years with very little. What makes me especially proud of you boys is that you persevered through some tough times. So, this is what we're going to do: We're going to take a vote. How many of you want to play tomorrow in the new uniforms?"

Eleven hands shot straight up.

"Come on, Roach," Jeff Brown snapped.

Roach quickly made the vote unanimous.

The players began removing the game uniforms and dressing for practice when Texas Tech coach Pete Cawthon walked in with a bundle of Red Raider jerseys.

"Coach Russell, we're proud to have your little team in our stadium," he said. "We were just wondering if your players wouldn't mind wearing the Tech jerseys during practice this afternoon."

It seemed that everyone wanted to dress up the poor orphans.

Russell gladly accepted the offer and said, "Coach, can you do me one little favor. Can you make sure that nobody spies on our practice today?"

"That's a promise," Cawthon said.

Russell planned to introduce a series of new passing plays that he hoped would surprise the Lubbock High defense.

It was an odd scene for the next two hours at Texas Tech Stadium. At one end of the field, fifty burly men knocked heads and prepared for a January 1 Cotton Bowl date against St. Mary's College of California. At the other end, twelve scrawny orphans scurried and dashed through various pass routines, while a lean, bespectacled coach in a three-piece suit and an old doctor looked on. Outside of the stadium, Tech student managers were busy shooing people away from the fence. As it turned out, most were Masonic Home fans hoping to catch a glimpse of their beloved Mighty Mites.

When practice was over, Cawthon led his Red Raiders in a boisterous gallop down the field to meet the orphans. The Tech coach was treating the orphans like royalty—the kind of football royalty that he would like to recruit for the Red Raiders.

"Coach Russell and the Mighty Mites," Cawthon shouted. "Texas Tech is proud to have the scrappingest team in Texas work out on its field. Everything here is at your disposal. We hope you enjoy your stay, and if you can show as much of a game against Lubbock as you have in the other games we've heard about, we hope you win."

The Tech players roared their approval and, moments later, the Mighty Mites floated back to the locker room for postpractice showers.

EACH DECEMBER, AN old Negro with thick curly hair showed up at the Home, walking up the redbrick drive in clean but unpressed coveralls, while the orphans whooped and howled their approval. Moses was as welcome around Christmastime as Santa Claus.

No one knew where he came from or what he did. No one was sure of his real name. But he always arrived in early December, just as the Mighty Mites were entering the Texas high school playoffs. Moses was the self-appointed "good luck trainer" of the team. Russell had befriended the man a few years earlier and, being the superstitious type, believed Moses must bring the team some luck.

On the day before the Highland Park game, Moses had wandered into the orphanage and over to the practice field where the Mighty Mites were practicing. That is when he bowed his head and the boys came running. Each one rubbed his woolly hair for good luck. Moses, a few days later, would stand on the sideline at Ownby Stadium and cheer on the Mighty Mites. "It's the poor kids against the rich kids!" he yelled. "It's the poor kids against the rich kids!"

When the bus left for Lubbock, Moses was expected to be on board. Russell held the bus for ten minutes, but no Moses. Everyone knew he would somehow make it to Lubbock, and he did—by hitchhiking. Two hours before kickoff that Saturday morning, he strolled into the locker room clutching a dead jackrabbit.

"What are you planning to do with that rabbit?" Russell said.

"Well, I'd skin him and eat him. But this time I plan to cut off one of his little feet and rub it for good luck."

Moses had stayed up half the night chasing the jackrabbit around the countryside beneath the light of the South Plains moon.

"I come here to help the poor little orphans," he said. "And I come here to help you, too, Mr. Russell."

"I just hope you caught a lucky rabbit," Russell said.

To the good fortune of the Mighty Mites, the morning had broken cool and clear, with a slight wind from the north. It was perfect weather, considering all of the ice and snow that had fallen in far West Texas the last two weeks. A treacherous field would have doomed Russell's boys. The Westerners were big and strong on both sides of the ball, and, without the passing game, the Mighty Mites might as well pack their new uniforms and head back to Fort Worth.

Maybe old Moses was lucky after all. He had brought with him a brilliant blue sky.

Warming up two hours before kickoff, the coach made certain to keep his players away from the Lubbock players, who looked like giants, compared to the Mighty Mites.

Russell focused on the north sky and said a brief prayer that the game could be completed in decent weather. Anything was possible on December 16 in Lubbock, where the Northers roared down from Colorado with powerful winds, snow, and ice. Russell had grown up in that part of the country, and knew to never turn your back on the weather. Opening the door to further disaster was that Texas Tech's horseshoe stadium was open on the north end.

A more suitable setting for the game would have been TCU Stadium, amid the rolling hills of Fort Worth, where the winter storms were more bearable. But Russell had lost the coin flip with the Lubbock High coach, and now his team was warming up on the vast plains. The only wind-catchers were fence posts, telephone poles, and sheep.

He approached little Gene Keel.

"Son, we've got to move the ball through the air. This Lubbock team has boys that could be playing in college right now. But they're not as quick as us."

Russell removed his team from the field thirty minutes before kickoff. This surprised the six thousand Masonic Home fans who had made the drive from Fort Worth. The coach wanted to limit the orphans' exposure to "Wild" Walter Webster, the 185-pound fullback, and Avon "Shakespeare" Sewalt, the 230-pound tackle. Sewalt got his nickname because William Shakespeare was born in Stratford-upon-Avon.

As the Mites trotted off the field, Doc Hall caught up with Russell.

"Coach, these Lubbock High boys are grown men. Hell, most of them got a beard thicker than mine. We need to check some of their birth certificates."

Russell chuckled. "It's a little late for that."

Sitting alone on a bench in the center of the Masonic Home locker room was Moses, tears streaming down his cheeks. He was rubbing the rabbit's foot and speaking in a low voice.

That morning, *Star-Telegram* sportswriter Frank Tolbert had written:

> Moses will be muttering mumbo jumbo gutturals of encouragement, squatting at the end of the Mighty Mites' bench with tears in his reamy old eyes and with the hind foot of a South Plains jackrabbit fresh-killed Friday night on the flats north of the Texas Tech campus clutched in his hand.

As the orphans lined up to rub Moses's head, the old man mumbled, "I want you orphans to win so bad today that I can barely stand it. I've been praying on it for several days. I just hope the weather turns out good."

"Weather don't matter," Jeff Brown said. "I'm going to clean their clocks with the Humper."

The Westerners had never experienced the Humper, but were familiar with all of the stories. The forearm shiver was known to wreak havoc. Brown had been teaching the Mites the brutal tactic all season. Teams in District 7A, along with the boys from Highland Park, had learned to stay on guard against the Humper. The governing body of Texas high school football down in Austin had threatened to outlaw the Humper, but at the moment it was still legal.

The weather was holding when Russell gathered the boys around him in the locker room. The more he talked, the louder Moses cried.

Roach patted the old man and said, "It's okay, Moses. We got this one."

The capacity of Texas Tech Stadium was twelve thousand fans. But nothing was going to stop the Masonic Mites faithful from seeing this state semifinal playoff game. One more victory, and the Mites would be back in the state championship game. The end zones and the sidelines were jammed with fans, and others were climbing fences and perching on light poles, as the teams sprinted out of the locker rooms and onto the brown grass. Ice and snow had rutted the playing surface, and Russell had made mental notes about which parts of the field to avoid.

According to the *Star-Telegram*, the Mites were thirteen-point underdogs among Lubbock bookmakers. The Masons, hoping to line their pockets, had been working the hotels, restaurants, and saloons since the previous night, loading up on all of the action they could find. As the teams trotted onto the field for the opening kickoff, Russell could hear the Masonic Home bettors working the sideline. In some cases, the Lubbock High backers were laying fourteen, fifteen, and sixteen points, and there were plenty of takers.

Jeff Brown booted the opening kickoff on a line drive between two Westerners and it bounced through the end zone. Wasting no time, Walter Webster rumbled around right end and received a rude welcome. Roach cut him down at the ankles and Wild Walter toppled over like a big oak tree, losing a yard.

"Hey, Walter," Jeff Brown said. "That's the littlest boy we got. Wait till *I* get ahold of you."

Webster, a dynamic package of muscle and speed, was rated by the sportswriters as the best player in the state. But as he settled into his three-point stance for the next play, his eyes surveyed the Mites defense for little number nineteen—Buster Roach. The Westerners would lose two yards on three plays, and the Lubbock High fans groaned as they retreated into punt formation.

Keel completed three of his first four passes, but the Mites' first possession also stalled, and Brown punted to the Lubbock thirty.

Through the years, Russell had become accustomed to relative calm on the sideline. Doc Hall was known to throw around an opinion or two, and to cuss the officials. But this day Russell could not help but hear the rants and raves of Moses, who stalked the boundary line stroking his rabbit's foot and hollering, "It's the little boys against the big boys! It's the little boys against the big boys!"

Moses's sideline commentary was not only entertaining, it was right on the mark. Lubbock High versus the Masonic Home looked like the high school varsity versus the junior high. Only Norman Strange appeared suited to be on the field with the Lubbock players that, in most cases, looked about a foot taller than the Mighty Mites. Strangely, the Westerners could barely budge the Mites off the line of scrimmage, and Brown, by the middle of the first quarter, had drawn blood three times.

Frustrated by the stalemate, Weldon Chapman reached into his own bag of tricks. Left end Buster Johnson, swinging left on the double reverse, took the handoff from Webster and hurled a deep pass to Allen Jackson that moved the ball thirty-two yards to the Home's twelve-yard line. The ice now broken, quarterback Rusty Wilson hit Webster in the flat and he sprinted to the five-yard line before four Mighty Mites shoved him out of bounds. The Westerners gained no yards on the next two plays, and it appeared the orphans' defense might hold. But Wild Walter carried four Mites on his back to within a foot of the goal. On the next play, the big man forced his way through the right side of the line into the end zone and Lubbock had a 6–0 lead.

Keel found his passing touch in the second quarter and began completing the quick hooks. Fullback Don Stephens got loose in the secondary, and it appeared he might break it all the way until his right foot was snared from behind by a defensive back and he tumbled down at the Lubbock forty-yard line. Then it was Keel to Roach to the twenty-eight, and Keel to Miller Moseley to the fourteen, and Keel to Moseley to the three. In a scene reminiscent of the Corsicana championship game in 1932, fans were beginning to cross over the sideline and onto the playing field, forcing the referee to halt the game. Many had been throwing back whiskey that morning on the special trains from Fort Worth. Heavy overcoats provided plenty of room for the pint bottles.

The whole scene was making Moses nervous.

"Gots to get out of the way of our little boys!" he yelled at the revelers. "Our little boys can't beat the big boys and the whole damn crowd, too!"

Finally, the fans retreated and the game was resumed. Keel had completed eight of twelve passes in the drive, and everyone in the stadium expected a quick toss to Moseley. From the shotgun, Keel raised his right hand as if to pass—and deftly slipped the ball into the gut of Stephens. He could have walked into the end zone, as the Westerners were scurrying to cover a total of six receivers.

Writers in the press box swore that either the stadium shook or the ground moved when Stephens tore into the end zone. It seemed that everyone in the stadium was on their feet and cheering the orphans.

"I could've swore we were in Lubbock," Pop Boone said quite loudly. "Is anybody in this joint pulling for the Westerners?"

Jeff Brown, with a chance to provide a lead, instead kicked the ball wide of the right post and the cheering died. The score was 6–6.

At halftime, as the teams trotted off the field, Russell set his eyes on the northern sky, where dark clouds were gathering in the distance. The wind had yet to kick up, and he felt reasonably confident that the game would be over before a storm came tearing down the plains. Just to be safe, though, he made the decision to give the ball to Lubbock to start the second half. That way, the Mites could defend the south goal in the third quarter and have the north wind at their backs in the fourth. The Mighty Mites had lost the coin toss to start the game and now could exercise any option for the second half.

Russell sent his captains to midfield with instructions to defend the south goal.

"We want the ball," Brown told the referee.

"No we don't," Roach said. "Coach said we defend the south goal."

"You're crazy, Roach. Coach said to always take the ball."

Brown had not been paying attention.

When Russell realized the error, he called the referee to the side-line and tried to plead his case. But the man turned a deaf ear and walked away.

"There's not a damn referee in this state that'll favor us in a big game," Doc Hall said. "I've been working for this orphanage since nineteen-aught-aught, and I ain't ever seen them give us a break."

As the ball was being teed up, the old doctor yelled, "You're a crooked bastard, and you know it!" The referee winked and smiled.

The Mighty Mites defense was nothing short of spectacular in the third quarter, as the welterweight defenders chopped at Wild Walter Webster's knees and ankles, and he gained only three yards. Jeff Brown had already loosened enough teeth to qualify for dental school.

From the Lubbock sideline, Weldon Chapman yelled, "They're a mean, rotten, dirty bunch of orphans. Why don't you throw a flag?"

"Coach," the referee shot back. "Every player on your team is two foot taller than them orphans. Why don't you just play the game?"

Neither team scored in the third quarter, and it was clear that the Mites had a fighting chance in a 6–6 game. Now it was time to brace for the gathering north wind.

In the blink of an eye, Russell saw the storm. Blackness blocked out the horizon from the sky to ground. The temperature dropped fif-teen degrees in about three seconds. Lightning danced in the belly of darkness and thunder shook the air.

"It's a goddamned black blizzard," Doc Hall howled. "You better tie down anything you want."

Russell did not have to be told about black blizzards. He had seen plenty during his days on the farm. Black blizzards were like hurri-canes on the prairie, unleashing death and devastation throughout the area known as the Dust Bowl. Lubbock was situated on the southern edge of the Dust Bowl.

Russell felt his heart sink as he studied the powerful storm. Black blizzards blackened the horizon and turned day into night. They ar-rived with a mighty turbulence, and rose like a wall of muddy water as high as eight thousand feet. Not only were these atmospheric events terrifying to behold, they caused utter destruction to what remained of the area's final layer of plantable soil. These hellish storms were much like snow- or ice-filled blizzards, in that they were pushed along by the polar continental air mass. Electricity from the atmosphere lifted the dirt higher and higher, as thunder and lightning accompanied the curtain of darkness, giving rise to predictions that the world was ending.

Russell also knew that black blizzards were known to rain mud.

The Mighty Mites passing game was now shot. Winds approaching sixty miles an hour made it virtually impossible to connect with a receiver. Even more disastrous, the powerful wind was now at Wild Walter Webster's back, and he was tearing through the Mites' defense as if running down a ski slope. Weldon Chapman was quick to add Shakespeare Sewalt to the backfield. The Mites were now up against twin battering rams, and even the Humper could not save them.

At a time when fans should have been running for the exits, several hundred shoved their way onto the Masonic Home sideline. Moses was feeling hemmed in. He took several steps onto the field and seemed ready to make a mad dash into the Mighty Mites' huddle. Instead, he dropped to his knees and rubbed his lucky rabbit's leg.

"Please, God, don't hurt the orphans," he prayed. "Let the little orphans be okay."

Doomsday finally arrived when Sewalt slammed into the end zone from the three-yard line. The extra point kick made it 13-7. Now the wind was blowing up huge clouds of dirt. The thick brown haze had made it almost impossible for Russell, with his limited vision, to follow the action. The referee set the ball at the thirty-yard line. Before he could walk away, it blew all the way to the fifty. Hundreds of hats bounded across the field like jackrabbits, as Russell held tight to his own fedora and desperately tried to imagine a way out.

The Westerners kept hammering. Shakespeare left, Wild Walter right.

The orphans dug in and refused to surrender. They never stopped plugging. Buster Roach turned Webster for a somersault, and then stood over the big fullback as if he had just felled the heavyweight champ.

The wind roared like a locomotive when Webster burst into the end zone from four yards out. The extra point increased the lead to 20–6. Fortunately for both sides, the final two minutes of the clock ticked away quickly. That is how it ended.

Mud was falling when Russell made the long trek to the locker room. He felt numb. They had been so close in three of the last six years, he could almost *taste* a championship. Now all he could taste was dust.

What buoyed the spirit was knowing that his greatest group of players would soon enter the system. Players like Hardy Brown, Ray Coulter, Dewitt Coulter, and C. D. Sealy were the next varsity stars.

Through the storm he could still see a championship.

Chapter 16

BOOTED

Thirty minutes before dawn, Rusty Russell stepped out of the little apartment attached to the dining hall and plucked the *Star-Telegram* from the back porch.

The headline on the front page above the fold almost took his breath away:

MIGHTY MITES KICKED OUT OF BIG-TIME FOOTBALL

Russell tucked the newspaper beneath his arm and, feeling a little lightheaded, tried to imagine he had not read what he just read. But it was too late. Hurrying across the campus with a slight limp was Doc Hall, and right behind him stormed William Henry Remmert. Both men were holding the newspaper above their heads and shaking it like a tambourine.

"What the hell does the Texas Interscholastic League think they are doing?" Doc Hall grumbled. "They're jacking with the wrong people."

In actuality, the powers in Austin had been trying to do it for years. Now it appeared that their latest little scheme might just work. The TIL had come up with a new classification for Texas high schools called "Double A," and the Masonic Home was not invited. The Mighty Mites' days of playing big-time high school football and competing for the biggest prize in the state were over.

"The sorry bastards down in Austin have been trying to get us kicked out ever since we got in," Remmert said. "They will never get away with this."

Russell chuckled. "They get away with just about everything else."

The TIL was a seven-member unit composed of athletic director Rodney J. Kidd, Roy Bedicheck, and five professors at the University of Texas. Since its inception at the state's biggest university in 1914, the TIL had ruled like a dictator. High school coaches across the state had spoken out against the TIL, saying the University of Texas should not play God with the rules of high school sports. Many claimed the TIL was started to help recruit athletes to the University of Texas. Several efforts to oust the committee had failed.

What chafed Russell was that, through the years the TIL had made no secret of its dissatisfaction with the Masonic Home's deal with District 7A. The TIL did not approve of a tiny school getting to play with the big boys in Class A. The orphanage in the high school grades had never come close to meeting the enrollment requirements for the biggest classification in the state.

Under the TIL realignment plan, only the schools with six hundred students would be allowed into the new Double-A class. The Home could count 157, sixty-eight of those being boys. Not only did the TIL rule that the Home could not compete in the major leagues, the orphanage was being kicked all the way down to Class B, the very basement of high school sports. In Class B, the postseason schedule ended with the quarterfinal round, and that killed Russell's dream of ever winning a state championship.

It seemed inconceivable that after playing in the upper division for six seasons, and rising to the pinnacle of Texas high school football, the Mighty Mites could be kicked to the curb. But the grapevine had been buzzing for months that the TIL was ready to take the orphans down a notch. In the words of TIL director Rodney J. Kidd, "This decision is final." There would be no special dispensation. No one seemed to care that Russell had consistently cobbled together one of the best teams in the state, or that the Mites had reached the state finals once and the semifinals twice. In Kidd's view, the orphans belonged in the minor leagues. Instead of playing against the New York Yankees of high school football, they would now compete against the likes of the Birmingham Firecrackers.

As the sun popped over the horizon, Russell finally was provided with enough light to read the entirety of the *Star-Telegram* article. He quoted Kidd aloud:

> We could give no consideration to football strength or previous records. If we make an exception in the case of the Masonic Home, we will have to make an exception for someone else.

Russell eyed the two men whose expressions suggested they were ready to fight.

"They might not have to make an exception for us," Russell said. "We might just quit their little league."

"Now we're talking," Doc Hall said. "Maybe we'll just form our own league." Russell's face was turning redder by the minute as he read Kidd's quote aloud:

> There are a lot of teams like the Masonic Home that want into the bigger classification because of the bigger gate receipts. But under the present arrangement, the Masonic Home is going back into Class B.

Parked about a hundred feet from where the men were standing was Old Blue. Russell thought about the sputtering, coughing antique, and how it compared to the streamlined buses that transported the other city teams. He considered the ragged uniforms and helmets. He remembered the sacrifices made by his family. At the moment, the coach had not a single dime in his own pocket. So, where had all the gate receipts gone? To other projects around the Home. Meanwhile, the football team plugged along as a second-class citizen.

"If we're all so rich, why am I living the in the poorhouse?" Russell said.

"They think we're all driving Cadillacs," Doc Hall spat.

Russell realized that his players, along with the rest of the orphans, had yet to be apprised of this troubling news. So the three men walked quickly to the big boys' dormitory and Remmert gathered the football team on the first floor.

The sleepy-eyed boys filed quietly into the room. Some, upon seeing the three stern faces, sensed that something bad was brewing.

"This doesn't look good," C. D. Sealy said to Hardy Brown.

"At least Remmert doesn't have his paddle," Hardy said.

Russell removed his glasses, rubbed his eyes, and delivered the news as gently as he knew how.

"Gentlemen, you came to the orphanage with nothing," he said. "That is the reason that we've fought for the right to compete in the highest level of football that Texas has to offer. We just found out that the TIL down in Austin has decided that we're not big enough to play big-time football. So, next season they're creating a new double-A division that requires all of the schools to have six hundred students. As you know, we're not even close. So they're knocking us all the way down to Class B. That's the bottom rung."

Little Gene Keel stood up.

"Mr. Russell, the reason we were able to play Class-A ball is because the district voted us in. Why can't that happen this time?"

"Because the bigwigs down in Austin came up with another new rule. You can only be voted into a double-A district if you have at least five hundred and fifty students."

There was a painful silence in the room.

Jeff Brown looked angry enough to unleash the Humper.

"That coach over at Poly High is causing all of this trouble, ain't he, Mr. Russell?"

Russell grinned. "There is no question that Luther Scarborough doesn't like us. But some people just don't like to lose."

Jeff Brown blurted, "I'd like to get my hands on those Poly Parrots one more time. They wouldn't have a football team left."

Brown and seven other Mighty Mites would be graduating in a month, and their high school football careers were over. But that did not soften the blow. Jeff walked to the front of the room and pointed to Hardy, his younger brother.

"What really hurts, Mr. Russell, is that my kid brother won't get to play for a championship. Hardy deserves a chance to show off his stuff. Is there anything that can be done to stop this?"

Russell had that look in his eye.

"We're going to try," he said. "We've got the backing of the Masons, and they are the most powerful group in the state. We're going to do everything we can."

The boys could tell that their coach was not ready to give up.

THE WAR OF words commenced within hours.

Luther Scarborough was the first to sound off.

"I don't think the Texas Interscholastic League did any injustice in removing the Masonic Home from top high school competition," he told the *Fort Worth Press*. "They have a twelve-month football team out there. The boys practice together, eat together, sleep together, and study together. Everything is coordinated around the clock when it comes to the football team. When my football practices are over, my boys scatter. At the Home, they all go to the dining hall together and eat a selected diet."

Reporters from the *Star-Telegram* and the *Press* worked around the clock, seeking opinions from everyone ranging from the police chief to a county judge to the pastor of one of the biggest churches in Fort Worth.

Hardly anyone agreed with Scarborough.

"If the Interscholastic League removes the Mighty Mites from top competition, then I will oppose the league," county judge Dave Miller said. "The boys from the Home form one of the most colorful aggregations in the state, and are followed closely by football lovers all over the state."

Police chief Karl Howard said, "Gate receipts will fall considerably if the Home is kicked out. Frankly, the only team in Fort Worth that everybody follows is the Masonic Home."

Rusty Russell jumped at the chance to air out his feelings. "I don't believe the fair-minded sportsmen of Texas will permit the ousting of our team. It's just like firing a man off his job because he doesn't have a dozen children. We're going to fight until the last ditch to keep our boys on athletic par with the other high school boys over the state. And fighting with us will be an army of Masons and an equally large number of fans who are not Masons. People all over the state believe that we are entitled to fair competition on the gridiron."

Telegrams began to arrive within hours. Members of the Grand Lodge of Texas were burning up Russell's phone. Each promised to challenge the committee's decision and to rally support in every sector of the state. A telegram sent by the High Noon Masonic Luncheon Club of Dallas to members of the TIL read, "All of the 400,000 Masons of Texas oppose this action. Every member has agreed to wire a personal telegram to Austin to protest this action."

Russell was offered space on the editorial page of the *Star-Telegram* and wasted no time firing off this commentary:

"School men like myself are asking for a vote in this matter, and since we are all Americans, it seems distasteful when an attempt is made to abrogate the principle of Democracy. Is it not unquestionable for the University of Texas, supported as it is by taxpayers, to maintain an autocratic department to work with all of the public schools. This is a great injustice to the boys, not only of the Masonic Home, but also the other schools being pushed out of the competition. The Interscholastic League committee jumped in and made this radical change without consulting anyone, and only public opinion can make them change. The imposition of this decision will be a further indication of the decreasing usefulness of the TIL in serving its members."

The statewide protest gained momentum with each passing minute and, according to the *Fort Worth Press,* was "gathering hurricane force." Flem Hall of the *Star-Telegram* wrote:

> The plan by the TIL might seem sound, but in some respects it is plain silly. Masonic Home is a very special kind of school and should be treated as such. It is really an academy, and if anything should be stepped up rather than down in the classification.

There was no more powerful political group in Texas in 1939 than the Masons. They owned the state legislature. The governor's mansion in Austin was occupied by a third-degree Mason, James V.

Allred, known for fighting monopolies, big businesses, and the Ku Klux Klan.

Masonic Home superintendent Thomas Fletcher, realizing that he had some serious backing, arranged a meeting with four of the TIL members. Before leaving Fort Worth, Fletcher huddled with Russell and Remmert and mapped out a plan that would heighten public attention. It seemed that Old Blue would also be making the 200-mile trek down to the state capital.

On a Wednesday afternoon down in Austin, Fletcher was given an audience with Rodney Kidd, Roy Bedichek, and two of the University of Texas professors. His voice rising, Fletcher threw open the curtains and pointed down upon Sixth Street, where the back of Old Blue was packed with members of the Mighty Mite team. On cue, the orphans looked up with sad eyes.

"Just look at those boys," Fletcher said. "You plan to deprive those little orphans of competing for the biggest prize in Texas high school sports. Tell me, gentlemen. Do you have no hearts?"

Just then, several hundred Masons began marching up Sixth Street, carrying protest signs.

It did not take an Einstein to realize that the TIL had a fight on its hands. The members could not deny the political clout already garnered by the supporters of the little orphanage. In voting to demote the Masonic Home, the TIL had failed to see the big picture. And the big picture was getting uglier by the minute.

The TIL had miscalculated what the ramifications might be of demoting such a popular team. They had bowed to the demands of some of the smaller schools around the state that were jealous of the Masonic Home.

For more than an hour, Fletcher twisted arms and hammered away in a loud voice. He managed to get all of his points across.

The next day, all four men at the meeting changed their votes. The Mighty Mites were reinstated into big-time football.

So what really turned the tide?

No doubt, the Grand Lodge of Texas had something to do with it. Fletcher knew that the Masons were his ace in the hole. Few people other than Fletcher were aware that Kidd, Bedicheck, and the two professors were long-time, dues-paying Masons. All he had to do was remind them of the problems they might face if the orphans were kicked down to Class-B football.

In truth, all that Fletcher had to do was play the hand that was dealt him.

Chapter 17

FORBIDDEN KISS

Pregnancy—just the mention of it caused stomachs to roil. It was the reason that doors to the girls' dormitory remained locked at all hours, why the window screens were nailed shut. Females were never permitted to stray into the back of the property to swim in Sycamore Creek or to pick peaches from the orchard. A Saturday morning trip to the moving pictures required at least one adult chaperone.

Thomas Fletcher demanded that every staff member be on high alert for boys and girls fooling around. Holding hands could get you kicked out. Pregnancy was the kind of scandal that could rock the orphanage, and, in the midst of the prudish thirties, could also shut the place down.

So it was little wonder that panic swept over the campus one evening when word spread that a boy had sneaked into the big girls' dorm.

In a matter of minutes, every staff member at the orphanage—including William Henry Remmert, Doc Hall, Rusty Russell, and Fletcher—descended upon the redbrick building in the center of campus. They searched each room and hallway, the basement, and the porches. They checked under bunks and desks. But they could not find Joe Davis, the alleged culprit. The men were about to give up when Remmert pushed deeper into one of the overstocked closets and found poor Joe pretending to be a mop.

Remmert dragged the boy out by his hair.

"You are expelled," the big man said. "The front gate is open. Do not ever come back."

It took Remmert less than five minutes to pack Joe's stuff.

"But, Mr. Remmert," Joe protested. "I haven't even had dinner yet. Can I at least get a bologna sandwich?"

"Not even a cold can of beans," Remmert said.

Hundreds of orphans watched from their dormitory windows as Joe, suitcase in hand, marched balefully toward his good-bye. Remmert was one step behind. It was a cold-hearted scene. Pitiable Joe was being cast out and there was nothing he could do about it. The message to the other orphans was that their worlds could come crashing down just as quickly if they chose to misbehave.

Two steps before reaching the front gate, Joe turned to Remmert and said, "Both of my parents are dead. I don't have nobody out there. Can I at least get train fare?"

"We called your aunt in Atlanta. She said she'd be to Fort Worth in a couple of days."

That was the end of Joe Davis.

DOUG LORD AND Opal Worthington fell in love in a moment of chance.

Lord, a young tackle on the football team, was sitting at the dining hall training table when Opal strolled into his life carrying a tray of mashed potatoes and cream gravy.

Opal had won the job as the football team's personal waitress because she had muscles befitting a wood-chopping, cotton-picking girl from West Texas. She was strong enough to arm-wrestle any boy. She had no trouble toting heavy trays of steak, mashed potatoes, rolls, corn, stewed okra, ice cream, and apple pie.

Thanks to Russell, the football team was afforded a reserved section in the dining hall and was served the best meals at the Home. Russell was trying to bulk up his little orphans, and no one could blame him.

Opal was also in charge of serving both milk and water. The boys had only one glass apiece, and were required to finish their milk before being served water.

At the moment, there were two drops of milk in the bottom of Lord's glass.

"Rinse," Opal said as she held out the water pitcher.

"What do you mean by 'rinse'?"

"Rinse out your glass."

Lord leaned backward and looked into her eyes. The boy's head bumped her chest and electric currents shot through his body. Words would not come out of his mouth. Lord was being flooded with emotions that he did not entirely understand. As Opal walked away, Lord turned to Chicken Roberts. "What's that girl's name? I'm in love with her."

"What took you so long?" Chicken said.

OPAL WORTHINGTON WAS the oldest of three daughters and the closest thing to a boy in the family. She was her father's right hand.

The Worthingtons lived in a ramshackle house planted so deeply between the cotton and the maize in West Texas that folks traveling Highway 208 between Colorado City and Snyder never dreamed it was there.

Charles Oscar Worthington could spare not a minute for his own farm because he was out chasing odd jobs, trying to keep his family fed. Twelve-year-old Opal was left to do almost everything—the milking, the planting, the cotton-picking, and the wood-chopping. Taut muscles sprouted on her lean arms and she was chiseled from head to toe. Everyone knew that Opal was destined to become the toughest girl in Scurry County. After all, she had been born in the midst of a blizzard on a day when the temperature dropped to five below. The high drifts made it impossible to seek a doctor's assistance, and Opal's twin brother did not survive being born.

Not a boy within twenty miles could swing an axe like Opal. What she really hated was that the wood-splitting had caused her to miss school that day. She promised herself that she would rise before the sun came up the next morning and walk three miles across plowed ground to the one-room schoolhouse.

It had been a long day of hard work. Now it was getting dark, and she hurried to milk the four cows before her daddy came home and it was time for supper. Opal had filled two pails to the brim when headlights pierced the rows of cotton and shadows danced across the back of the farmhouse. This seemed impossible. Oscar Worthington would be on foot. Not a soul he knew owned an automobile.

But Opal was certain she had heard the automobile tires breaking up clods along the sun-baked road. She could never remember anything but a horse or a mule approaching the Worthington shanty. The slamming of the car doors jolted her heart. She stepped from the shadows and did not recognize either of the men. They were large and seemed menacing in the twilight. Her daddy was not with them.

"Who are you?" one of the men said.

"I'm Opal Worthington. I live here."

"Is your daddy Oscar Worthington?"

"Yes sir."

"I have some bad news, little girl. Your daddy won't be coming home."

"Why not?"

"He's dead."

Opal's heart turned to putty. She glared at the men and said nothing. Then she walked over to the pails of milk she had just filled and pushed them clattering into the bin below.

THE SIGHT OF the dilapidated Worthington house made the two men shake their heads. The rotting door almost came off the hinges when they tried to open it.

"Ma'am, we found your husband dead in the backseat of a car about three miles from here."

Opal stomped her feet.

"My daddy doesn't own a car."

"Opal, be nice," Bernice Worthington said.

"Ma'am, he put a bullet in his own head."

"My daddy doesn't own a gun!"

Tears streamed down Opal's face.

"I don't understand," she said. "My daddy had no reason to kill himself. He *loved* us."

"I'm just giving you the facts, little girl."

"Are you the sheriff?"

"No, but I know the sheriff."

"Then you tell him I want to talk to him. My daddy didn't kill himself."

The men shuffled their feet and stared at the crumbling floor. Opal knew they were lying. Many years later she would learn the truth. Somebody indeed wanted Oscar Worthington dead because the Worthington farm was sitting on a mother lode of oil. It was the lure of easy money.

THE EXTENDED FAMILY filled up the little farmhouse an hour later. They had turned the place upside down looking for money and found less than a dollar in coins.

"You really have no choice," Aunt Bertha said to Bernice. "The kids will go to the Masonic Home in Fort Worth. And you, Bernice, will have to become a ward of the county."

Bernice was going to the poorhouse.

In spite of the family's destitute condition, Oscar Worthington had kept himself in good standing with the local Masonic Lodge. Some theorized he paid his dues because his plan all along was to put a bullet in his brain. At least that was the story that circulated around town.

They buried Oscar Worthington on the family farm, and three days later a shiny blue Packard with two well-groomed men in the front seat pulled into the driveway. They were Masons from Fort Worth.

The three girls told their mother good-bye and cried. They knew they might never see her again.

The large sedan sat idling outside the front door. Not in her wildest dreams did Opal envision a backseat so large and comfortable or a ride so smooth. She had never set foot into an automobile. They rolled through Sweetwater and Abilene and Cisco. Approaching Ranger, the man in the passenger seat turned and said, "You kids ready for some pop?"

"What is 'pop'?" Opal asked.

"Kind of like Coca-Cola, I guess."

None of this registered. But Opal smiled anyway.

"Why, yes, sir, we would love to have some pop."

They pulled into a gas station outside of Ranger and the three girls peered into a large steel box filled with bottles of many flavors. Each one pointed to a bottle with red liquid—strawberry.

Opal had never tasted anything so sweet in her life and was not sure she liked it. But she drank it out of politeness. Her sisters downed theirs in a matter of seconds and smiled to reveal red teeth.

Two hours later, the Packard approached Fort Worth and Opal marveled at a skyline that was beyond the imagination. They traveled east on Highway 287 before turning off onto a dirt road that passed a creek and wound up a hill.

The girls could see the orphans playing beyond the fence.

"What's that thing they are kicking?" Opal said.

"That's a football."

"I think I want to play football."

"You'll get to play tennis."

"Oh, goody. What's that?"

At the moment, the orphans were kicking and throwing, chasing each other, tackling each other, and punching each other in the mouth.

"Is there a school here?" she said.

"Of course. You'll go to school every day."

"That's exactly what I'd been hoping for."

Opal watched the children playing and then felt the sun on her face. This was the most exciting scene she had ever set eyes on.

Then she spotted the redbrick road.

"I want to walk on the redbrick road," she said.

"Go right ahead, little girl," the man said.

She followed the redbrick road straight to the little girls' building, where her dorm mother was waiting.

She turned again and watched the kids playing in the sunlight. She soaked up everything.

"I am in heaven," she said.

*   *   *

THAT OPAL WORTHINGTON would become the happiest girl at the Masonic Home in the coming weeks and months came as a major turn of events. Her heart had been shattered when her daddy was murdered. But the orphanage had sparked a revival of her spirit and her feet rarely touched the ground.

Opal would never forget the first day at the Home, when Mrs. McClendon, one of the dorm matrons gave the three Worthington girls a tour of the place. Each of the dormitory floors contained a community bathroom, and Opal, age twelve, was amazed at some of the equipment.

"What is that?" she said, pointing to a commode.

Mrs. McClendon was speechless, until she pulled out the background report on the Worthington girls and read it carefully. They had grown up dirt-poor, in a two-room house surrounded by miles of cotton fields. The two youngest Worthington children slept in cabinet drawers.

Before the matron could respond, Opal pointed to a sink and said, "What is that?"

Things really got confusing when Mrs. McClendon handed the three girls hygiene packs that included toothbrushes.

"What do you do with this?" Opal said, holding up the toothbrush.

There had been no modern amenities back on the farm. Teeth were brushed with a rag and baking soda. Clothes were dried in the wood-burning stove. The girls walked three miles to school. They had never ridden in an automobile until the two Masons picked them up in Dunn for the four-hour drive to Fort Worth.

No child, however, had made a smoother adjustment than Opal Worthington. She made new friends at every turn. She loved going to school every day, along with the strict supervision of the teachers. Back on the farm, her education was often interrupted. Schoolwork could wait. The cotton picking could not.

A few weeks after reaching Fort Worth, Opal could not wait to tell Mrs. McClendon just how happy she was.

"When I got here, I thought the Pearly Gates had opened up," she said. "I thought the redbrick road was the road to heaven. I really felt a lift in my heart. I knew when I got inside the grounds at the Home that everything in my life was going to be all right."

Mrs. McClendon and the other dorm matrons soon discovered that Opal possessed a fun-loving urge that rarely slept. Her imagination could not be harnessed. Especially on the day when she made a rather cunning connection with a boy named Leonard Hutto.

Opal was walking—practically skipping, actually—up the redbrick road when she was approached by Hutto. The boy was in the midst of performing his daily chores of carrying lunch trays to the nurses at the infirmary. He looked around, reached into his pocket, and stealthily handed over the contraband.

"What do you plan to do with it?" Hutto whispered.

"Smoke it," Opal said.

It was a cigar.

This rendezvous had been planned for several days. Leonard had managed to appropriate the cigar from a drawer inside one of the doctor's offices. Opal had gotten her hands on some matches and could not wait to light the big stogie and take a long drag.

A few minutes later, when she got back to the dorm, Opal approached her best friend, Anne Phillips, and pointed toward the community bathroom. The two girls locked themselves inside one of the stalls and Opal fired it up. She took a long drag and on the cigar and handed it to Anne. They were laughing and smoking up a storm when the door to the urinal swung open and there stood Mrs. McClendon.

"What in the world?" she said.

"We never thought you would know," Opal said weakly.

"I could smell that thing into the next county."

The matron actually laughed. "You girls are greener than my garden vegetables." They both hopped off the commode and started to throw up.

When they were finished, Mrs. McClendon delivered the bad news.

"You girls won't be going to the Saturday moving pictures for awhile. You know why?"

"Why?"

"Because you're going to be scrubbing kitchen floors every Saturday morning until the cows come home."

Their cigar-smoking days were over.

SATURDAY MORNINGS AT the Poly Theatre usually included a newsreel and a Western B movie. Not exactly fuel for the libido.

But if you were willing to roll the dice and sneak out after William Henry Remmert went to bed, you were likely to get an eyeful. Many of the boys were obsessing over a movie filled with chorus girls that sang and danced in various stages of undress.

All the rage at the time was a musical comedy entitled *Gold Diggers of 1933,* that starred blonde bombshell Joan Blondell, the Marilyn Monroe of her era. Magazines were filled with risque photos of Blondell, who probably showed more skin than any female of the thirties. Her role in *Gold Diggers* was enough to cause a young orphan to have heart palpitations. Blondell and the other chorus girls appeared in scenes wearing only coins, some large and others quite small.

One of the highlights of the movie was Ginger Rogers singing "We're in the Money," an ironic title for the Depression thirties.

Orphans Bill Mercer and Horace McHam sat through the movie twice late one night, even though they knew a butt-whipping was waiting for them when they got back to the dorm. They would never sneak this one past William Henry Remmert.

Remmert, as expected, was waiting for the boys with the paddle in hand when they got back to the dorm. But neither seemed fazed.

"You know, Mr. Remmert," McHam said. "I'd take another paddling for a chance to see that movie again."

In February of 1940, another movie of a different ilk captivated the orphans. There was not an empty seat inside the Poly Theatre when *The Wizard of Oz* was playing. It had been released in late summer 1939. The orphans laughed and cheered and found plenty of comparisons to the Home.

Toto, the little cairn terrier, was actually Ziggy.

The singing Munchkins from Munchkinland were the Mighty Mites.

The "Yellow Brick Road" was actually the redbrick road at the orphanage.

The "Great and Powerful Oz" was William Henry Remmert.

Ray Bolger, playing the scarecrow, bore a resemblance to C. D. Sealy.

The highlight of the film was Dorothy, wearing the ruby slippers, clicking her heels three times, saying, "There's no place like home. There's no place like home."

All the way back to campus, the orphans recited that line with one minor change.

"There's no place like *the* Home. There's no place like *the* Home." It became their mantra.

A YOUNG BOYS' time was usually occupied around the Home. There was football and the milking barn and the boxing team and trips to Sycamore Creek. They also shucked corn and picked peaches and sneaked around the neighborhood chasing Poly girls.

Naturally, the girls wanted to have fun, too. But they were locked in their dormitory much of the time, which inspired a need to create. They were willing to try anything to beat the boredom. They tried to cook soup over candles and crack walnuts by slamming the window down on them. Actually, the only thing that cracked was the window.

The best imagination belonged to Opal Worthington. She was a leader inside the big girls' dorm from the day she had arrived. She was the one who set up the Victrola on the front porch for all the all-girl dances.

"They won't let us dance with the boys," she said. "So we might as well dance with each other."

One of the most popular songs of the day on the radio was "By the Light of the Silvery Moon" performed by Ada Jones. The overly sheltered orphan girls rarely even saw the moon—or the stars, for that matter. But down in the basement, where there was nothing but bare walls and a concrete floor, all dreams were possible. With a little imagination, you could actually see the light of the silvery moon. It

was a naked light-bulb hanging from a long electrical cord. Opal and
the girls would circle around it, hold hands, and sing their hearts out:

> *By the light of the silvery moon*
> *I want to spoon*
> *To my honey I'll croon love's tune*
> *Honey moon, keep a-shinin' in June*
> *Your silv'ry beams will bring love's dreams*
> *We'll be cuddlin' soon*
> *By the silvery moon.*

OPAL AND DOUG decided after a couple of conversations at the dining
hall that they were meant for each other. They decided to go steady.
Never again would they pass notes to anyone else of the opposite sex.

The writing and passing of notes was a small industry inside the
orphanage. It required both courage and great timing. Teachers were
always on the alert. The best chance for communicating through the
written word was study hall late in the day, when one teacher had to
watch over about fifty orphans.

Opal would write something like, "I saw you on the practice field
today and you looked like a real man. I can't wait till we get married."

And Doug would write back, "I think I'll go shopping for a ring tomorrow."

The notes were tucked inside the unabridged dictionary that acted
as a makeshift post office at the front of the room. Upon delivery, Opal
would silently mouth the letter in the dictionary where the note had
been stashed.

If the teacher on duty happened to be heavy on the radar, a sub-
terfuge was employed. Doug might yell out, "Hey, there's a rat running across the dang floor!" The teacher would climb up on the desk
and miss everything.

If that trick failed, Doug knew some others. He would light a fire-
cracker.

One afternoon, Doug delivered a note that gave Opal goose bumps.

She was so excited about his little scheme that she blushed. She winked at her boyfriend across the room and Doug knew that he had scored.

It behooved the young lovers that the tennis team and the football team practiced at the same time every afternoon. The tennis courts and the practice field were side by side, and both were bound on the south end by the peach orchard.

Opal would keep one eye on her boyfriend through the tall fence surrounding the tennis court. Doug's plan was to kick the ball deeply into the peach orchard. Then he would yell, "I'm going after the ball." At that point, Opal would knock her next tennis shot over the tall fence and holler, "I'm going to get the ball."

It happened in the blink of an eye. Deep in the trees, far from the view of everyone, the young girl in the white tennis dress would bend to retrieve her tennis ball just as the big football stud reached for his. No one would see the forbidden kiss. For one tender moment, the young boy and girl would float away on silvery clouds, somewhere over the rainbow.

Naturally, it would not be their last kiss.

Chapter 18

LONESOME COWBOY

U nlike the ragged, skinny kid that had scrambled through the front gate back in the summer of 1928, Hardy Brown now walked the orphanage like he owned the place.

He was a six-foot-one, 195-pound package of muscle and momentum. He was broad-shouldered, with a square chin and the face of a young Douglas MacArthur. Nothing could stop the boy, not the memory of his father being brutally murdered, not the absence of his mother these past dozen years.

Football was his life. It had been since age six, when he first put on the shoulder pads, pulled on a leather helmet, and climbed aboard Old Blue, the truck with mechanical bronchitis. Not in eighteen years of coaching had Rusty Russell seen anything like him. Hardy had grown up ramrod-straight, with slabs of muscle. He ran like the wind and hit with the force of a Joe Louis uppercut. There was even a rumor he had steel in his shoulder pads.

It was late July and the Mighty Mites were on the practice field, the hot Texas sun burning their faces as they prepped for the start of the 1940 season. Twenty kids, wearing only gym shorts and grim faces, ran wind sprints barefooted across a land covered with rocks, gravel, and sandspurs. Most were short or skinny and lacking in muscle. But nobody noticed or complained.

Not a single cloud infringed upon the hard blue afternoon sky. Texas was in the grip of yet another drought as cattle spent the better part of the day seeking shade and water and the grass around the orphanage had turned to ash. That morning, Rusty Russell had watched a starving jackrabbit stripping bark from a cedar fencepost.

The coach of the Mighty Mites stood on a hillside about a hundred feet from the edge of the practice field and watched the sweat pouring off his players' backs. Rules of Texas high school football forbade Russell from either organizing practice or instructing the players until the middle of August. The Mighty Mites, however, had been working out as a team on a daily basis, excluding Sundays, since early June. The coach had spent most of his time standing on the same hill, watching. Nothing in the rule book could stop him from either observing practice or having contact with his players during the long summer break. After all, he was the head coach *and* the principal of the entire school system, and these were his orphans.

Russell could only shake his head when he thought about Luther Scarborough, the coach of Polytechnic High, which was just a mile from where he was standing. The bane of Luther's existence was Russell's year-round access to his players. Luther was lucky if he could spend two hours a day with his team. The Poly Parrots were now long gone on summer break, working on oil derricks, chasing girls at the Dairy Queen, or flopping about in the Trinity River.

For the last two hours, Russell had studied the Mighty Mites as they practiced his spread offense—quarterback C. D. Sealy tossing passes to Snoggs Roach, Ray Coulter, and Teague Roberts. He had smiled when Hardy Brown took a handoff from Sealy and ripped through the line, his bare feet kicking up dust and rocks. The orphans took these summer workouts as seriously as they did the practices in pads leading up to games. There was a sync and a rhythm to the passing game. Most impressive was the cohesion in the line that included Ray and Dewitt Coulter, Brownie Lewis, Crazy Moseley, Walter Finnegan, Curtis Robbins, and Billy Joe Cagle.

The heat congealed in the Texas sky and a thermometer on a nearby oak tree registered 101 degrees. But the Mighty Mites worked harder as the day wore on. Russell was proud to watch this superbly conditioned and finely tuned team. His only wish was that they could hold onto the weight they gained at the training table during the winter months. In seasons past, they had been outweighed by thirty to forty pounds a man. But things were going to be different this year with Hardy Brown in the backfield and the lanky Coulter brothers lining up at tackle and end.

For Russell, it was hard to focus on the players from such a distance with eyes that had been so badly damaged by the mustard gas at St. Mihiel. The coach knew that he was lucky to be watching at all. Doctors at the Paris hospital, back in September of 1918, had initially said that he would never see again, and when his vision slowly began to return, he was overwhelmed with joy.

It was the winter of 1919 in Paris when he began go see the world again through a thick soup. He would walk to the window and try to make out images on the street. He asked the nurse if he was seeing the Eiffel Tower in the distance, but she said it was just another tall building. *Aha,* he said to himself, *at least I'm seeing "just another tall building."*

When faces and objects and buildings started coming back into focus, so did his life. Simply knowing that he was going to be able to live fully again made his heart rush with joy. There were so many things he wanted to do. He wanted to coach. He wanted to work with children. There was something special about being around a football team. He had almost missed out on the opportunity as a kid. His father had laid down the law when little Rusty said he wanted to practice with the high school team after school. A farm boy in the afternoon was expected to pick cotton until his hands bled. Finally, his father relented, saying he could pick in the morning, and Rusty was up at three, fumbling around in the dark, filling up the long cloth bags with pounds of cotton until the bus driver sounded the horn at eight.

After the war, when his eyes were good enough for the trip back across the Atlantic, young Rusty gazed at the great expanse of blue water and thought about his life replenished. It was a second chance. He held the world in wonder.

Russell had scoffed at the notion that because of his damaged eyes he should never play football again. Honestly, though, he could not imagine playing with lenses almost as thick as beveled glass. He had never seen anybody playing football wearing glasses.

But nothing was going to stop a man who had stared down death.

Russell would forever remember rolling on the muddy, blood-stained ground at the Battle of St. Mihiel, a badly injured medic still desperately rendering aid, praying that the thick, gray, stinking gas would somehow dissipate. He remembered the concussion of the bombs and being carried away on a stretcher. He remembered opening his eyes in the hospital. And the total darkness.

No wonder he thanked his lucky stars each day for the wondrous world his eyes could now see.

POP BOONE DROVE an old Buick that he called Blue Baby. He left the offices of the *Fort Worth Press* around noon that day for the short drive out to the Masonic Home. This was to be a surprise visit.

"Caught you," Boone said as he came over the hill and found Russell intently watching the unofficial practice. "Boy, if Luther Scarborough could see you now. Coaching up these little boys in the middle of the summer. He'd write a letter to the Texas Interscholastic League and have you tossed out of high school football."

Rusty Russell smiled.

"Popper," he said. "You look like you've been working out."

"Yeah, I went fishing down in Mexico last month and ate up all the tacos they had."

Pop had sweated through his gray suit.

"Think we could find us a place in the shade," he said. "I hate to sweat all over my notebook."

"This should be interesting," Russell said.

"Actually, I've got some bad news, Mr. Russell. I've decided to write a column that says your orphans are going to win state this year. What do you think about that?"

"Nobody'll believe you. We've had three chances and blown them all."

"It'll happen and I'll tell you why," the old sportswriter said. "You'll do it because you've got a tough bunch of resilient cusses on this team. Hell, the Texas Interscholastic League's tried to kick you out of big-time football twice and you just kept fighting. The last time they tried to kick you out, the whole state, the whole country revolted."

Russell studied the sportswriter's face as he pulled deeply on a stubby cigar.

"You got something else up your sleeve, Pop," he said.

"Yeah, I guess you could say so. You see, I got this theory. People've been telling me things. I'm hearing this'll be your last year at the Home."

Russell chuckled. "Popper, you tried this trick on me a couple of years ago."

"Yeah, but I think I'm right this time. I'm hearing more rumors from those rich folks over in Dallas. They're saying Highland Park's going to hire you away."

"Hold on—"

"Now wait a minute, Mr. Russell. Everybody knows that you're sick and tired of fighting the Texas Interscholastic League. Every time you turn around, they're trying to screw you. Every time you turn around, Luther Scarborough is trying to screw you. You're just like a country dog in the city. Every time you turn around, somebody's trying to screw you."

Russell shook his head.

"So I suppose you're going to write a story about this."

"I know what I know," Pop said. "And I've been around a long time, Mr. Russell. I know the rich people at Highland Park are putting together a kitty to hire you away."

Russell pointed toward the practice field where the boys were running the final gassers.

"That's one of the best football teams I've ever coached," he said. "That boy down there, Hardy Brown, is the best football player in the whole state. I've got the Coulter boys and C. D. Sealy and—"

"I'm not arguing with you, Mr. Russell. But Hardy Brown and C. D. Sealy and the Coulter boys are almost graduated. I'm hearing you ain't got that much talent behind 'em."

Boone had some of his facts straight and the coach knew it.

"Look," Russell said. "We've got football players all through our system. You never know which of the little boys is going to come up."

"Mr. Russell, the Depression is almost over. Enrollment at the

Home is going down. The Germans have already overrun France. The Japanese won't stop until they take China. And we're all headed for another big war."

"I know."

"So this is what I need to ask you: Do you think this season will be your last shot at the championship?"

Russell gazed at the cloudless sky, his mind drifting away. He did not know what to say.

AWAY FROM FOOTBALL, Hardy Brown rarely stopped smiling. Girls at the Home thought he was the sweetest boy they had ever met. The boys knew differently.

One Saturday morning at the moving pictures, Hardy went to the restroom and was preparing to return to the theater when one of the ushers, a student at Poly High, committed the cardinal sin.

"Don't they teach you orphans to wash your hands after you take a piss?"

Hardy walked up to the boy.

"No, but they do teach us not to piss on our hands."

As he said "hands," Hardy hit the boy with a pile-driving right that turned him into a wet noodle. He was unconscious before his head smacked the cold concrete floor.

Standing nearby was Doug Lord with his mouth agape. He knew from years at the orphanage that Hardy Brown was never to be crossed. But he had never seen anything like that punch.

"Hey, Fairbanks," Hardy said, using Lord's nickname. "If this guy doesn't wake up in fifteen minutes, come get me."

Lord stood over the limp usher for five minutes. That was all he could handle. He dashed through the front door of the theater and ran straight for the orphanage. He feared the poor kid might be dead.

Boys around the Home never stopped thinking about Hardy Brown. Of course, he was always around, just like the others, eating at the same table, sleeping in the same room, milking the cow right next to you.

But Hardy was different from all of the others. He was fearless and he scared the hell out of every team they played. You could see the opposing players eyeing Hardy as the Mighty Mites warmed up for a game at La Grave Field. You could hear them talking.

"Somebody's got to block that boy," they would say, "or our quarterback's gonna get killed."

Hardy was now making good use of the Humper, a blocking technique that had been introduced by his brother, Jeff. Being on the wrong end of the Humper in the age of leather helmets and no face mask was like taking a Dizzy Dean fastball off the chin. Jeff Brown delivered the blow like no other. That is, until his brother Hardy came along.

The Humper had initially been used strictly for blocking. But Hardy was now taking it to a new level on the defensive side of the ball. Throwing his shoulder into running backs and quarterbacks, he was sending them into orbit. Some did backflips. Coaches around the state had decried the Humper and claimed it to be illegal. But the orphans had yet to be flagged for using it.

"Those orphans are cheating," Luther Scarborough would yell at the officials. "That Hardy Brown needs to be kicked out of the game. He can't do that to my players."

From the day he suited up with the little orphans, Hardy had played like he was boiling over with rage. Kids from Riverside and Poly and North Side avoided him like a water moccasin. They would never forget the Saturday morning, down at Sycamore Park, when the Riverside boys taunted Hardy and the gang and called them orphans. This so incited Hardy that he leaped from the back of Old Blue while the truck was still moving. He knocked one of the offenders to the ground with a punch that would have made Max Baer smile.

When it came to fighting around the Home, Hardy Brown was at the head of the class. The Masonic Home seemed to be the fistic center of the universe, and William Henry Remmert, in spite of the presence of his giant paddle, could never beat it out of them.

The pecking order at the Home was established by your pugilistic abilities. The alpha male always sat at the head of the training table, and that person, of course, was Hardy Brown. It was his job to arrange for most of the fights that took place down at the water tower. If Hardy gave orders, you took orders.

As the boys gathered in the dining room for the evening meal, Brown looked across the table to Crazy Moseley.

"Crazy," he said. "Tonight you are going to fight Dewitt Coulter right after dinner. Got it?"

Crazy, who rarely spoke, simply nodded.

Still chewing his mashed potatoes, Dewitt looked up from his plate and glared at Hardy.

"Oh, so you want to fight me, do you, Dee-Witt?"

Dewitt held up a big paw like a stop sign.

"Hold it, Hardy," Dewitt said, his mouth full of potatoes. "I'll fight Crazy."

Snoggs Roach laughed.

"Hell, Dee-Witt, I could beat you up," he said.

Hardy said, "How big are you, Snoggs? About a hundred and thirty pounds?"

"That's what the football program says. I'm more like a hundred and twenty."

Dewitt Coulter was the biggest kid to ever hit the orphanage. At 210 pounds, he was a giant, compared to most of the Mighty Mites, a team that had averaged 147 pounds per man the previous season.

After dinner, all of the boys walked down to the water tower, and as the sun was setting over the eastern hills of Fort Worth, Dewitt Coulter and Crazy Moseley squared up to fight. Fists began to fly. Giving up almost sixty pounds, Crazy waded in and popped Coulter three times on the forehead, raising red welts. Two more shots and the big boys' eyes were swelling shut. Dewitt now whaled wildly at the air as a right uppercut caught him on the chin and knocked him to the ground.

"Get up, you big sissy," Hardy hollered.

Dewitt staggered to his feet just as Remmert came around the corner with paddle in hand.

"Y'all stop picking on poor Dee-Witt," the dean hollered. "You know he ain't nothing but a big *sissy*."

Fortunately for Dewitt, that is where the fight ended.

*   *   *

SUMMER VACATION FOR the orphans always started the first week of August and lasted until the middle of the month. It meant that an aunt or an uncle, or maybe an older brother or sister, would be at the front gate to pick you up. Many of the kids had lost both parents, although in some cases the mother was still alive. The Grand Lodge, with financial assistance from the Eastern Star, years earlier had constructed a widows' home in nearby Arlington, and some of the kids would be visiting there.

Hardy Brown was sitting on the edge of his bunk when Brownie Lewis walked up. Brownie's bags were packed. Hardy's were not.

"Hardy, is your mama going to pick you up this year?"

"I haven't heard from her."

"Hardy, where are you going for summer vacation?"

"Nowhere, I guess."

"Where's your mama?"

It was a look that Brownie had seen before, and he did not like it. It was like a dark cloud had descended over him. His face was sad, aching, brooding. Hardy looked straight ahead and seemed to be looking at something or someone that did not exist. Gone was the fun, animated boy.

"I know what you're going to ask me?" Hardy said emptily.

"What's that?"

"You want to know if my mama killed my daddy. I don't know, Brownie. Nobody ever told me. I don't know if I really want to know."

"What really happened to your mama, Hardy?"

"She took off running for the train right after they killed Daddy. We haven't seen her since."

Brownie shook his head.

"What are you gonna do while everybody's gone?"

"Sit around, I guess."

"My uncle's picking us up and we're going down to the Hill Country to do some camping. There's a big lake down there. Wish you could come."

"Me too."

As Brownie walked away, Hardy looked up and smiled.

"Don't get out of shape, Brownie. Football season's right around the corner."

Soon the big boys' dormitory was empty, with the exception of a solitary figure sitting on his bunk. Hardy knew this was going to be the toughest summer vacation of all. In the other years, Hardy had his brothers and sisters—Jeff, Rebe, and Katherine—to play with.

Two months ago, Jeff had graduated from the Home and taken a football scholarship at Rice University. He was down in Houston, working out on campus and getting ready for the upcoming football season.

Katherine had quit school the previous year and, much like her mother, Maggie Ann, had taken off without any explanation.

Rebe never adjusted to the Home. The kids chided him about his wandering right eye. Jeff beat up any kid that messed with Rebe, but it did not help. The boy had a learning disability and the teachers did not know what to do with him. Mr. Remmert pulled him out of school and gave him a full-time job working around the Home, and for a while, Rebe liked it. He was handy with his hands. He could paint and do carpentry work and he even liked to plant corn. But soon he was wandering through the front gate and running away. Fort Worth police would pick him up and bring him back, pick him up and bring him back. Rebe drifted farther and farther away. They found him one day down in Galveston and brought him home.

"If you find him again," Remmert told the cops. "Don't worry about bringing him back."

That was three months ago.

Hardy picked up a notebook from his bunk and began to draw. Looking through a four-year-old's eyes, he drew a picture of his dad. He was tall and dark, with big, friendly eyes. He remembered his dad carrying him around the backyard on his shoulders. That is when the pain hit his heart. He recalled the hot August afternoon back in West Texas when the Gossett brothers sneaked up behind them with shotguns.

He could still remember the look in Maggie Ann's eyes when he told her.

"I'll be back," his mother had said, throwing clothes into a bag. She ran for the train station as if her dress were on fire.

Years later, young Hardy finally learned that his daddy had been a fearsome bootlegger in the little town of Kirkland. There had been clan wars in Childress County. The Gossett brothers were getting even with Hardy Brown Sr. That is why his mother had fled. She feared for her own life.

A week later, the Brown kids were on the train traveling south to Fort Worth, where life would begin anew. Through the years, there had been football and fun and Mr. Russell and a letter jacket that he wore even on the hottest days of summer. There had been friends that had never left his side.

But today—well, it hurt.

Breaking the silence were footfalls on the stairwell. Sauntering into the room was a tall, thin man with thick glasses.

"Hardy, Mrs. Russell is cooking fried chicken," the man said. "I was wondering if you'd like to join us for dinner."

"Mr. Russell," Hardy said, "that's the best offer I've had all day."

Chapter 19

FIGHTING BACK

With summer vacation winding down, C. D. Sealy stood at the front gate of the orphanage and watched tears rolling down his mother's face.

"I love you so much," she said. "I want you to come with us, so we can be like a family again."

Widowed ten years earlier, Wanda Sealy had recently remarried. Now she wanted her youngest boy back.

"I never should have let you go," she told him. "It was the worst mistake of my life. I want you to come home."

C.D. pointed to the redbrick buildings.

"Mom, this is my home. It has been for ten years. We're starting football two-a-day practices tomorrow morning. And besides, this year we're going to win state."

Wanda Sealy Jones released her son's hands and tearfully walked away. She turned one last time.

"I'll come to all of your games," she said. "You play good, C.D."

Sunrise the next morning brought a surge of adrenaline to the orphanage. There was nothing like the first day of fall football practice. It lifted the spirit of every kid, all the way down to the five-year-olds, and sent an electric wave across the campus. Rusty Russell could feel it the moment he walked out of his little apartment into the bright sunshine. Too bad his mood had already been ruined.

That morning, a telegram had arrived from the Texas Interscholastic League, and, once again, the news was not good. The power brokers down in Austin had decided to reduce the age limit of the athletes competing in high school sports and once more their "decision was final." There would be no vote of the membership. There would be no reprieve this time around.

"They are dictators," Russell had said to Juanita that morning. "We no longer live in a democracy. Sometimes I wonder what we were fighting for over in France."

That year, high schools in Texas were expanding from eleven to twelve grades. So, with the addition of the extra grade, the TIL had decided it was appropriate to reduce the age limit for athletes from nineteen to eighteen years of age. To schools like Amarillo and Abilene and Fort Worth Paschal and Highland Park, this meant virtually nothing. But to a tiny orphanage, it meant that Russell was losing seven players—most of them starters. Anyone celebrating their nineteenth birthday before September 1 was off the team.

Now he had to break the news to the team. Hearts were going to be broken.

"Boys, I need you to gather around," he told the players. "There is some more bad news from Austin. No, they're not kicking us out of Double A. But I'm sure they would like to try. Instead, they're saying that anybody who turns nineteen before the start of next month is off the team."

The players looked at each other. Most of the stars were safe— Hardy Brown, C. D. Sealy, Brownie Lewis, Snoggs Roach, the Coulter brothers, Crazy Moseley, Basel Smith, and Teague Roberts. But seven others who had contributed to the football program since the age of six were out.

Bill Roberts broke down and cried, as did Willie Smith.

"Coach, is there anything we can do?" Roberts said.

"I'm afraid not this time. It looks like they've got us this time."

"But, coach, I haven't even graduated."

"We're going to make sure that you do," Russell said convincingly. "It is far more important to walk out of here with a high school diploma than with another letter for your jacket."

Russell studied all of the sad faces and felt his own heart starting to melt. Here were seven kids that had lived for this moment, for the chance to play on a championship team. Now their dreams were as dead as the scorched grass of the practice field.

That morning, the *Star-Telegram* reported that the hardest-hit team by the new ruling would be the Mighty Mites. Conversely, Amarillo would be reduced by about ten players to forty-five and the same could be said for Highland Park and Abilene High. The big-city schools were so well-stocked with players that losing a handful of nineteen-year-olds meant virtually no erosion.

Russell, a man of principle, was fuming. His disdain for the TIL could not be disguised. He told the *Star-Telegram,* "It seems to me that school men have three choices. We can oppose this rule and fight for one that actually serves the schools, we can be content with whatever the league dictates and support the league, or we can start to operate our schools in a sound way, in a way best to serve the interest of our students. I hope that we do the latter."

Again, Russell supported a movement to break away from the TIL and to start a league where the members would be able vote and therefore control their fate. Once more, he knew in his heart that he was fighting an uphill battle.

But that would never stop him from fighting.

Chapter 20

CAUGHT IN THE ACT

After a full day of practicing football beneath a hot August sun, the boys were thirsty for grape juice.

They were lying on their bunks at the big boys' dorm, when Hardy Brown informed C. D. "Wheatie" Sealy they were going to sneak into the dining hall that night for the purpose of stealing their favorite refreshment.

"We've already done that three times this week, and pretty soon we're going to get caught," Wheatie said.

Hardy laughed. "So you're not going with us?"

"Actually," Wheatie said. "I'm sneaking out tonight and taking my girl to the movies. Besides, I'm tired of grape juice."

Wheatie, the quarterback and cocaptain, was one of the smartest and toughest boys on the team. But Hardy knew there were plenty of football-playing milk slimes willing to make a ten o'clock run on the dining hall.

Already, Hardy had lined up Teague Roberts, Crazy Moseley, Snoggs Roach, and his best friend, Brownie Lewis. They would wait until the lights went out in William Henry Remmert's room and then sneak through the backdoor and out into the night.

"Let me give you one little piece of advice," Wheatie said to Hardy. "I've been hearing that Mr. Lynn and Mr. Bodiford are going to be laying for you guys tonight. They are pretty mad that so much grape juice has been disappearing. You better wait for another night."

Frank Lynn managed the dining hall and Earl Bodiford was the chief cook. Word around campus was that the two men had taken a recent inventory of the grape juice and discovered that several cases were missing. Hardy and the boys had been stealing the stuff for the last couple of weeks and transporting it to the darkened and remote practice field, where they drank it by the pint jars.

They actually thought they could get drunk off the stuff.

"There're grapes in wine, right?" Hardy said. "And you get drunk on wine, don't you? Why can't we get blasted on several pint jars of grape juice?"

Indeed, the boys had been slugging back the purple concoction and then howling at the moon until well past midnight. But since none of them had ever tasted alcohol—or been inebriated, for that matter— they did not know the difference between a wine buzz and a sugar rush. They were convinced that this wildly energetic feeling was the same intoxication all drunks felt after several bottles of wine.

Then, the next morning, when diarrhea struck, they thought it was just the ill effects of a full-blown hangover.

"God, I love getting drunk," they often said. "But the morning is hard on a drinking man."

Hardy, Teague, Brownie, Crazy and Snoggs tiptoed through the backdoor just past ten o'clock and then double-checked one of the rear windows to make sure that Mr. Remmert's lights were out.

"I think I can hear him snoring," Snoggs said. "He won't have any idea what we're up to."

The night was pitch-black, with no moonlight to guide them. Of course, they could have found the dining hall blindfolded after eating three meals a day there the last ten years.

Not a word was spoken as they sneaked across campus, until they bumped into Wheatie Sealy, who appeared like an apparition from behind a massive oak tree.

"Look, fellas," he whispered. "I scouted the whole place out for you and there are no cars parked around the dining hall. It looks like Mr. Lynn and Mr. Bodiford have gone home. But I still think it's a trap. Better save your thirst for another night."

"Nah," Hardy said. "Mr. Lynn and Mr. Bodiford got to be at work at five in the morning. No way they're hanging around the dark kitchen at this time of the night."

Hardy and the other milk slimes knew the exact time when Lynn and Bodiford arrived for work. Milk slimes started squeezing nipples at four in the morning and delivered the product to the backdoor of the dining hall at five-thirty. That is why they knew about the secret door to the basement that led to a staircase that would take them straight into the rear of the kitchen, where the grape juice was stored.

As they rounded the corner of the dining hall, they discovered that Wheatie was right. All of the parking spaces were empty. They also realized that Wheatie had vanished as quickly as he had materialized. They were now on their own. They just hoped that Hardy knew what he was doing.

"There is no reason to be scared, fellas," Hardy said. "If we get caught, I'll take the rap."

In truth, the boys were afraid of nothing. Living at the orphanage, tolerating Remmert's paddle, playing football, milking the cows, and chasing the Poly girls at all hours had turned them into a fearless bunch. They had learned to trust each other. The orphans stuck together, helped each other, covered for one another in a jam. It was the code of the Home. Besides, it was much easier to take a beating from Mr. Remmert than an ass-whipping from Hardy Brown.

The boys would never rat each other out, even when Remmert threatened them with twenty-five licks. Remmert, of course, had his ways when he suspected a crime. He would gather the boys on the sidewalk and say, "Okay, Hardy Brown, tell me who did it?"

No response.

"Okay, Sealy, tell me who did it?"

No answer

"Okay, Crazy, who's the culprit."

Crazy never talked.

Exasperated, Remmert would hand the paddle to Hardy. "Okay, you give Sealy twenty-five licks." Then Sealy would paddle Crazy and on down the line. But never in a million years would they give each other up.

The five boys moved like an infantry unit approaching a sleeping enemy camp. Not a word was uttered as they crept toward the rear of the dining hall.

"I'm going in first," Hardy said. "I'll do reconnaissance. If Mr. Lynn and Mr. Bodiford are in there, I'll yell 'Beat Poly!' If that happens, I want all of you guys to run for the hills."

According to the lingo of the Home, the basement back door was known as a "trap door." The dark wooden stairwell was called the "tunnel." Hardy was approaching the top of the stairs when he was grabbed from behind by two men.

"Beat Poly!" he yelled.

"Shut up," Lynn said. "You're in a lot of trouble, boy."

As instructed, the others bolted. Hardy could hear them running down the sidewalk and felt relieved.

Hardy was shoved down into a chair by Lynn, whose teeth were clenched in anger.

"Your ass is already grass," Lynn said. "We know you been stealing grape juice. If you don't tell me who the other boys are, I'll make damn sure you don't play a down of football for the Mighty Mites this season."

"No way," Hardy said.

Lynn was now madder than a wet hornet.

"I'll call Mr. Remmert over here right now and we'll see just how tough you are," Lynn said.

"Call him," Hardy said.

A few minutes later, a sleepy-eyed Remmert walked into the kitchen and yawned.

"What's the problem here, chief?" he said to Lynn.

"Problem is these boys have stolen ten cases of grape juice out of this kitchen the last three weeks. There's twenty pint-bottles per case. That's two hundred pints."

"That's a helluva lot of grape juice," Remmert said. "What have you boys been doing with it, Hardy—bathing in the stuff?"

"Drinking it," Hardy said.

"No wonder there's so much diarrhea going around."

Lynn pointed at Hardy and said, "If this boy doesn't come clean right now, I'm going to have him kicked off the football team. And I've got the backing of Mr. Fletcher."

Remmert placed his hand on Lynn's right shoulder. "Why don't we take a walk?" he said.

The two men headed for the kitchen office and Remmert quickly shut the door. But Hardy could still hear every word.

"Looky here, you dumb bastard," Remmert said. "If you think you can single-handedly kick the best football player in the state off the Mighty Mites, you got another thing coming. Now I'll handle the punishment on this matter. You can be sure there will be no more stealing of grape juice. But don't ever tell me you can kick Hardy Brown off the Mighty Mites. This might just be our last chance to win a state championship, and you can be damn sure he'll be playing."

Remmert walked out of the office and grabbed the boy by the collar. "You come with me," he said jerking Hardy out of the chair.

It was a long walk back to the dorm. Remmert told Hardy to wait on the sidewalk while he walked to the window on the first floor and yelled, "Brownie, Teague, Crazy, Wheatie, and Snoggs. Get your asses out here. And somebody fetch my paddle."

Five boys were now lined up on the sidewalk, facing one angry dean.

"First, I want y'all to know that Hardy did not turn y'all in. But I have my ways of finding these things out. I know that all of you have been stealing grape juice. And let me say that I'm sick and tired of it."

Remmert paused. "Where the hell is Wheatie Sealy?"

The quarterback slowly walked out of a long shadow and into the light.

"Where have you been?" Remmert demanded.

"Oh, just around, Mr. Remmert."

The big man actually smiled. "Okay, this is how we're going to do it. Each one of you will give Hardy five licks apiece. And then he's going to beat your butts twenty-five times. Any questions?"

It took the boys almost twenty minutes to finish their work. The *whop, whop, whop* could be heard all over campus and managed to awaken every orphan. But none of the football players/milk slimes uttered a sound. Nobody cried or moaned or even breathed hard. That was yet another part of the code.

When it was over, Remmert smiled broadly.

"Okay, boys, get your blistered butts to bed," he said. "If I hear about one more grape juice binge, you boys won't be going to the moving pictures till Christmas. Now get out of my sight."

The late-night plundering was officially over.

Chapter 21

I WANT MY MAMA

While the other boys were running from trains and bolting off Black Bridge into Sycamore Creek, Dewitt Coulter hauled railroad crossties around on his shoulders.

"It takes two of us to carry one of those big logs," Wheatie Sealy said. "That boy totes around two like they were toothpicks."

Rectangular railroad ties were six feet long, as thick as a tree trunk, and weighed close to a hundred pounds. Laid down side-by-side, they provided a foundation for the steel tracks that were the super-highway for trains thundering along at sixty miles per hour. Treated with creosote, the ties were built to withstand heat, rain, blizzards, earthquakes, tornadoes, and Indian raids.

Wheatie Sealy was splashing around in Sycamore Creek one afternoon, when he spotted Coulter jogging with a railroad tie on his shoulder.

"Dewitt, why don't you put that thing down before you hurt yourself?" he yelled. "Why don't you learn to act like a regular kid?"

At fifteen, Dewitt Coulter was a child inside a lumberjack's body. He stood six feet tall, with a head like an oaken bucket. You could fry a half-dozen eggs on his forehead.

Dewitt knew that toting railroad ties would build muscle, and compared to the other orphans, Dewitt looked like Paul Bunyan. He walked for hundreds of yards down around the creek with the railroad tie balanced on his shoulder. Later in the day, he would also work out with the Charles Atlas weights that had been left behind by Bob Hall. Like Hall, Dewitt developed an obsession for the twelve-pound steel ball called the shot put. When the others took off for Poly

Theatre on Saturday mornings, Dewitt stayed behind to throw the shot. When they returned, he was still grunting and heaving and throwing the thing at astronomical distances.

Dewitt, pronounced "DEE-Witt," was born in tiny Red Springs, about twenty miles north of Tyler in East Texas, where the Texas twang was thicker than honey. Tires were "tars" and pecan pie was "pee-can pah." He was the youngest of the Coulter clan, and entered the Home at age five, on Oct. 29, 1929. His brother, Ray, was two years older, and his sisters, L.E. and Ima, were in their early teens. Dewitt was the baby of the family.

That first night at the home, when they separated the Coulter kids, due to gender and age, Dewitt cried his eyes out.

"Can I sleep with Ray?"

"No, Dewitt," said Mrs. Thannish, the dorm mother.

"Then, can Ray sleep with me?"

"No, Dewitt."

"Then I want my mama."

A few weeks after their father died of tuberculosis, the four kids packed their bags for the orphanage. Maggie Coulter was not going to be able to run the farm and feed a family of six. She had a seventh on the way. So she kissed her four oldest kids good-bye one morning and put them on the train headed west. No one hated the situation more than Dewitt, who told everyone that he wanted to go home.

"I want my mama," he told everyone.

Tough kids like Hardy Brown, Brownie Lewis, Wheatie Sealy, and Arizona Pete tortured him about his homesickness. Crazy Moseley just laughed.

"I want my mama," the boys said. "Boo-*hoo*."

The Coulter boys grew faster than the other kids. Several inches of skin was exposed from the bottom of their overalls to their ankles. They were wearing big boys' clothes by the fourth grade.

Ray was an easygoing boy who adjusted well to Home life and all of its idiosyncrasies. Never one to shed a tear, Ray took to the game of football like a farmer to the plow. He could handle himself with the big hitters like Hardy Brown, and his hands were perfectly suited to catch the ball. The first play of each game was Sealy over the middle to Coulter. He would snag the ball at full stride and usually turn the short completion into a big gain. Russell noted the fluidity of the boy's stride and the softness of his oversized hands.

Dewitt was stronger and actually faster than Ray, but lacked his football IQ. He was awkward and tended to draw penalty flags. He could also be a crybaby when things did not go his way.

One day during practice, Wheatie Sealy broke a sixty-yard touch-down run, only to find a flag on the field. As usual, it was clipping—on Dewitt.

"What the hell is wrong with you, orphan?" Sealy yelled.

Dewitt might have been four inches taller, but Sealy shoved him backward like a bag of feathers.

"You ain't nothing but a big sissy," Sealy said.

Russell, the master psychologist, tried just about everything to help Dewitt. The coach hated to pull out his paddle. But Dewitt gave him no choice. He needed to get the boy's attention. When the boy was slow out of his stance, Russell whacked him on the butt. Then he would chase Dewitt down the field, yelling and waving the paddle until he got the message: *Do not clip.*

"Mr. Russell hits me more than any other boy on the team," Dewitt told his brother.

"And you got it coming," Ray responded.

Dewitt was a popular boy during his early years at the Home. But as he grew older and stood taller, he started to feel alienated. He was the only starter on the football field that had quit the milking team, in spite of it being the coolest clique on campus. Dewitt did not want to fiddle with a bunch of cold, wet nipples at four in the morning.

This annoyed Wheatie Sealy to no end. "You're the biggest boy in this school, and I honestly think that you're afraid of a bunch of old milk cows," he said. "Good thing you didn't have to grow up on a farm."

One night when the boys sneaked down to the dairy, a distrustful Dewitt tagged along. Dewitt walked into the barn and caught the boys in the midst of an uncivilized act with one of the cows. He took off running for the dormitory and never came back.

Dewitt was not a mental giant. The boys were always poking, prodding, and capitalizing on his intellectual deficiencies. But no one could ever get his goat.

Dewitt sneaked away from the Home one night with Doug Lord and Wheatie Sealy. They searched the Poly area for young girls willing to be kissed and fondled. But Dewitt's lack of wit managed to dissuade the local maidens.

The boys returned to the orphanage around midnight and managed to skirt the eagle eye of the night watchman. They were walking up the hill toward the big boys' dormitory when Lord spotted a red flicker.

"Cigarette," he gasped.

William Henry Remmert was on the prowl.

"Get down," Lord said hoarsely. "Mr. Remmert knows that somebody's sneaked out."

Fortunately, the grass had grown high behind the dormitory, so the threesome hunkered down. They watched Remmert pace and smoke, pace and smoke. His eyes scouted every inch of the property, and it was obvious he was not trying to walk off some sleepless anxiety. He lit up another cigarette and continued his watch. The boys were beginning to tremble with fear. It was only a matter of time before Remmert would beat them senseless.

A few minutes later, the big man sauntered down the hill toward the boys. All the while, his eyes were locked on the distant fence. Maybe, just maybe, he was waiting on someone else. Lovesick orphans made their getaway practically every night.

Standing in the midst of the tall grass, Remmert unzipped. Then came a long, arcing stream that seemed to last for ten minutes. Never looking down, he let out a short sigh and zipped back up. Then he lit another cigarette and strolled through the backdoor of the dormitory. Seconds later, he flipped off the outside light.

Feeling somewhat safe, the boys moved into the crouch position and finally stood up. Dewitt Coulter was soaking wet from head to toe.

"I really don't think he saw us," Dewitt said.

"Why's that," Wheatie responded.

"Because he pissed all over me."

Lord and Wheatie laughed.

"Orphan," Wheatie said "You are dumber than a bag of hammers."

WHAT HAUNTED DEWITT was the fearsome presence of Hardy Brown. They had been best friends as kids, but Hardy was now the biggest bully at the Home. No one questioned his place as the bell cow of the entire orphanage. Now Dewitt was avoiding Hardy like a cold shower. But there was nowhere to hide when the football players sat down at the training table.

"We're all going down to the water tower after dinner," Hardy would say. "Dewitt, you're fighting Brownie tonight."

"But Hardy—"

"If you don't want to fight Brownie then you'll have to fight me."

"Okay. I'll fight Brownie."

Through it all, Dewitt toted his railroad ties, lifted weights, and threw the shot put at near-record distances. Some of the smaller orphans had started shagging the twelve-pound ball for him. Dewitt threw it so far that it took three throws by the other guys to get it back to him.

Dewitt's dedication did not go unnoticed. There was no question that the big boy loved sports. But out on the football field, he was rapidly losing ground.

"I actually think that Dewitt is going to be a great football player someday," Rusty told Juanita. "He's just got to get tougher."

Unlike the other orphans, Dewitt seemed timid. He could not bring himself to mix it up with the other boys, and no one knew why. He did not fit the stereotype of the brave little orphan.

Orphans were fearless because they had nothing to lose. Parents, uncles, aunts, cousins, friends, dogs, cats, horses, and home, sweet home had been snatched away in the blink of an eye. Orphan boys became calloused, and some were meaner than a snake. Earl Bodiford's theory about the arousal of anger following the loss of a mother or father rang true. Hardy had suffered a double whammy in watching his father die and his mother run away. There was not an orphan on the grounds that would fight him.

So, what was wrong with Dewitt? Why would a boy already six feet tall cower on the football field?

Russell was trying to find out.

THE FIRST DAY of summer two-a-days was a journey through hell. The boys were in shape because of the practices in June and July. But Russell knew his team would have to be supremely fit. Many of the games would be won in the fourth quarter.

Because they had lost seven players to the new age-eligibility rule, the Mites would practice with twelve players. That meant the right side of the line would have to practice blocking against the left side of the line. It meant there would be only two players in the offensive backfield and two in the defensive backfield. It was not exactly game-like conditions.

Most of the day, Russell focused his eyes on Dewitt. On the first play, he jumped offside. He was then beaten on a block that allowed the defender to body-slam Wheatie Sealy. He missed tackles and was rewarded with a kick in the butt from Hardy Brown.

That evening, Russell sat down at his typewriter and composed a long letter to his overgrown man-child.

"Dewitt, I honestly believe that you are afraid of hurting the other boys. You are the strongest player on our team, but you seem to be holding back. Football is a tough sport and you're going to have to be a tough player. Otherwise, you will be the one getting hurt."

The father-son connection between Russell and the orphans was shatterproof. It did not matter that the boys had no fathers. Russell would forever be their father figure. Dewitt knew he was lucky to have someone like Mr. Russell watching over him.

The next day, Dewitt came out of his stance like a raging bull. He hit the boy across the line so hard that he flew backward. Hardy Brown patted Dewitt on the helmet.

"Now that's what Mr. Russell is talking about."

But two plays later, Sealy spotted Dewitt up to one of his old tricks, clipping one of the defensive backs. In just seconds, Sealy's index finger was an inch from Dewitt's nose. "That will get us a fifteen-yard penalty every time," Wheatie yelled.

Before Wheatie could finish the sentence, though, he was stumbling backward and landing on his butt. This time, Dewitt was doing the shoving.

Every day at practice, most of Wheatie's passes went to either Hardy or Ray Coulter, the right end. But the next one landed softly in Dewitt's mitts. He bowled over Crazy Moseley and Brownie Lewis and dragged Snoggs Roach more than fifteen yards down the field.

"Looks like I got a new receiver," Wheatie said. "Thank God that boy finally woke up."

WHEATIE SEALY WAS a rail-thin boy just short of six feet tall. He had gone through seventeen years of life believing that he did not have a real name. Only initials. Teachers at the Home often asked, "What does C.D. stand for?"

"Nothing," the boy would say. "My mama and daddy didn't give me a name. Just two initials. I don't know why."

His parents had never told him the reason.

One day, Wheatie was thumbing through the *Grand Lodge* magazine, when he came upon a roster of Masonic Home students. He decided to check if C. D. Sealy was on the list. Much to his dismay, he found no C.D. at all. Then he looked closer.

"My God," he yelled. "I've got a name after all. My name is Charles Drew Sealy. It says it right here in this magazine."

Hardy Brown cuffed him on the head and the two boys had a big laugh.

"I wonder why my parents never told me about my name," Wheatie said.

Hardy shook his head and chuckled. "I guess because they didn't want anybody calling you something stupid like Charles Drew."

The new Mites quarterback was filled with nervousness as the new season approached. He knew that he could never replace little Gene

Keel as a passer. In truth, Wheatie had little passing form. His long arms were like windmill paddles. His passes fluttered like a duck lifting off from a pond.

The loss of Gene Keel created a hole in the lineup. He had staked a claim as one of Texas's best quarterbacks in 1938, when he completed 21 of 40 passes against Highland Park. In ten games in 1939, he completed 146 passes for 1,959 yards. That was an average of 14.6 completions per game, in an era when most teams threw the football, on average, only ten times per game. But twenty-one thousand fans, most of them rooting for the Mites, saw the orphans lose to Woodrow Wilson 14–6 in the 1939 state quarterfinals.

Keel was not the only star player lost to graduation. Also departed were two of the best ends in the state, Miller Moseley and Norman Strange. Jeff Brown was playing college football at Rice Institute.

In spite of two straight 8–1–1 records, the 1938 and 1939 seasons had ended in bitter disappointment. The Mighty Mites were becoming known as the team that could not win the big game. They had captured five district titles under Russell, but the postseason was a hill they could not climb.

Still, no one ever questioned Russell's record at the Home. He could count one hundred and eleven wins and twenty-six losses during a dozen seasons, most of them against the toughest competition in Texas. His only disappointing season was 1937, when the Mites finished 5–4. They still outscored their opponents 178–58.

The 1940 season was supposed to mark the end of the Mighty Mites' fantastic run. At least, that was the opinion of the sporting press. Most of the writers were picking the Mites to finish no higher than second or third in District 7AA, and there was no promise of a playoff berth. Losing a third of your team to a new eligibility rule, along with breaking in a new quarterback, was not the best way to launch a championship season.

But, during that summer of 1940 Russell's confidence grew a little with each passing day. Big Ray Coulter, after catching seven touchdown passes in 1939, was already emerging as one of the best tight ends in the state. Ray had shot up to six foot four in what seemed a matter of days. College recruiters were already coming around to see the gangly orphan with hands like catchers' mitts.

"That Coulter kid is like a big octopus," Michigan coach "Fritz" Crisler said. "He's all arms and legs on defense. He really puts on the maul."

There was no denying Coulter's pass-catching talents. He also punted and handled place-kicking duties. Coulter and Hardy Brown had been elected team cocaptains, and Russell could not remember a better pair of leaders at the Home.

Losing eight starters from the previous season, either to graduation or the new eligibility rule, was tough. There was much work to do. Russell decided to move Dewitt Coulter from end to tackle, making room for Snoggs Roach to play left end. Brownie Lewis would be the right tackle, lining up next to Ray.

At left guard, Crazy Moseley, like his brother, Miller, was afraid of no one. He blew open huge holes in the offensive line and was like the immovable rock on the defensive side. Curtis Robbins was replacing all-district center A. P. Torres, and Billy Joe Cagle had taken over at right guard.

For the first time, Russell's team boasted some bulk. Hardy Brown weighed in at 185 pounds, Dewitt Coulter at 195, and Ray Coulter at 200. But the other starters were mostly midgets. Soaking wet, Snoggs Roach or Basel Smith could barely make 125.

On the afternoon of the first game, Pop Boone delivered as promised in the *Fort Worth Press*. He wholeheartedly disagreed with the other writers in town by picking the Mighty Mites to win their first state championship. As he had pledged, Pop also predicted in the same column that Russell would move on to Highland Park in 1941. The Scots were prepared to offer a bundle of money, along with some terrific young talent. It would be more than Russell could possibly turn down.

Pop wrote, "The sad part for the Mighty Mites is that when Rusty Russell wins that long-awaited state title this year, they can kiss the best coach in Texas good-bye. The man, in spite of his love for the little orphanage, will be hotter than the bakery down at Mrs. Baird's."

Rusty just smiled when he read it.

WHEATIE SEALY HUNKERED down in the back of Old Blue and heard the rusting engine growl to a start. From his nervous look, the boys instantly knew that something was wrong.

"God, I've never started a high school game in my life," he said to Hardy Brown. "I don't know what I'm going to do."

A dozen Mighty Mites in football uniforms were spread across the long bed of the Dodge, and most seemed relaxed. But not Wheatie. His eyes registered pure anxiety. His throat was dry and he could barely swallow. The Mites were about to open the season against one of the most revered football programs in the state. Nothing would come easily against the Wichita Falls Coyotes on their home turf. The Coyotes were ranked number-two in the state in the preseason polls. This is how the rest of the top ten shaped up:

1. Amarillo
2. Wichita Falls
3. Big Spring
4. El Paso
5. Paris
6. Greenville
7. Masonic Home
8. Dallas Sunset
9. Stephenville
10. Temple

Late that afternoon, Rusty Russell, decked out in a dark suit with a blue tie, spun the wheel, hit the gas, and guided the coughing old-world truck onto the winding asphalt strip known as Highway 287 toward Wichita Falls. Some wondered if Old Blue could last the hundred-mile journey through Rhome, Decatur, Bowie, and Henrietta. Sack lunches had been packed for all of the boys by Earl Bodiford.

An extra pint of grape juice was stashed in the bag belonging to Hardy Brown. It was old Earl's way of making a joke.

Wichita Falls was situated just south of the Red River, across the border from the towns of Waurika and Geronimo, Oklahoma. Football fever never died in Wichita Falls. The West Texas state of mind had seized its citizens back in the early twenties, about the time that oil geysered from the hard, red earth. Wichita Falls was really no different than Amarillo, Abilene, Breckenridge, Odessa, or Midland. Every business in town would be closed and locked up, every highway deserted, every man, woman, and child seated inside the stadium when Friday night's game kicked off.

Standing at the geographic center of the Red River badlands, Wichita Falls' football team supplied a pipeline of football players to Texas and Oklahoma. The Comanches ruled the territory in the early 1800s.

As the truck sputtered northwest, Wheatie Sealy was looking more pale by the minute.

"Those Wichita Falls boys are going to look like giants up against us," he told Hardy Brown.

"Not any more. Not since Dewitt woke up."

At that moment, Dewitt was sacked out next to one of the side-boards. He could not hear the horns braying from the drum-and-bugle corps just two cars back.

"How can a boy be sleeping at a time like this?" Wheatie said.

Hardy chuckled. "Let's just hope that he wakes up in the same world that he left from."

Russell checked the side mirrors to see hundreds of headlights trailing the Mighty Mites.

Fans could barely wait for Labor Day to crawl by, so the orphans could start playing football again. Almost nine months had passed since the 1939 season had cratered in disappointment. Most had read Pop Boone's column that afternoon and knew the stakes were high. This might be their last chance for a state title.

As usual, Doc Hall was riding shotgun. Russell was glad that he had company. But he wondered if the kindly old doctor ever went home. He officially worked out of Harris Methodist Hospital in downtown Fort Worth, but he usually pulled into the orphanage at sunrise and never left. You could almost set your watch by him. He was always packed and ready to go when Old Blue pulled through the front gate on Friday night.

"Did you read Pop Boone's column this morning?" Doc said to Russell. "Did you believe any of it?"

"Are you asking me if this is our last shot at state?" Russell replied. "Are you asking me if I've got my bags packed for Highland Park."

"Both, I suppose."

"Well, then, the answer is no and no. We've got a pretty young team, and I don't know what I'd do without you."

After three solid weeks of preseason practice, Russell was not overly worried about starting the season with a new quarterback, or with a young, raw player like Dewitt Coulter at left tackle. The offense was built around the running and receiving of Hardy Brown, along with the long legs and sticky hands of Ray Coulter. The defense was solid, with the Coulter duo taking up as much space in the line as four orphans used to.

"The only thing that worries me," Russell said, "is that we don't have enough bodies. We could've used those seven kids they took from us."

"Don't worry," Doc said. "I can mend a boy in no time."

Ahead they could see the bright lights of the stadium. Wheatie's stomach was churning again. The new Mighty Mites quarterback could already hear the Wichita Falls band playing from the stadium, and it was almost enough to make him throw up.

"Stop fretting so much," Hardy said. "Just give the damn ball to me and get the hell out of my way."

Wichita Falls was about as close as Hardy Brown would ever come to his old childhood home. Kirkland was just up the highway, on the other side of Electra, Vernon, and Quanah, the latter named for the great Comanche chief, Quanah Parker.

Hardy tried not to think about the little farmhouse, the bass-filled stream, and the sight of his daddy dying and his mother deserting the kids. Some days were better than others. He just wished Hardy Sr.

could be driving down for the game with a car filled with family members. Most of all, it would be great just to see his mother again.

Soon after the team's arrival, Russell stood in the middle of the field while his team warmed up and gazed upon the fans decked out in orange shirts, sweaters, and jackets, waving orange pennants. It still baffled him that so many people could care so much about this little football team. Fans of the Mighty Mites were spread across the state, and some even lived in Wichita Falls.

Russell had heard about the legions of followers from across America that worshipped Notre Dame. Most of them had never attended a single class on campus. Football, as America was finding out, attracted a passionate breed of fans, and the Mites had more than their share. At that moment, Russell tried to estimate the number of Masonic Home fans inside the Wichita Falls stadium. He actually thought they outnumbered the local fans.

Just minutes before kickoff, the coach put his arm around Wheatie Sealy's shoulders. "Don't worry, son," he said. "We're not going to do anything fancy tonight. Give the ball to Hardy and throw the quick slant to Ray. You don't have to win the ball game all by yourself."

Wheatie knew the best way to calm his own nerves was to carry the ball and take a big hit. So he called his own number on the second play of the game. He glided around right end, followed a block by Basel Smith, and burst into the open field. All he could see was an open field, and he was shocked it had happened so quickly—sixty-seven yards and a 6–0 lead.

But as Sealy turned around in the end zone and looked back upfield, he could see a flag on the ground. Dewitt Coulter was standing next to it. He could see Mr. Russell shaking his head. He could see the official tapping the back of his leg with an open palm—*clipping*.

Sealy ran toward Dewitt, waving his arms wildly. "What the f——," he yelled. Then he saw the rage in the big boy's face and decided to give him a wide berth. He did not want to be knocked on his butt in front of ten thousand fans.

"Look, Dewitt," Hardy said. "If you see somebody's back, don't block him."

"He turned around on me," Dewitt said. "I couldn't help it."

Another opportunity like that would not present itself again in the first half. The defensive units took control of the game, and Wichita Falls did not even cross midfield in the first two quarters.

Late in the second quarter, Doug Lord noticed blood running down the back of his leg and hoped the officials would not notice. He had been gashed by a flying cleat and knew that he needed stitches. Lord told no one about his injury at halftime. On the second play of the third quarter, the referee stopped the game and pointed at Lord.

"You can't be out here bleeding like that," he said. "Get to the bench."

Head down, Lord approached Doc Hall, who scowled at him.

The old doctor gritted his teeth and measured his words."Lord, did you know about this cut at halftime?"

"Yessir."

"Then why didn't you ask me to fix it then. Now I'm going to have to miss some of the game."

Doc Hall hated to miss a single play. He instructed Lord to stand on the bench so he could position himself behind the player and catch snatches of the action while he sewed. Lord looked down at the doctor to see if he was paying attention to his work.

"Can you go a little faster?" Lord said. "I want to get back in the game."

"No, Lord. And the next time something like this happens, you'll tell me at halftime that you're hurt."

Wheatie Sealy had completed a handful of passes in the first half without an interception. Now, as the game moved deeper into the third quarter, it was time for his bread and butter—the quick slant to Ray Coulter.

The big tight end was just five yards down the field when he cradled the high pass. His legs started pumping as he tore through two tacklers. Now the Coyotes were chasing him and the big orphan was not slowing down. Russell was amazed at how Coulter seemed to gain speed with every stride. He made it to the end zone before anyone could lay a hand on him. The roar inside the stadium told the story about the number of Mighty Mites loyalists in the crowd. They refused to shut up, even when Coulter's extra point kick sailed under the crossbar.

Charlie "Two Guns" McCoy sneaked out of the stands and was doing handsprings across the end zone before the Wichita Falls cops could react. He made it from one end of the field to the other before the local lawmen managed to escort him away.

"I think we got more fans here than the mighty Coyotes," Pop Boone announced to everyone in the press box. No one disagreed.

At that point, led by Hardy Brown, the Mighty Mites defense took charge of the game. Not until midway in the fourth quarter did the Wichita Falls offense cross midfield, and that drive stalled at the Home forty-one-yard line.

That was the closest that the Coyotes came all night to the end zone, and the frustration was evident on every face as the clock ticked to 0:00. The Mites had won 6–0.

Several members of the Masonic Lodge, dressed in dark suits and ties, strolled onto the field at the end of the game and started passing out dollar bills. Local bookmakers had been kind enough to offer the Mighty Mites and ten points. Once again, the Masonic Home bettors had made out like bandits.

Opening the season with a victory over the second-ranked team in the state put a smile on Russell's face and provided a badly needed hit of confidence for his players. The wind in their faces, they celebrated on the back of Old Blue all the way back to Fort Worth.

Russell thought about Pop Boone's column and knew he might be right about one thing.

A state championship was not out of reach.

Chapter 22

HARDY RULES

Even in the middle of September, with temperatures hovering in the nineties, Hardy Brown was rarely without his wool letter jacket. He wore it morning, noon, and night. Some of the orphans wondered if he slept in it.

It was his identity.

Just one game into the 1940 season, Hardy already had earned movie star status around the orphanage. His thundering tackles and his powerful inside running against Wichita Falls had merely fueled this image. The previous Friday night, every girl at the orphanage past the age of twelve had stayed up late waiting for Old Blue to roll back through the front gate. They wanted to catch a glimpse of Hardy Brown.

The two most popular citizens in Fort Worth at the time were Rusty Russell and Hardy Brown. This might seem hard to imagine, with a colorful character like Amon G. Carter strutting about town in cowboy duds and a pair of six-shooters on his hips. But the Mites were getting more ink than Carter, in spite of the fact that he owned and operated the most widely read newspaper in the entire South.

Now it was a laid-back Sunday around the Home, and the girls were hoping to see Hardy strolling across campus, or hanging around the redbrick circle, where couples were allowed to stroll for one hour without touching.

William Henry Remmert stood on the top step of the boys' dorm and kept an eagle eye on the boy-girl carousel.

"Get some air between you," he yelled. "Let me catch you holding hands and you'll be scrubbing floors till July."

Some of the orphans gathered on Sunday at the home of Superintendent Thomas Fletcher to listen to *The Jack Benny Program.* But Hardy had other plans. He was feeling bulletproof after surviving the grape juice scandal, and that was why he was waiting at the front gate at one o'clock that afternoon, his eyes intently focused on Wichita Street.

She would be coming in a red Cadillac convertible with the top down, her blonde hair flying. Her expensive French fragrance, her deeply tanned legs, and her perfectly sculpted body were certainly enough to turn the boy inside out. And, of course, no one at the Home—not Remmert, nor Russell, nor Fletcher—were going to stop the Paschal High School homecoming queen from driving straight into the little orphanage and picking up everyone's favorite football player. All were looking the other way when she arrived. They certainly did not see Hardy hop into the Cadillac with a smile wider than West Texas. They did not see the long, deep kiss.

They did not see Doug Lord running down the sidewalk in pursuit of the Cadillac, yelling, "Hardy, can I go with you?"

"What do you think, Lord?"

"No, I guess not."

Hardy Brown and the mystery girl, the daughter of a wealthy Fort Worth doctor, would glide down the winding, tree-lined road, as Lord watched them fade into the distance. They were the most beautiful couple in Fort Worth, Lord thought.

That night, Hardy Brown would have no curfew.

AS IT TURNED out, there was still one boy at the Home dumb enough to challenge Hardy.

His name was Red Webber, a nonfootballer who was growing more jealous of the football hero by the day. Webber was something of a physical specimen; at six feet, he packed plenty of muscle, and his temper had led to a number of scrapes.

Webber could stand it no longer when he spotted Hardy late one hot afternoon strutting across campus in his letter jacket.

"Hardy Brown, you think you're pretty cool, don't you?" Webber said. "But I'm tougher than you."

Wheatie Sealy stepped between the two boys and looked straight at Webber.

"Orphan, you've got to be out of your mind. This boy will whip your ass all the way back to Waxahachie."

Big Red had not come to talk. He had come to fight.

"Let's go up to the top floor," Hardy said.

"Why don't we go down to the water tower?" Webber responded.

"Because, orphan, I don't want the whole school to see me knock you colder than a Christmas turkey."

Minutes later, on the fourth floor of the big boys' dorm, Hardy connected with a left-right combination that sent poor Red sprawling across the floor. He staggered to his feet and Hardy knocked him down again.

That is when Hardy revealed his reason for fighting on the top floor. He grabbed Red's ankles and yelled, "Open the window!"

Wheatie's face turned ashen. "You're not going to throw Big Red out the window," he said.

"Just open the window, Wheatie."

Wheatie knew he had no choice. He just prayed that Hardy was no killer.

Hardy carried the kid over to the window and, with a firm grip on his ankles, dangled him upside down for all to see. A crowd quickly gathered below and the boys let out a long *ohhh*. One slip, and Red Webber was going to be a smashed bug on the sidewalk.

"Okay, Red," Hardy said. "Tell me who's the toughest boy at the Home?"

Red did not hesitate. "You are, Hardy," he blurted.

"No. I want to hear you say it loudly: 'Hardy Brown is the toughest boy at the Home.'"

The boy complied and Hardy nodded his approval.

"Now, Red, I want you to yell it as loud as you can. Twenty straight times without stopping. Or I'm going to drop you four stories headfirst."

Red's voice could be heard all over campus. "Hardy Brown is the toughest boy at the Home! Hardy Brown is the toughest boy at the Home! Hardy Brown is the toughest boy at the Home!"

Somehow, it was enough to pacify the heavyweight champ.

*   *   *

RUSTY RUSSELL WAS overwhelmed with all the hundreds of telegrams addressed to him since the *Fort Worth Press* hit the newsstands the previous Friday. Pop Boone's theory that Russell would soon bolt the Home for Highland Park had all of Fort Worth up in arms. Harold Ratliff picked up the theme and trumpeted it across the Associated Press wire. Now the missives were burning up Western Union from all over America. A fat sack was arriving each day.

"Let them talk," Russell said to Doc Hall during the afternoon practice. "Pop Boone is just trying to sell newspapers."

The Mighty Mites would wallop North Dallas 19–0 in the second game of the season, as Wheatie Sealy threw two touchdown passes to Ray Coulter and Hardy broke four tackles on a twelve-yard touchdown run.

The following Monday, you could feel the electricity on the practice field, even as the boys were warming up. Highland Park was the next opponent, and the Mites under Russell were 4–0 through the years against the rich kids from Dallas.

Thanks to Pop Boone, the newspapers in Dallas had seized the Russell-to-Highland-Park angle and run with it. Reporters were ringing the coach's phone and asking questions he did not care to answer.

"I have a great team here at the Home," he said. "I've been here thirteen years and I feel pretty darn comfortable. This is my home. I doubt that I will be going anywhere next season."

Russell stepped back and took the time to consider all of the forces at work against the Mighty Mites. Was it possible that he could be feeling any more pressure? The Mites were going up against one of the biggest and most resourceful football programs in the state. Again, Russell would be trying to outwork head coach Red Hume and a staff of five assistants. And, no doubt, the Highland Park players would be emotionally charged up, with revenge on their minds after losing the 1938 playoff game to the orphans.

To complicate matters, the Mites had a new quarterback whose passes sailed about as capriciously as the Texas wind. The 2–0 record really meant nothing. This was Russell's most inexperienced team in years, and there was no telling how they would handle the crazy scene over in Dallas.

Thirty thousand fans showed up at SMU's Ownby Stadium on a warm Friday evening, and the fans of Highland Park were calling for blood. "Orphans! Orphans! Orphans!" they yelled, as Old Blue pulled into the stadium.

Highland Park fans were surprised to see that the orphans were not wearing their expensive new uniforms. Hardy and Ray Coulter had called a team meeting the previous week to discuss the uniforms. The vote was unanimous. They were going to pack up the fancy duds and go back to the old, ragged stuff.

Hardy explained the team's feelings to Russell.

"The boys don't want to feel like we're getting a handout," he said. "We might be orphans, but we're not a charity case."

Russell had nodded his approval and pulled the old stuff out of storage.

Wheatie Sealy opened the game by tossing six straight incompletions. But in the second quarter, he returned an interception twenty-seven yards to the Scots' seventeen-yard line. On the next play, Hardy broke through a hole opened by Crazy Moseley, ran over the linebacker, and dragged two defensive backs into the end zone. Ray Coulter's extra point kick made it 7–0.

In the second quarter, Hardy took the pitch around right end and, with two blockers leading the way, seemed poised to power his way down the field. The Highland Park safeties turned upfield and braced themselves for a mighty collision. But just before reaching the line of scrimmage, Hardy set his foot and uncorked a perfect spiral that sailed into the hands of Louis Burress in the end zone. Ray Coulter missed the extra point and the Mites led 13–0 at halftime.

Nothing was going to stop the orphans in the second half. Russell went against his own coaching philosophy and sent in his only reserve, with the hope that game experience would pay off later in the season. Tackle Doug Lord made a smashing tackle at the line of scrimmage and failed to rise from the ground. Hardy stood over him and yelled, "Get up, Lord. We don't need any loafing."

"I can't get up," Lord said. But Hardy lifted him by the shoulder pads anyway, until he realized that his right leg had snapped in two places. The bone was sticking through the skin.

"Lay back down, Lord," Hardy said. "I'm sorry."

Doc Hall and Russell sprinted onto the field and could not believe the bloody mess that was Lord's right leg. They both felt nauseated. Doc Hall tried to shift the bone back into the skin, but the bone would not cooperate.

"Oh, my Lord," was all he said.

AFTER LORD WAS carried away by ambulance, the Mighty Mites scored twice more on a twenty-five yard reception by Ray Coulter and a one-yard run by Hardy Brown. The 25–0 victory was dominating and quite satisfying. Wheatie Sealy completed only 4 of 16 passes. But the Scots were trampled in total yards 188–38 and first downs 16–3. They crossed midfield only once.

The Highland Park fans uttered not a single word about orphans as Old Blue carried the Mites away from the stadium and into the Dallas night.

Chapter 23

THE HOUSE THE ORPHANS BUILT

Fort Worth, since the oil explosion of 1917, was a magnet for hustlers, gamblers, con men, grifters, swindlers, floozies, and the filthy rich.

Colorful cats dotted the landscape even during the hard years of the Depression. Amon G. Carter was the ringmaster for the grand circus that was Texas. He sold Fort Worth to outsiders the same way a carnival barker sold the naked ladies—loudly and incessantly.

In the fall of 1940, with the Depression fading fast, Fort Worth boasted a righted economy. The stockyard area was a bustling, thriving machine that ranked second behind Chicago in cattle population. A new building spree was on. This did not mean that Cowtown had lost its taste for the nonsensical.

Holding down the governor's mansion in Austin was a Fort Worthian that topped them all.

His real name was Wilbert Lee O'Daniel. But that would never do. He called himself Pappy O'Daniel, as in "Please pass the biscuits, Pappy."

Pappy had stunned the political analysts in 1938 by utilizing campaign tricks that resembled old-fashioned tent revivals. He played gospel music, then passed collection plates in the form of barrels labeled "Flour, not Pork." He was merely copying the strange act that brought him fame and fortune back in Cowtown. A widely known radio personality, he sold O'Daniel's Hillbilly Flour with a three-man band known as the Light Crust Dough Boys. He also enraptured his audiences with his poetry. His favorite: "The Boy Who Never Got Too Old to Comb His Mother's Hair."

Between Pappy O'Daniel and the Mighty Mites, something was always cooking in Fort Worth. How else would a tiny orphanage with a bunch of skinny kids convince the city to construct a brand new stadium across the street from the fabulously successful performance hall known as Casa Mañana?

Farrington Field was built in the shadows of downtown on prime real estate. The city really had no choice. Five-thousand-seat La Grave Field down on the Trinity River could no longer satisfy the masses. Tens of thousands were now flocking to see the Mighty Mites, and too many monied people were being turned away.

When it opened on April 18, 1923, Yankee Stadium was known as "The House that Ruth Built." Farrington Field became "The House the Orphans Built." Ironically, Ruth, at the age of seven, had been sent away to St. Mary's Industrial School for Boys, a reformatory and orphanage. One of his favorite pastimes was fighting, just like the little boys from Fort Worth.

On the evening of October 12, 1940, every police officer in Fort Worth was on the clock. Most were assigned to traffic duty, hoping to sort out the mess around the new concrete fortress situated at the corner of University Drive and White Settlement Road. When gridlock seized the city at five o'clock that afternoon, Old Blue was still huffing and puffing up Main Street, trying to deliver its cargo to Farrington Field.

The opponent would be the North Side Steers, another undefeated team with great aspirations of humbling the little orphans. The Steers had beaten the Mites only once in the last eight years and were madder than hell about it.

In the preseason, the sportswriters had overwhelmingly voted the Steers as the district favorite. Now the bookies were calling it an even game. There was plenty of money on both teams. This game approached the status of the annual backyard brawl between Texas and Texas A&M, and flaunted the same rocking enthusiasm as Texas-OU in Dallas on the second Saturday of October each year.

This was a classic matchup of what the orphans liked to call the "Home Guys versus the City Guys." These were two distinct classes of people. Of course, the "Home Guys" were the good guys. They believed in the rights of kids, dogs, and flag-waving, God-fearing Americans. "City Guys" were mostly punks. They had never been taught manners, values, or the right way to kiss a pretty girl. They were certain to bolt the country when the next big war hit.

"Home Guys versus the City Guys" was the embodiment of the "Us Against Them" mentality. It had been ingrained into every orphan. William Henry Remmert lectured on this subject every chance he got.

"You keep screwing up, orphan," he would say. "And I'll put you outside that fence with the City Guys."

Nothing sent shivers down an orphans' spine like those five words: "Put you outside the fence." It was one of the great ironies of Home life. The orphans, upon first arriving at the compound, could barely stand the thought of living there. It was almost like walking into prison. It was an environment they had never imagined and certainly never wished for. It was cold, dark, and creepy inside that fence.

Over the years, though, the Home would become a warm blanket. As the years passed, the orphans would come to distrust the outside world. Remmert had drilled it into their brains that life on the outside was cruel and uncaring. Thanks to Remmert, thought processes were altered. He was pleased to see their frightened looks when he said, "I'll put you outside that fence."

The "Us against Them" mentality was as old as the Tablets of Stone. Warlords had used it for centuries. Adolf Hitler, at that very moment, was stirring up hate in Germany with the same psychological tool.

In 1940, a popular approach with football teams all over America was to turn all outsiders into enemies. Opposing teams possessed cruel intentions, just like the people outside the fence. It was a rallying cry that the orphans could readily identify with.

Old Blue, the victim of a traffic jam, was now stopped at the corner of Main and Houston Streets, several blocks from the stadium. Cars loaded with Home fans stretched for as far as the eye could see. A flatbed truck transporting the drum-and-bugle corps was filled with musicians in funny hats. They belted out something that sounded like the school fight song.

Hardy Brown decided to seize the moment. It was time to light a fire under his teammates. Hardy stood up on the back of the truck and leaned against the cab.

"Everyone knows that we're the Home Guys," he told the boys. "We stick together through thick and thin. We play football together. We eat, sleep, and milk cows together. We never rat each other out. We believe in each other. Tonight, we got a game against the City Guys. The City Guys hate us. They call us orphans. They don't like it when we steal their girls. They don't like us period. How many of y'all really would like to be City Guys?"

"None of us," shouted Brownie Lewis.

"Good," Hardy said. "Because we probably got the most important game of the year tonight. We been playing the North Side Steers since we were little orphans down at Sycamore Creek. We've beat them every time. We know every player on that team. They hate us. We hate them. We hate them because they're City Guys."

City Guys was actually pronounced as one word. It came out as "SITeeguize." Saying it was like spitting it out. *SITeeguize.*

As Hardy delivered the pregame pep talk, Dewitt Coulter was just waking from a nap. His head was actually clearing.

"Hardy, I hate the City Guys."

"Aw, hell, orphan," Hardy said. "You don't even know what day it is."

The Mighty Mites through the years had always been regarded as the underdogs. It was easy to exploit that stereotype when your players were small and your student body small enough to fit into three or four phone booths. Now, though, North Side was trying to trade places with the Mites. One of the biggest high schools in Fort Worth wanted to see if the glass slipper might fit.

At that very moment, North Side coach Hugh Smith was standing in the middle of the locker room at Farrington Field, yelling his lungs out.

"Those little bastards beat y'all every time," he shouted. "They own you. Are you going to let it happen again? Next thing you know, those orphans are going to be trying to steal your girlfriends. Hell, they probably already stole your girlfriends, for all I know."

It was a little early in the season to call Masonic Home–North Side the biggest game of the year. With both teams undefeated, though, the winner would have a clear shot at the district title.

There was not an empty seat at Farrington Field as kickoff approached. The fire marshal was allowing fans to gather behind the end zones, just as they had done at old La Grave Field. Hundreds were sitting in the aisles. Seating capacity was fifteen thousand, and that would be the official announced attendance. In truth, it was closer to eighteen thousand.

Russell peered across the field at the North Side Steers jumping up and down and pounding each other on the shoulder pads, and he knew this was going to be a long night and a very tough game.

The first play caused Russell's heart to sink. Wheatie Sealy to big Ray Coulter was an automatic first down. But not this time. The little Steers jammed Coulter at the line of scrimmage, and when he did get free, two more defenders blanketed him. Sealy wisely tucked the ball beneath his arm and took the three-yard loss.

The Mites ran three plays and punted. Russell prayed the defense could hold.

North Side quarterback Elmer Moseley did not see Hardy Brown dropping into pass coverage. He tried to float a high pass to his tight end, but Brown intercepted at the Home's forty-five-yard line, tucking the ball beneath his right arm and taking off like the running back he was. He broke three tackles, dodged a couple more, angled to the sideline, picked up a block from Ray Coulter, and sprinted into the end zone. Russell's heart soared. Until he saw the flag on the field.

The referee dashed over to the Masonic Home sideline.

"Coach, the clipping is on number forty."

"How did I ever guess?" Russell said.

It was Dewitt.

Russell asked himself if the boy was ever going to learn. *I can't do anything with him,* he thought. He had lectured him and paddled him and written him a long letter. But it seemed that Dewitt was never going to stop hurting the team.

Out in the middle of the field, in plain sight of eighteen thousand fans, Hardy Brown walked up to the big tackle and glared at him. Then he planted his right foot in Dewitt's butt.

Russell decided it was time for a substitution and sent Teague Roberts in for Dewitt. The big boy looked like he was going to cry.

To win this game, Russell knew that he was going to have to make offensive adjustments. The Steers, having played the Mites every season, were just too familiar with the offensive scheme. With Ray Coulter bottled up, Russell turned to the running game. Hardy and Basel Smith were picking up big yardage. But two drives stalled inside the North Side twenty, as Ray Coulter missed both field goals.

Fortunately, Moseley, the North Side quarterback, kept throwing interceptions. Hardy again was the recipient, this time returning it just beyond midfield.

The Steers were putting three and four men on Ray Coulter. But Wheatie was not about to give up on completing passes to his number one target. He decided to throw a jump ball to Coulter at the North Side twenty-four, and the big tight end seized it like a hoops center ripping down a rebound. Wheatie then faked a pass and sprinted around right end to the sixteen. Hardy's four-yard plunge gave the Mites a first down at the twelve. On a quarterback draw, Wheatie powered his way down to the six. Then he turned the show over to Hardy, who gained three yards to the three, two more to the one, and, on fourth down, carried half the Steers' line into the end zone. Ray Coulter made the PAT kick for a 7–0 lead. That was the score at halftime. But Russell knew the game was far from over.

Neither team scored in the third quarter, as the North Side offense seemed to be going nowhere, with Moseley throwing his fifth interception of the game. Then he inexplicably started completing passes to his own team. The Steers moved the ball forty-two yards to the Home's twenty-six in just five plays. But Hardy intercepted his third pass on the night, and the Steers were all but finished.

The Mites powered down the field on a drive of some seventy

yards, with Hardy carrying the mail. Late in the game, Wheatie Sealy dived into the end zone from the one-yard line and Ray Coulter's kick made it 14–0. That would be the final score, as the Mites cleared one of the biggest obstacles of the season.

Once more, the Home Guys proved that the City Guys did not deserve the girls.

IT COULD BE said that a trend had been established when the Mighty Mites defeated Riverside High 18–0 the following week. None of the first five opponents had scored a single point.

Then it happened again in week six, as Fort Worth Tech fell 27–0.

Ditto for week seven. Paschal, normally one of the powers of the district, did not even cross midfield in a 19–0 loss.

The Mites were throwing more shutouts than Cleveland's Bob "Rapid Robert" Feller, who, in 1940, led the Major Leagues in wins, strikeouts, ERA, and shutouts.

As the season progressed, so did Wheatie Sealy's passing. The offense still focused on the running of Hardy Brown and the receiving of Ray Coulter, who was unstoppable when Sealy threw the ball high enough. Hardy and Ray were tied for the team lead with seven touchdowns.

Russell could not remember a better defensive unit at the Home. Brown dominated the games with tackles from sideline to sideline, and his eight interceptions in seven games led the entire state. The opposition knew not to overlook little guys like Basel Smith and Snoggs Roach. They were chopping the big boys down at the ankles.

Remaining on the regular schedule were Arlington Heights and Polytechnic High. Both were still in the thick of the district race, Arlington Heights with one loss and Poly, like the Home, still undefeated.

"Arlington Heights will be one of the most physical teams you've ever played," Russell told the Mites minutes before kickoff. "They're a lot bigger than us and you'd better buckle up your chinstraps."

Fifteen thousand showed up in spite of temperatures in the twenties. The Mites moved the ball to the Arlington Heights eleven, thirteen, and seventeen, only to be stopped each time. Twice, Ray

Coulter's field goal attempts flew wide of the right post, and a Coulter fumble killed the third drive.

But the Yellow Jackets could not dent a defense that had yet to allow an opponent to cross the twenty-five all season. The Jackets reached the Mites' forty-three on a punt return, but fumbled on the next play. Later in the game, a ten-yard sweep moved the Heights all the way to the Home's thirty-six, but it was nullified by a fifteen-yard penalty.

It was Russell's strategy to throw the ball, and Wheatie did the best he could against the north wind. After a Hardy Brown fumble recovery, Wheatie hit Teague Roberts in the left flat, and Snoggs Roach managed to floor two defenders with a cross-body block. Roberts weaved his way all the way to the end zone, and Coulter's extra-point kick made it 7–0.

Frank Tolbert's game story reinforced Russell's pregame prediction in the *Star-Telegram*:

> It was a tribute to the excellence of both teams that the Masonic Home Mighty Mites and the Arlington Heights Yellow Jackets played the most all-around magnificent football game of the season here Thursday night, even though bitter north winds where whistling through the Farrington Field ramps and it was colder than an Amarillo well-digger's shoulder blades.

Eight games and nobody had scored on the Mighty Mites.
But one hurdle remained. This hurdle was huge.

Chapter 24

MAN OF STEEL

Most people spent the thirties railing against the Great Depression. Luther Scarborough saved his venom for the Mighty Mites.

Scarborough, the coach at Polytechnical High, was the lone rebel among the Fort Worth coaches that voted every year to drop the Masonic Home from District 7AA. Two years earlier, Russell had gotten fed up with his archnemesis.

Russell rarely gave high voltage pregame pep talks, but Scarborough's threats of sending the Mighty Mites back to the minor leagues had sent him over the edge.

"Go out there and beat the Parrots team by forty points," he told the boys before the 1938 game. "We need to send these people a message."

The Mites fell short of Russell's wish. They won 39–zip.

Scarborough and the Poly Parrots could not wait for Thanksgiving Day, 1940, to finally arrive. It would be their day of reckoning, they thought. Through the years, they had been bruised and humiliated by the little orphans up on the hill. To compound their misery, everyone knew that Poly High, with more than a thousand students, was the biggest high school in Fort Worth. The Masonic Home could count about one-fifth that total population.

The fans of Poly were deeply incensed that the Parrots had not beaten the little orphans since the teams started playing in 1932. The teams did tie twice in 1934, with the Mighty Mites taking both games on penetrations. The second meeting had broken the tie for the District 7A championship and catapulted the Mites all the way to the state semifinals.

Poly had plenty of reasons for frustration. They had scored but twelve points in nine games against Russell's team. But the biggest bone of contention was that the orphans had been stealing the Poly players' girlfriends. Late-night raids into the neighborhood had been fruitful, and many a Home boy had gotten at least one kiss.

Years earlier, Jeff Brown had passed along some juicy advice about the Poly girls to the young milk slimes. The orphan boys were never going to have sex with the orphan girls locked down each night in the dormitories. But the girls out in the Poly area could show them a thing or two about the birds and the bees. No wonder the boys were sneaking out of the orphanage every night.

What really fueled the rivalry was the close proximity of the Masonic Home and Poly High campuses. Both were situated on hilltops, so when the autumn leaves fell, the schools were visible to each other.

Polytechnical was a proud neighborhood, filled with some of the most respectable, hardworking folks anywhere. The post-Depression recovery had filled the area with brand-new three-bedroom brick homes and shiny new cars. There was folding money again, thanks to the abundance of jobs, and parents were proud to send their children off to school in new blue jeans, saddle oxfords, and cotton dresses.

So, why were the girls of Poly so engrossed with the downtrodden orphans, when right there in their own backyard they could find so many big, strapping, hairy-chested football-playing boys?

Poly parents were perplexed. This rich girl–poor boy infatuation made no sense. It was yet another reason that the fans and supporters of Poly were running out of patience with Scarborough and why they were contemplating running him out of town. The orphans needed their comeuppance and they needed it sooner than later.

That Thanksgiving morning, traffic began to percolate up and down Highway 287 not long after dawn. Fans had been advised to leave early for the game, scheduled to kick off at one o'clock. Everyone in Fort Worth was trying to get their hands on a ticket. The streets were going to be unbearable.

Why not? The Mites and the Parrots were both 8-0. The winner took away the District 7AA title. The loser missed the playoffs entirely.

Right after breakfast, the orphans started climbing onto the back of Old Blue, as Russell wanted to arrive early at the stadium.

Doug Lord, with a fresh cast on his broken leg, had planned to ride with the boys to the game. But the previous day he had noticed blood oozing from his cast.

As Russell cranked Old Blue at nine that morning, he was surprised to see two black-and-white Fort Worth police cruisers creeping up the hill. Normally, the cops came to the Home to return wayward orphans. This visit caught everyone off guard.

One of the officers stepped out his car and approached the cab of the truck.

"Mr. Russell, we're here to give you an escort to the game," he said. "It's Thanksgiving, of course, and the streets of Fort Worth are going to be pretty doggone crazy."

Russell laughed. "We don't get a lot of favors around here. So I guess I won't turn you down."

Doc Hall tried to focus on the cop, but his crazy right eye would not cooperate. It shot off in the wrong direction. As the cop walked away, the old doctor blurted, "Sir, could you do me a favor. Would you mind turning on the siren?"

With a broad smile, he said, "We'll turn her on when we get downtown."

On game day, most fans headed straight for the stadium. But the Mighty Mites loyalists were a different breed. They wanted to be close to the orphans at all times. Cars had begun lining up on Wichita Street for over an hour. Tires on the flatbed truck carrying the drum-and-bugle corps were ready to pop. The musicians were now entertaining the crowd with some Tommy Dorsey swing that sounded more like polka. Russell, as he swung the big rig onto Highway 287, peered into the side mirror and knew he could not possibly calculate the number of cars that were on his tail. One thing was for certain, they were all getting a police escort. And nobody knew at that particular moment just how badly they were going to need it.

As the cop predicted, the downtown streets were already jammed. Cars were now backed up for three miles. Highway 287 was the only artery into downtown from the east side, and in a matter of minutes, Old Blue would be idling on the highway, stuck in a long line of cars.

Doc Hall gazed at the trouble that lay ahead, thumped a cigar ash out of the side window, and said, "Looks like we might as well get out and walk."

Several miles away, Fort Worth police were frantically working the downtown streets, diverting traffic, rerouting cars. Somehow they had managed to clear Main Street, and that allowed Highway 287 to flow again. The Poly team bus and Old Blue managed to reach the stadium in plenty of time for kickoff, and that was something of a miracle. But there were so many fans ringing the stadium—searching for tickets and drinking beer—that the players on both teams needed another twenty minutes just to reach their dressing rooms.

The day had broken clear and bright, with temperatures now pushing into the fifties. The downtown sidewalks were filled with revelers headed to Farrington Field. It was reminiscent of December 26, 1932, when practically everyone in town was headed for the Texas and Pacific train station, in hopes of catching a ride down to Corsicana for the state championship game.

Eighty percent of the crowd was decked out in orange and waving orange-and-black banners. Most were from Fort Worth, but they had also come from the Panhandle and East Texas and the Gulf Coast to cheer for the Mighty Mites.

Poly fans occupied a small percentage of the seats, but there was a fire in their bellies and revenge on their minds. There was plenty of talent on the Poly team and many reasons to believe they could finally take down the Mites. Running back C. D. Allen ranked among the best in the state, and he lowered his shoulder and ran with the same bruising style as Hardy Brown. Sportswriters had been comparing the two all season.

Poly tight end J. C. Phillips was a couple of inches shorter than six-four Ray Coulter, but could go up for the ball and make the big catch just like the big orphan. Phillips was a terror on defense. In scouting the Parrots that season, Russell had made several notations about Phillips and his ability to single-handedly shut down a running attack.

As the game approached, Fort Worth officials estimated attendance at eighteen thousand fans. It was actually closer to twenty-five, with fans sitting in the aisles, ringing the field, and perched upon anything that would hold them, including telephone poles. Several hundred were standing on cars and buses outside of the stadium, hoping for a glimpse of the action. Any school in the Southwest Conference would have been proud to have a crowd of that size.

Just before kickoff, Charley "Two Guns" McCoy decided to get a jump on the cops and started doing handsprings across the end zone as the teams ran onto the field. Men wearing the dark blue uniforms turned a blind eye. This time, anyway.

The Parrots were dressed in dark green jerseys and pants, with gold helmets. The Mites donned their ragged orange jerseys with white patches on the shoulders, white pants, and helmets.

As Russell gathered his team around him, Hardy Brown yelled, "Let's beat the crap out of these SITeeguize."

Across the field, Luther Scarborough was not as tactful. "How much longer are you going to let these little bastards steal from you?"

The Parrots really needed no pep talk. This was the day they had been waiting for, and it was time to take care of business.

The Mites were lining up to kick off, when Ray Coulter began scooping up dirt to build a tee for the football. That is when Scarborough tore onto the field and got into the face of referee Jack Sisco.

"That is illegal, dammit," he yelled. "We got a rule that says you can't kick the ball off a tee."

Scarborough had gone into the same rant two years earlier when Jeff Brown sculpted a tee out of dirt. He also won that argument.

Russell looked across the field at the angry banty rooster of a coach. "Here we go again, " he said.

On the second play of the game, Hardy Brown hit the line like a battering ram and ran over three defenders, including Phillips and Allen, en route to gaining twenty yards.

Again, Scarborough sprinted onto the field and grabbed Sisco's sleeve.

"I want you to stop the game," he said.

"You want to tell me why?" the referee said.

"Because I want you to check Hardy Brown's shoulder pads."

"For what?"

"Steel."

Sisco laughed.

"I'm serious as a heart attack," Scarborough said. "People've been telling me all year that he's got steel in his shoulder pads. Why else would he be knocking all these kids cold?"

Sisco chuckled to himself and trotted across the field to break the news to Russell.

"We have a slight problem," Sisco said. "Coach Scarborough is claiming that Hardy has something in his shoulder pads."

"So you're going to undress the boy right here in front of twenty-something thousand people."

"No. We're going to take him under the stands. It'll just take a minute."

"Then I'm going with you."

Beneath the west stands, Hardy Brown pulled off his jersey to reveal a worn pair of shoulder pads that probably should have been replaced years earlier.

"Son, those are a pitiful set of shoulder pads," Sisco said. "What happened to the stuff that Highland Park bought y'all a couple of years ago?"

"Kids won't wear it," Russell said. "They don't like handouts."

Sisco returned to the playing field and approached the Poly sideline.

"Coach Scarborough, Hardy Brown has no steel in his shoulder pads. In fact, he's wearing the most raggedy set of shoulder pads I've ever seen."

"What happened to the Highland Park stuff?"

"The orphans refuse to wear it."

"I guess they like steel better."

Sisco laughed as he walked away.

The purported scandal not only backfired, it served to fire up the Mighty Mites. Hardy strolled back into the huddle with a smirk on his face and told his teammates, "These city guys think I've got steel in my shoulder pads. They just won't admit that we're tougher than them. Hell, I could run over those fags in my overalls."

Hardy set out to prove it. He hammered the right guard for six yards and swept left end for thirteen. Dewitt Coulter had yet to draw a flag.

The Mites were at the four-yard line, with enough power in their legs to break down the concrete barrier behind the end zone. Hardy smashed into the line with head down, shoulders cocked, and legs churning. Then something happened that no one could have predicted. Poly's C. D. Allen broke through the other side of the line, drove his helmet into Hardy's chest, and the ball came flying out. Phillips recovered for Poly at the one, and you could feel the momentum swing.

Nothing was going to stop the Poly Parrots now. Allen repeatedly drove into the Masonic Home line, as Hardy stuck his shoulder into the boy's shoulder and face. But Allen kept powering forward. Reaching midfield, the Parrots were forced to punt. But the Mites gave the ball right back to Poly, and Allen returned this punt seventeen yards to the Masonic Home thirty-nine.

On third down from the thirty-four, quarterback Frank Smith flicked a pass over the middle to Phillips, who whirled through the arms of Snoggs Roach. He angled for the right sideline and picked up a key block from an unexpected source—the back judge. The man in stripes was scrambling to get out of the way when he managed to knock Basel Smith off his feet. Phillips was now in the open field, and he cruised the final twenty yards to the end zone.

Allen's kick flew wide of the post and Poly led 6–0.

Russell could not recall the Mites playing so poorly in a first half all season. The Parrots had become the first team to cross the twenty-five-yard line and the first to score against his team. The Home fans were befuddled and atypically quiet.

It seemed that C. D. Allen was everywhere the Mighty Mites turned. He did it all. He averaged fifty yards per punt. He returned punts at twenty yards per pop. He was mauling the Mites' line. Even Hardy Brown was having trouble bringing him down.

The Mites were in a pickle to begin the second half. For the first time all season, they were behind. The passing of Wheatie Sealy was not likely to bring them back, as the Poly defenders were sticking like glue to Ray Coulter. Sealy had completed only two short passes to the big tight end.

Now the Parrots offense was rolling again.

Allen tore off gains of five, six, and seven yards on each carry. Poly was at the Masonic Home twenty-yard line when Allen hammered the line and met Hardy Brown helmet to helmet. For the first time anyone could remember, Brown did not get up. It was like Joe Louis hitting the canvas. The stadium fell silent. Finally, he staggered to his feet and stumbled back to the huddle like a wobbly drunk.

Russell quickly called a time-out.

Brown was down on one knee when Wheatie Sealy decided to have a word with him.

"Hardy," he began. "I hate to tell you this, but C. D. Allen is laughing at you. He's over there right now laughing his guts out at you."

Hardy's vision was too blurred to see more than five yards. Otherwise, he would have seen that Allen had also been dazed by the collision and was being attended to by one of the trainers. Wheatie had made up the whole story.

Doc Hall waddled onto the field.

"Do you need to come out of the game for awhile?" he asked Hardy.

"Hell no," Hardy snapped. "I got steel in my head, you know."

Neither Allen nor Brown left the game. When action resumed, the big Poly back slammed into the line and never saw the Humper. Hardy Brown delivered it like a sledgehammer. Blood spurted from Allen's nose as he crashed to the ground.

Allen was unconscious for several minutes, and when he did come to, the Poly team doctor straightened his nose with a pair of tongue depressants.

"That boy's nose is crookeder than my right eye," Doc Hall said from the sideline. "Hardy flat turned out the lights on him."

Remarkably, Allen missed but two plays. But when he returned to the game, he was not the same ball of fire that had torched the Mighty Mites. It seemed that he did not want to carry the ball any more. When the Home punted, he strayed away from the ball and let it hit the ground. Instead of gaining huge chunks of yardage off tackle, he was being stopped dead at the line on every carry.

"C. D. Allen wants nothing to do with us," Wheatie yelled for all to hear. "That boy can't wait for this game to be over."

It hardly mattered. The Mighty Mites offense could barely put together three good plays. It was still 6–0 as the game moved deeper and deeper into the fourth quarter.

Poly was trying to run out the clock at their nineteen-yard line, when Allen made the biggest mistake of his entire football career. He fumbled and Ray Coulter recovered.

From the sideline, Scarborough instructed his defense to be alert for trickery. But Russell had nothing but old-school football on his mind. Hardy Brown left, Hardy Brown right, Hardy Brown up the middle.

From the three-yard line, Brown plowed into the end zone and the crowd sounded like a seventy-car freight train roaring by at full speed.

But there was one last piece of business to take care of. Ray Coulter had made about half of his PAT kicks all season. Miss this one and the season was over. The Mites trailed 4–2 on twenty-yard-line penetrations.

As Coulter lined up for the kick, nobody breathed. The greatest season in the history of the Masonic Home was on the line.

Folks in the upper rows said you could feel the stadium rock when Coulter's kick split the uprights. It was the most beautiful sight Mighty Mites fans had ever seen.

Up in the press box, Pop Boone blew out a thick cloud of cigar smoke.

"Right now," he said with a grin, "I'm looking like a damn genius."

Chapter 25

OH, LORD

The afternoon practice began precisely at four o'clock, with Rusty Russell tooting the whistle and the orphans breaking into side-straddle hops. Milk slimes would be a little late, but Russell expected to see Hardy Brown, Wheatie Sealy, and the gang sprinting down the hill any minute with leather helmets in hand.

Russell could not recall the last time he had started a practice without Doc Hall. In spite of his crusty exterior, the old doctor loved football. Nothing thrilled the man more than watching the little orphans scratching and clawing their way to victory. Who else would have labored for forty years—fixing broken bones, extracting tonsils, patching up battered boys—without ever taking a nickel from the orphanage?

Russell never thought he would feel lonely without Doc Hall by his side. Normally, at this part of the day, his focus was riveted to the action on the field. Instead, his eyes were now scanning the entire compound, from the milk barn to the peach orchard to the infirmary. No sign of Doc Hall. This worried him.

Russell thought about sending one of the team managers to fetch him, then realized he might be in surgery.

This Monday afternoon practice was the start of preparation for the first playoff game against the Sunset Bisons. The luckless Russell once again had lost the coin toss and the Mighty Mites would be traveling to Dallas for Saturday's bi-district game. When it came to heads and tails, why did Russell always lose? *Good thing I don't gamble,* he thought.

Most of the realists gave the Mites little hope of defeating the state's fourth-ranked team. The Bisons had survived a powerhouse district, a record that included four rugged wins at the end of the season against Woodrow Wilson, North Dallas, Dallas Tech, and Adamson.

One thing was certain about Saturday's game at Dalhigh Stadium. Every seat in the twenty-four-thousand-seat complex would be filled. Mighty Mites fans from all over the state would arrive early and stay late. They would be coming by train, bus, and broken-down jalopies.

Harold Ratliff of the Associated Press knew the subject better than anyone. This was part of his advance story on the game:

> This year, in their march to the district title and another shot at the state crown, the Mighty Mites have played before a hundred thousand fans, despite miserable playing conditions for several of their games. The fans believe that this is the year when they finally get the coveted title. If they get to the finals again, it's going to take the Cotton Bowl at Dallas (seating 47,500) to handle the crowd.

Simply beating Sunset on Saturday was going to be a tall order. There was no guarantee that quarterback C. D. Sealy would be ready to play. He had sprained his right foot late in the Poly game, and Russell noticed that the boy was still limping when he ran down the hill with the milk slimes. Now he was gimping about the practice field like an old man with the gout. Doc Hall had fashioned a brace for the foot, but at the moment, the good doctor's whereabouts were a mystery.

"Sit down and take a rest," Russell said to Sealy. "Snoggs Roach will take over at quarterback today."

Snoggs stepped into the huddle and, before he had a chance to call the next play, Hardy Brown tried to take over.

"Just give me the damn ball, Snoggs."

"Shut up, Hardy," Snoggs shot back.

"What do you mean, shut up?"

"I'm telling you to shut up. I'm the quarterback now and I'm calling the plays."

Snoggs had been suiting up and knocking down bigger boys since the little orphans started playing football as first-graders down at Sycamore Creek. He was afraid of no one. At age six, Snoggs had to tie a rope around his oversized pants to keep them from falling down. But nobody, absolutely nobody, called him "Shorty."

The new quarterback was now ready to call the first play.

"Quick post to Ray," he said. "On two. Ready, break."

Snoggs retreated three steps and fired a perfect strike over the middle to Ray Coulter. The lanky tight end caught the ball in stride for a twenty-yard gain.

Russell marveled at the sight. Snoggs had taken about three snaps in four months of practice, yet handled the position like it belonged to him.

Little Snoggs was not the only orphan putting a smile on Rusty Russell's face. Left guard Cecil "Crazy" Moseley had been tearing up the competition all season. At one hundred and forty-five pounds, Crazy was overmatched physically in every game. He normally faced boys in the two-hundred-pound range. But he handled them all.

Just a few days earlier, Russell had told Pop Boone, "Cecil Moseley, pound for pound, is the best lineman in the state. I've never seen a kid that can whip the man in front of him on every play."

Pop scribbled down the quote and then cocked his right eyebrow.

"Is Cecil as good as his brother, Miller, was?"

"Just about," Russell said.

Miller Moseley, the valedictorian of the 1938 class, was considered a mathematical genius. Crazy, in the eyes of his teachers, possessed the same kind of brainpower. But for some reason the boy never opened his mouth.

"Cecil, I know that you are no dummy," Miss Billingsley often said. "Why you refuse to share your thoughts, I will never know."

Crazy just smiled.

Russell had called the boy into the principal's office one afternoon to inquire about his apathy in the classroom.

"Cecil, I have an observation that I would like to share."

No response.

"Cecil, I think that your number-one goal in life is to be one of the boys. You want to make Cs just like everybody else."

No response.

"Well, let me show you something, Cecil."

Russell pulled a list of names from his top drawer and placed it in front of the boy. "These are the football players who made the straight-A honor roll last semester."

Crazy's eyes grew wider as he read each name: Hardy Brown, C. D. Sealy, Leonard Roach, and Walter Finnigan.

"Wow!"

Russell smiled.

"Thank you, Cecil," he said. "At least I can now go to my grave knowing I heard you say one word."

The boy smiled.

Crazy Moseley was a silent tribute to a great American colloquialism: Actions speak louder than words. Play after play, he opened holes in the defensive line for Hardy Brown, and the big fullback responded with huge gains.

After carrying the ball for a big gain, Hardy liked to cuff Crazy across the top of the helmet and say, "I just wish you could teach Dewitt to block like that."

Practice was almost over, and the sun was setting behind the downtown Fort Worth skyline, when Doc Hall sauntered in from the gloaming. The muscles in his jaw were tight and he looked like a man in need of a stiff drink.

"I suppose that you've had better days," Russell said.

"It's Doug Lord," the old doctor sighed. "A couple of weeks ago, I had to set his tibia in three places. Today, I had to rebreak it. The bone went through the skin just below his knee. But it's even worse than that."

"What is it, Doc?"

"Gangrene."

NOTHING SET OFF alarms inside a hospital in 1940 like the mention of gangrene. It was the disease that confounded medical practitioners and sent thousands to their graves. Alexander Fleming had, by accident, invented penicillin in 1928, but the antibiotic was still a slippery eel some twelve years later. Some experiments in humans had worked, others had failed. America might have been on the threshold of the "age of antibiotics," but in late November of 1940, there was nothing on the market that was certain to cure Doug Lord's swollen and blackened lower right leg.

Lord lay on a hospital bed on the first floor of the Masonic Home Infirmary. He was about ten feet from the emergency room. Doctors had stationed him where they could check his condition night and day.

No one was certain how gangrene had set in. But if Lord had not spoken up—and spoken up loudly—he might already be gone. Days earlier, Lord had informed Doc Hall about a blood pool gathering in his cast.

"It's just perspiration," Doc Hall said.

"No, it's not. It's blood."

"No, Lord, you're just sweating in there."

"I know the difference between sweat and blood. I can feel it. It's blood."

"I'll take off the cast," said Doc Hall. "But if it's just perspiration, you'll admit you're wrong."

Doc Hall was aghast at what he found. Not only was the cast filled with blood, one of the fractures had been rebroken and now the skin was torn again. The leg just below the knee was greenish yellow, with the lower part turning black, signifying an advanced stage of gangrene.

"Oh, Lord," exclaimed Doc Hall.

"How bad is it?" the boy said.

"Bad enough that we're going to have to operate."

THE INFIRMARY AT the Masonic Home had opened just after the turn of the century with the hope that the orphanage could be medically self-reliant. Sending kids to medical facilities all over the city was certain to bankrupt the place.

Thanks to two widely respected physicians—Dr. Skink and Doc Hall—along with a talented staff of nurses, the infirmary ran like clockwork. Tonsils and spleens were removed, broken bones fixed, gashes stitched, and late-night stomach aches relieved.

As with all parts of the orphanage, boys and girls were segregated—girls on the third floor, boys on the second floor, and intensive care patients on the first. Smallpox, chicken pox, and mumps were quarantined in the basement.

Most of the young orphans would never forget that first trip to the infirmary to have their tonsils removed. It was one of the scariest days of their lives. The little boys had to file past the big boys' dorm en route to the infirmary, and what they heard sent chills down their spines.

"They're going to *cut your throats out,*" the big boys yelled. "Run! Run! Run!"

The little boys were crying by the time they reached the front door of the infirmary.

Naturally, the same kind of anxiety swept through the little girls' dorm when word got out that tonsils were being removed.

One night, seven-year-old Virginia Claypool had been tipped to the pending surgery coming up the very next day. One of the older girls told her, "They give you ether and sometimes you don't come out of it."

Virginia decided to take matters into her own hands. She packed a bag, sneaked out the back door, and made it through the back gate. She was headed to her older sister's house located in the Poly neighborhood when a stranger approached. "Young lady, you are out very late, or very early." Virginia took off running and made it to her sister's house just past daybreak.

Her sister was standing at the front door with a scowl on her face. Virginia was escorted back to the orphanage, apologized to Mr. and Mrs. Fletcher, and, a few days later had her tonsils removed.

DOUG LORD DID not know what to think about his predicament, or all of the attention he was receiving.

Opal Worthington came to visit every day and brought magazines.

As she was leaving one morning, Lord said, "I want to thank you, girlfriend."

Seconds later, Nurse Fleming stormed into the little room and set her blazing eyes on poor Lord. "I don't want to ever hear you calling a female around here your girlfriend," Miss Fleming said. "We do not have boyfriends and girlfriends around this orphanage. That kind of thing does not *exist.*"

"But Miss Fleming—"

"No, you listen to me, Doug Lord. You say that one more time and Opal Worthington does not visit you again."

Lord learned to cool it around the nurses.

What surprised him was the constant stream of football players coming to his bedside. Lord was among the youngest players on the team, and not exactly all-district material. But the Mighty Mites paid regular visits. Even Hardy Brown was nice to him.

"Fairbanks," he said. "You're going to be a big-leaguer someday. You're not the fastest or the strongest kid on the team. But I'll give you a lot of credit. You've got a lot of spunk."

Lord felt a lump in his throat. "That's the nicest thing anybody's ever said to me, Hardy."

Hardy smirked. "Well, don't let it go to your head."

It was William Henry Remmert who gave Lord the nickname "Fairbanks." The dean tried to act like he did not like the boy. But, just the same, he made regular visits to the infirmary while he was there.

One day, Lord had heard rumors about a fire being started by some orphans on the south side of the property. The fire had burned the entire hillside. Lord knew that Remmert would round up the usual suspects, and, thankfully, he would not be one of them this time.

That afternoon, Remmert strolled into the infirmary and looked Lord squarely in the eye.

"Actually, I know that it was you that started the fire," Remmert said.

"No way, Mr. Remmert. I've been in this bed for over a week."

Not surprisingly, Lord had a pretty good idea of how it started. Months earlier, he had taught some of his fellow orphans how to catch mice and rats. At the time, Remmert was paying a penny for any mouse and three cents for any rat they caught. So Lord came up with a sure-fire plan to snare the little buggers. He would set a fire on top of the hill that sent mice and rats running downhill—straight into his burlap sack. The boys thought Lord was brilliant. What they underestimated was just how quickly a fire could spread.

Naturally, when the hill burned, it did not take a rocket scientist to sort it all out. Lord was at least partly responsible.

"I know you burned that hill, Lord," Remmert repeated.

"Impossible, Mr. Remmert. Just look at me." Sweat was beginning to form on Lord's brow.

"Oh, don't take me too serious," Remmert said. "I was just trying to get a laugh."

Remmert actually smiled. Then a dark cloud slowly passed over his face. It was the look of sadness that Lord had not seen since little Missy Lou got hit by the train.

The boy's heart sank. Remmert's expression said it all. Lord's broken leg was not healing and Remmert sensed the worst.

"I hope you will be okay soon, I really do," Remmert said as he turned and walked away.

LORD AWOKE THE next morning with bright lights in his face. Standing over him with a grim expression was Doc Hall.

At first, the boy thought it was all a dream. Then he heard the old doctor's voice and knew it was real.

"We're going to give you the ether and put you under," Doc Hall said.

"Why is that?"

"Because we're going to have to amputate your lower right leg."

Lord felt every muscle in his body freeze. His fingers dug into the mattress and his throat released a long "Nooo!"

"Doug, we've got to do it," the doctor said. "Your life is on the line, son. This gangrene is spreading out of control."

The boy shook his head violently.

"You can't do this, Doc. I need my left leg. I'm getting married, you know. I'm marrying Opal Worthington and she doesn't want a one-legged boy. You can't do this, Doc."

The last thing Lord remembered was floating away on light clouds and the expression on Doc Hall's face.

How could he ever forget it?

Chapter 26

DREAMING OF "STATE"

I t was now the Mighty Mites against the world.

Rusty Russell could not deny it. You either loved the Mighty Mites or you hated them. And the haters were making life more diffi-cult by the day.

Now it was a man named P. C. Cobb taking out his frustration on the little orphans. The blustery, cigar-chomping athletic director of the Dallas school district was tired of the Mighty Mites beating up on his football teams every year. He wanted revenge and he wanted it now. He was calling upon every resource available to find a way to stop the mad bomber known as Rusty Russell. More than a half-dozen coaches from various Dallas football programs had been assigned by Cobb to scout the Mighty Mites, with all of the information being fed to Sunset High coach Herman Crowell. The Dallas people had but one goal in mind: Stop Russell dead in his tracks.

Thanks to Cobb, Crowell now had more assistant coaches than any head coach in the National Football League. Russell, meanwhile, had none.

This was no longer the Masonic Home versus Sunset. This was the Masonic Home versus the entire city of Dallas.

"They are not scouting my team," Russell had told Juanita. "They are spying on my team. They can't beat me. So they've decided to gang up on me."

On a cool, windy, and cloudless day, Old Blue carried the twelve boys from Fort Worth to Dallas for a two-thirty kickoff against Sunset High. The game was set for Dalhigh Stadium, located in the shadows of downtown Dallas. More than twenty thousand would be shoe-horned into the place.

Old Blue sputtered into the parking lot just past noon, and the Mighty Mites headed straight for the visitor's dressing room. Russell decided to take a look around the stadium. He stood in the middle of the field and gazed into the stands. Mighty Mites fans were already arriving in huge numbers, and the drum-and-bugle corps was playing something that no one could make out. Russell could also see Charley "Two Guns" McCoy sitting on the front row near midfield, and from his expression, Russell knew the handspring champ was about to make his move.

The coach could already feel the tension in the air. This enmity between the fans from Dallas and Fort Worth had been building for years, and there was little doubt that the Dallas fans were jealous of the Masonic Home's success. Dallasites and Fort Worthians were as different as silk stockings and cow patties. Dallasites flocked to the symphony. Fort Worthians watched fireflies from the front porch. Dallas boasted Neiman Marcus. Fort Worth had "Two Guns" Mc-Coy. Dallas's best football team resided in the monied neighborhood of Highland Park. Fort Worth's hailed from an orphanage.

Making all of this quite gratifying was Russell's 9–2 record against the Dallas teams the past nine years. Neither Highland Park nor Sunset had ever defeated the Home.

No wonder that P. C. Cobb was pacing the sideline as the minutes ticked down to kickoff. He was gunning for an ambush. Nothing would have been more satisfying to Cobb than the humbling of the "mighty" orphans.

Russell smiled as he watched Cobb pacing and puffing. Recently, Cobb had headed the fund-raising for the construction of Dalhigh Stadium, a place that one day would be named after him. Now he needed a big coming-out party.

Breezey Carroll of the *Fort Worth Press* watched the pregame warm-ups from the press box and began to compose tomorrow's story in his head:

"When the little Mighty Mites trotted out onto the field Saturday afternoon, their adversaries, the Dallas champion Sunset Bisons, were already on the field going through warm-up exercises. The common reaction of sportswriters, scouts, and fans alike was 'How can those boys do any good against that mighty Sunset team?' "

The Bison players were huge when measured against the little orphans. They had suited almost fifty players—almost five times as many as the Mighty Mites—and, wearing their new jerseys and helmets, they looked like a college team, compared to a junior high outfit. Anyone attending a Mighty Mites game for the first time would have been convinced that the little boys were about to get pushed around.

Crowell's game plan was to pound the little orphans into submission and to keep the ball out of the hands of Russell's outstanding offense. It was not the first time, nor would it be the last, that an opponent would take advantage of the great size advantage.

The Mighty Mites held their own at the line of scrimmage in the opening minutes of the game and actually seemed to be the more physical team.

Sunset needed a break for their first score, and the Bisons got it when the Home's Louis Burress intercepted a pass at the twenty-six-yard line and started weaving back and forth across the field. Burress retreated all the way to the nineteen, where he fumbled and the Bisons recovered.

On Sunset's first offensive play following the turnover, halfback Bill Blackburn swept left end, found a crack in the secondary, and sprinted all the way down the sideline to the end zone. Lee Forrest added the extra point for a 7–0 lead. In the press box, *Star-Telegram* sportswriter Amos Melton described P. C. Cobb's celebration as a "man trying to imitate a flock of Comanches."

Cobb was still going strong at halftime, with Sunset ahead by a touchdown. He grabbed one of the press box phones and started dialing the number of Paris High School head football coach Raymond Berry. Paris was scheduled to play the winner of Sunset–Masonic

Home, and Cobb was of the opinion that his team had already won the game. He was not willing to wait around to see what happened in the second half.

"We will meet you at ten o'clock tomorrow morning in Commerce for the coin flip," Cobb said jubilantly. "We can't wait to play your football team next week."

There was a pause on the line. Finally Berry said, "I've been listening to your game on the radio. Best I can tell, Mr. Cobb, it's not over yet."

"Oh, it's over," Cobb said. "We're kicking the orphans' butts. See you tomorrow." He quickly hung up.

Cobb should have paid more attention to the book-size scouting report he had ordered from the Dallas coaches. He would have learned that the Mighty Mites were a strong second-half team. In fact, the Mites scored in the final minute the previous week to beat Poly 7–6.

From the opening minute of the second half, it was obvious that the orphans were not yet ready to surrender. Hardy Brown returned the kickoff to the thirty-five, and, on the first play, Wheatie Sealy bootlegged around right end and completed a thirteen-yard sideline pass to Ray Coulter. Wheatie and Hardy alternated carries all the way down the field, gaining six and seven yards a pop. The brace that Doc Hall had made for Wheatie's sprained foot was working wonders. The Mighty Mites quarterback was a determined runner, lifting his knees high and powering through tacklers. From the Sunset four-yard line, he slipped two tackles and was stopped a foot short of the end zone. Then Hardy blasted in for the touchdown and Ray Coulter kicked the extra point that made it 7–7.

The Mites led in penetrations 2–1. Soon they would start treating the twenty-yard line like the goal line. Sunset would not cross the twenty for the rest of the game, and lost the contest on penetrations. Naturally, the Mites were more than happy to settle for this kind of outcome and to move one step closer to a state championship. They were also quite pleased to leave P. C. Cobb with a broken heart. The big man avoided the press after the game and slipped down the back stairway of the press box.

But Amos Melton did have one last parting shot for him. He wrote:

> After all these years, it was our impression that everybody knew about the Masonic Home Mighty Mites. Folks from as far away as New York do. They'll tell you that when Rusty Russell puts on the orange uniforms that his team might get knocked around some. But the game is never over until the ushers start picking up the seat cushions. Saturday, Dallas athletic director P.C. had a lapse in memory and it cost him.

As Melton was typing, Charley "Two Guns" McCoy was still doing handsprings across the field.

Folks from Dallas were quite surprised their team had lost. But they were also quite amazed that Charley's cowboy hat never fell off.

FOUR DAYS LATER, a blizzard crashed into Fort Worth, knocking out power lines and paralyzing the streets.

The orphanage was blanketed beneath ten inches of snow in a matter of hours, as visibility was reduced to about two feet. Everything stopped moving—trains, buses, and even Old Blue.

The only place the Mites could simulate a decent practice was the chapel. Pews were pushed back and Russell began introducing a new series of passing plays that he was certain would never work in the snow. But the players still needed to pass some time.

Ironically, Russell had finally won a coin flip, bringing the game to Fort Worth. As it turned out, the weather in Paris, located about a hundred miles due north of Dallas, was clear and dry, with a temperature in the midforties. In just a matter of hours, the mercury would plummet all the way to eight degrees in Fort Worth.

The Mighty Mites hardly needed another weather obstacle. Sportswriters were comparing the Paris Wildcats to the great Amarillo teams of the past, and that was enough to make anyone pay attention. Tailback Buryl Baty was the second-leading rusher in the state, behind

Amarillo's Myrle Greathouse. *Star-Telegram* sportswriter Frank Tolbert had called Baty the "heart, soul, and gizzard of the Paris offense."

Paris also boasted one of Texas's best high school coaches in Raymond Berry. Years later, his son, Raymond Berry Jr., would earn all-America honors at SMU and become a Hall of Fame wide receiver in the Johnny Unitas era of the Baltimore Colts.

The temperature thankfully rose into the low thirties Saturday morning, as the ground at Farrington Field turned to frozen goo.

At first, the Mighty Mites played like a team from the polar region. They took the opening kickoff and drove all the way to the one-yard-line. Then something happened that the fans had not seen all year. On first down, they could not budge the Wildcats line. It happened again on second and third downs. On fourth down, Hardy Brown smashed head-first into the center of the line and hit a wall. No gain. Paris had fashioned a butt-kicking goal-line stand in the early minutes of the game that totally silenced the Farrington Field crowd.

Not to be deterred, the Mites again powered their way down the field minutes later, with Brown and Sealy doing most of the heavy lifting. After thirteen plays and seventy-three yards, they set up at the Paris one. But four straight rushing plays netted zero yards. Again, the frustrated Mites could not push the ball into the end zone, and the game was still scoreless.

Midway through the second quarter, Buryl Baty sent nervous chills through Farrington Field when he broke two tackles and galloped twenty-two yards to the end zone. A gust of wind pushed the extra point kick wide of the right post, but Paris still led 6–0.

Everyone knew that the Mighty Mites, trailing by six points, would somehow pull it together at halftime. After all, Russell did have his magical ways. The game was there for the taking and all they needed was that one last push when they reached the one-yard line.

Winds howled even louder in the third quarter. Water boys were replaced by "fire boys." During the breaks, the fire boys dashed onto the field with small kerosene stoves as the players huddled around to warm their hands.

Once again—this time in the middle of the third quarter—the

Mites started marching. Brown left, Sealy right, Roach around end. Ray Coulter picked up thirty-three yards with a quick pass over the middle. A couple of more running plays and the orphans were back to a familiar place—the one-yard line.

Surely it could never happen again. Or could it? The crowd groaned when the muscled-up, raw-boned Paris boys stopped the Mites once more on fourth down, just inches from the goal.

So, yes, the game would come down to the fourth quarter once more. Fans prayed the Mites would come through, just as they had against Poly and Sunset. With the sun now perched on the rim of the horizon, and most of the field refrozen, Russell chose to stay on the ground. Hardy started eating up big yards behind Crazy Moseley. Sealy hit Teague Roberts in the right flat and the little halfback was knocked out of bounds at the three. Hardy dug his long cleats into the hard ice. On fourth down, with two minutes to play (it was now or never), Hardy followed Crazy's trap block, squeezing his shoulders between the guard and center, and bowling over the linebacker into the end zone. Relief swept over the stadium.

Few people expected Ray Coulter to make the extra point kick from the icy surface, and it really did not matter. The Home led on penetrations 4–1. Furthermore, Paris had lost Baty to a bone-rattling tackle by Ray Coulter back in the third quarter. As expected, Coulter's kick missed badly, but the 6–6 tie was as good as a win. In fact, two straight ties would qualify the Mites for the state semifinals for the fourth time in eight years.

When it was over, Charley "Two Guns" McCoy, wearing work gloves, did handsprings across the frozen field, and the Masons, thanks to Paris being a seven-point favorite, passed out dollar bills to the Mighty Mites.

Ahead was the roughest sledding of all. Amarillo was up next. The Golden Sandstorm had defeated El Paso and Wichita Falls in the first two rounds of the playoffs by the combined score of 74–6.

Up in the Panhandle, they were saying that this was the greatest Amarillo team of all time.

The Mighty Mites had heard it all before.

Coach Rusty Russell. *(Portrait by Dewitt Coulter)*

Coach Rusty Russell. *(Masonic Home Museum)*

Dewitt (left) and Ray (right) Coulter, as shoeless orphans in the late 1920s. *(Masonic Home Museum)*

They're Coming Material for the 'Little Rascals' Varsity

l team of Texas, the "Little e at Fort Worth, have just one (Rusty) Russell. He's been the sole coach for 12 years. Here he is with the 75-pound team, the youngsters who'll grow up to get on the varsity. These lads are seven to nine years old and act as reserves.

A. P. Wirephoto

Coach Rusty Russell with a number of little orphans in 1930. *(AP Photo)*

The Moseley family in 1928, just before the three kids are shipped to the orphanage. Left to right: Miller Moseley, Mildred Lucille, Dorothy, and Cecil. *(Tom Kellam Collection)*

Heavyweight champ Jack Dempsey at the Masonic Home in 1932. The child at the right is Betty Russell, daughter of Rusty Russell. The child at the left is unidentified. *(Masonic Home Museum)*

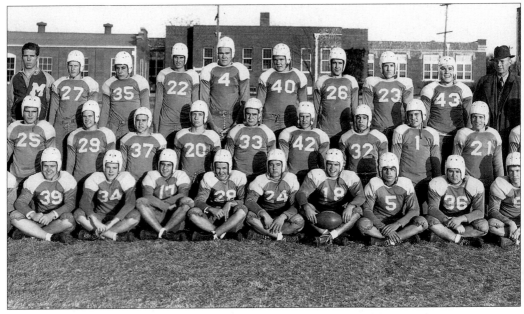

1940 team picture. This included the junior high and junior varsity teams.
(Masonic Home Museum)

Doc Hall (right) cheers from the bench along with Masonic Home fan A. H.
Odom. *(UTA libraries)*

Hardy Brown breaks through the North Side line. North Side player 51 is Bobby Putnam. Basel Smith is on his knees. *(UTA libraries)*

Hardy Brown (43). *(UTA libraries)*

Hardy Brown making a tackle against a Carter-Riverside running back. Ray Coulter (40) trails to the play. *(UTA libraries)*

1940 Masonic Home line. *(UTA libraries)*

Hardy Brown running the ball in a staged shot. *(UTA libraries)*

Rusty Russell (center) with two of his best players, Dewitt Coulter (left) and Ray Coulter (right). *(UTA libraries)*

The Mighty Duck standing in front of the 1934 Mighty Mites line. *(Masonic Home Museum)*

Leonard "Snoggs" Roach making a speech during a public-speaking class at the Masonic Home. Hardy Brown is sitting at the desk. *(UTA libraries)*

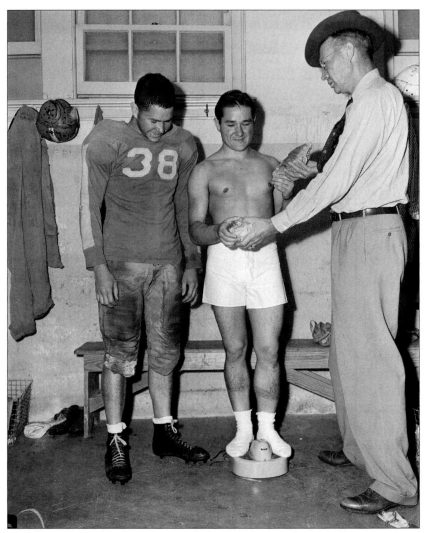

Rusty Russell hands some rocks to Lester Villines, a 141-pound tackle, with hopes of making him heavier. Cecil Moseley watches. *(UTA libraries)*

Opal Worthington, Masonic Home student. *(Doug Lord Archives)*

Opal Worthington with Doug Lord's football jacket. *(Doug Lord Archives)*

Doug Lord and Opal Worthington holding hands as they walk down a downtown Fort Worth street.

Dewitt Coulter (left) and Ray Coulter shoulder a number of orphans after a big win over Dallas Woodrow Wilson in 1940. The boy at top left is B. J. Hogan. The boy at top right is Donald Roach. The boys at bottom right are Eugene Clayton and Floyd Gunn. *(Masonic Home Museum)*

Hardy and Jeff Brown, the great brother duo. Hardy went on to stardom in the NFL and is still considered by many to be the meanest man to ever play football. Photo taken by family member, 1950. *(Masonic Home Museum)*

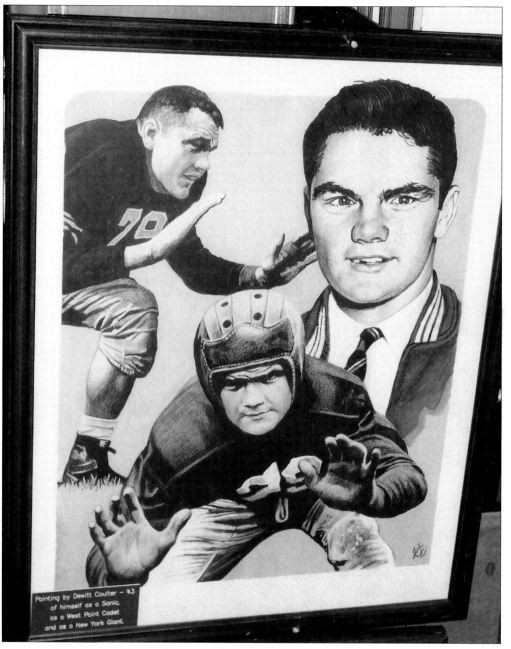

Painting by Dewitt Coulter – '43 of himself as a Sonic, as a West Point Cadet and as a New York Giant.

Three faces of Dewitt Coulter. Left as an Army tackle, center as a New York Giants tackle, and right as a Masonic Home student. *(Portrait by Dewitt Coulter)*

Rusty Russell (left) shaking hands with Heisman Trophy winner Doak Walker at his 1970 induction into the Texas Hall of Fame. At right is Juanita Russell. *(Masonic Home Museum)*

The 1932 team picture of the Mighty Mites, who shared the state Class A championship with Corsicana. Fifth from the left in the first row is Leon Pickett, the only living player from that team, and fourth from the left in the third row is Abner McCall, who became the president of Baylor University. *(Jack Evans Collection)*

Chapter 27

ESCAPE

The chartered bus sat humming outside the dormitory before daybreak, as William Henry Remmert marched from bunk to bunk, rousting the Mighty Mites from their warm beds.

"Where are we going?" Hardy Brown said, cracking open one eye.

"You're going to play the biggest football game of your life."

"But Mr. Remmert, it's only *Tuesday*. We don't play Amarillo till Saturday."

"Y'all have got a lot of work to do between now and then."

Rusty Russell had informed only his wife and a couple of key people around the Home that the Mites would be leaving town early for the trip to Amarillo. The press, the fans, and the drum-and-bugle corps would have to find out on their own.

Christmas break had begun at the orphanage the previous day. The team would be on its way to West Texas before the sun came up, and could practice in privacy for at least two days. They would need the time to polish some of their trick plays, if they were to defeat the over-grown, corn-fed boys of the Panhandle.

Russell had learned a great lesson from playing in big games. The faster he could get his team out of town, the faster they would focus on the task ahead. The coach had begun to draw up a travel agenda a few hours after defeating the Paris Wildcats in the state quarterfinals. Telegrams had come pouring in Monday morning, and it seemed that every little town between Fort Worth and Amarillo wanted the Mites to stop and shake a few hands. It reminded Russell of the whistle-stop tour by Seabiscuit a few years earlier, before the match race against War Admiral.

Russell, wrapped in a full-length overcoat, walked onto the bus and dropped a sack of telegrams on the seat next to Doc Hall.

"I've never seen anything like it," the coach said. "If we made every stop the fans wanted us to make, it'd take three weeks to get to Amarillo."

Truth be known, they were not headed to Amarillo. Not yet, anyway. Leaving Fort Worth, the bus took Highway 180, traveling west through Mineral Wells and Abilene. Soon they would be angling southwest on Highway 351, all the way to the little town of Sweetwater.

The Mighty Mites were in for a surprise in Sweetwater. They were going to spend a couple of hours with "Slinging" Sammy Baugh, the legendary quarterback who had just finished his fourth pro season with the Washington Redskins. The former TCU All-America quarterback had led the NFL that year in passing and punting. Most players went both ways during the 1940 season, and Baugh also managed eleven interceptions, the most by any player in the league.

The meeting with Baugh had been set up by Russell. The two men had been friends since Baugh quarterbacked TCU to the national championship in 1936. But Russell did not want anyone to know where they were going. All the players were sitting on the edge of their seats when the bus turned off at the little farmhouse in Sweetwater.

Baugh stepped out onto the porch and all of the boys recognized him immediately. Of course, no one could miss the all-pro quarterback whose picture had adorned the cover of the sports section for years and years.

"My God, that is Sammy Baugh," Wheatie Sealy said, pointing at the man. "Where'd he come from?"

"He lives here," Russell said.

The boys started bounding down the steps of the bus and running toward Baugh.

"Don't hurt the man," Doc Hall yelled "He's still got a lot of football playing to do."

Baugh shooks hands with everyone.

"I've been looking forward to meeting you boys for a long time," Baugh told the orphans. "Your coach and I are good friends. Mr. Russell called me the other day and asked me if I'd say a few words to you.

I understand you've got a pretty big football game coming up Saturday in Amarillo."

"Yessir," Brownie Lewis said. "And those boys from Amarillo are mighty big."

"Yeah, I know," Baugh said. "I knocked heads with the Golden Sandies a lot in my high school career. I can tell from looking at you boys that most of you are going to be outweighed pretty bad. In fact, some of you boys are the littlest football players I've ever seen."

Picnic tables were set up behind the farmhouse and everyone ate peanut butter sandwiches made by head cook Earl Bodiford. There was plenty of grape juice.

Baugh told the boys about one of the most remarkable seasons in the history of the NFL—his rookie year of 1937.

Baugh was known by his teammates as "Fighting Legs" because he never gave up. It was a notable accomplishment that he even survived that championship game against Chicago that year. The game was played at wind-whipped Wrigley Field, with ice covering the south end of the field. The Redskins had never won a championship and were heavy underdogs against the greatest team in the history of football, led by Bronko Nagurski.

Bears coach George Halas had told his players, "I want you to hit that sonofabitchin' Baugh until blood is coming out of his ears."

They hammered Baugh and piled on. But he kept coming back. An early touchdown pass gave Washington a 7–0 lead. In the second quarter, Nagurski got free into the secondary, and the only man standing between him and the goal was the rail-thin Baugh. Without thinking, the Washington safety lowered his head. Nagurski pile-drived over the top of Baugh and knocked him unconscious. Finally, the smelling salts brought him around and Baugh said, "That sonofabitch ran plumb over me."

Baugh laughed when he told the Nagurski story. "That Bronko Nagurski was the biggest, strongest, meanest football player I ever met in my life," he said. "But you couldn't let yourself be afraid of him. If you did, he would kill you."

Baugh was still woozy at the start of the third quarter, but he threw a touchdown pass to tie to the game. The fourth quarter started with the Bears ahead 21–14, and it looked like Halas and Nagurski would win their fourth NFL title of the past seven years.

But Baugh threw two touchdown passes in a span of three minutes and the Redskins upset the Bears 28–21. That day he completed 17 of 34 passes for 356 yards, in the greatest passing performance in the history of the young NFL.

"That is the greatest story I've ever heard in my life, Mr. Baugh," Hardy Brown said. "Now, can you tell us what happened against the Bears a couple of weeks ago?"

The Redskins had lost that championship game 73–0—the largest margin of victory in the history of the NFL.

"Football is a funny game," he said. "The Bears were still mad at us from the thirty-seven game. I think that's the biggest reason they beat us seventy-three to nothing."

Hardy shook his head. "So it's always the maddest team that wins the game."

Baugh smiled. "Let's just say that it's the team that's the most motivated. If you guys are fired up Saturday against Amarillo, there's a pretty good chance you'll win. Remember. It's not always the best team that wins. It's the team that wants it the most."

After lunch, the boys reboarded the bus and waved good-bye to the greatest football player they had ever seen.

They were now ready to tackle Amarillo.

THE ORPHANS WOKE up Wednesday morning in Lubbock and did not know why. "Why are we not in Amarillo," they asked. The whole set-up seemed pretty confusing.

The boys were rising from their beds when they heard the voice of Doc Hall out in the parking lot.

"It's time for breakfast. Everybody get your behinds to the dining hall."

Russell chuckled. "That would be the hotel restaurant."

"Aw, hell," the old doctor said. "I want them to feel like they're still at home."

The sun was rising over the Western Hotel in Lubbock when the twelve orphans began to file into the restaurant. Each was dressed in pressed clothes, with their hair combed and teeth brushed. They sat down in unison and each boy placed a napkin in his lap.

People all over the restaurant were watching them.

"That's the best-behaved group of kids I've ever seen," said a local farmer sitting across the room. "Where did they come from?"

The orphans silently passed bowls of sausage, eggs, and fruit to each other. Each boy chewed with his mouth closed and nobody spoke until the meal was finished.

Russell then noticed that a man across the room was trying to get his attention.

"Looks like the hotel manager wants to talk to you," Doc Hall said. "One of our boys must've messed something up."

Russell walked across the restaurant and the two shook hands.

"Mr. Russell," the man said. "I need to ask you, sir, if you realize that you're staying in a hotel."

"Well, I guess that's pretty obvious," Russell said.

"Well, sir, I just spoke to one of our maids. And she tells me that your boys got up this morning and made up their own beds. They cleaned the room. They even hung up their clothes and towels and cleaned up the bathroom."

Russell could not keep from laughing. "Well, these boys are orphans. They've lived in an orphanage most of their lives. They've all got a lot of self-discipline. Right now, if I told them *not* to make up their beds, they'd do it anyway."

The manager shook his head.

Doc Hall was patting his foot when Russell came back to the table. "What the hell did he want?" he said.

"Well, it seems he's never been around a bunch of orphans."

RUSSELL'S PLAN THAT day included a closed-door practice at Texas Tech Stadium. He had arranged it through Tech coach Pete Cawthon, just as he had done back in 1938. Cawthon also stationed several of his team managers outside of the stadium to shoo away potential spies.

Doc Hall cringed as he watched the Mighty Mites slamming into each other that day. Not in his long history at the orphanage had Hall witnessed a more brutal practice. It was Russell's opinion that you had to keep your team in "pounding shape" all season, otherwise the big boys from Amarillo would run over the Mighty Mites.

That evening, the first reporter from Fort Worth finally caught up with the Mighty Mites at the team hotel. It had taken Frank Tolbert almost two days to track down the mysterious little traveling show. Tolbert needed to file a story quickly for the Thursday editions, and he was lucky to run into Doc Hall at the hotel. He needed a few quotes.

"Those kids are hitting each other so hard that I can not bear to watch," Hall told the reporter. "What would we do if we got one of the twelve hurt?"

THURSDAY MORNING, POP BOONE aimed Blue Baby north toward the Panhandle.

"I don't know where the Mighty Mites are," he said to himself. "But I know that I'll catch up with them sooner than later."

In his possession were a suitcase, a box of cigars, and the best moonshine licker in Tarrant County.

About two hours later, Blue Baby was topping a hill on the other side of Bowie when the old sportswriter's heart accelerated. He prayed that he could get the big Buick stopped. He knew the odds were against it. But at least it gave him something to write about in his Friday column:

> As usual, I was making one of those conservative drives. You know me—safe and careful, but steady. I come over a hill around fifty miles per hour and saw a small chicken coop ahead. Nothing strange about the coop—it was just ambling along as small coops will.
>
> I have a driving habit that isn't bad—I take my foot off the accelerator just about when I'm about to pass a car and let the engine brake me down a little. It's a good rule. It was a particular good rule in this instance. I was running maybe forty-five when I pulled over to pass the coop.

I reach for my horn just as the gent in the coop made up his mind to turn left. Bing, just like that, with no preliminary warning whatsoever—a sudden left turn right smack dab in front of me and me not more than thirty feet away, already on the left side of the road.

Naturally, a guy first hits his brakes. I did. Very surprising, I did not get too excited. I was going too fast to swing to the right, which would have brought three or four somersaults to Blue Baby. I wasn't going to miss him to the left, as he was going that way. Nothing to do but hit him.

He heard my brakes so he turned a little right. It gave me a chance to sock him in the rear. Believe it or not, I almost laughed when I saw the gentleman's head almost snap off. That coop leaped forward like a shotgun shell and it took a hundred yards to get it stopped. I stopped dead like a pool ball with the English put to it.

When the gent finally stopped his coop and came back to where I was getting out of Blue Baby, I grinned at him. He had come back reluctantly, feeling guilty and expecting me to start shooting at him with verbal if not actual lead bullets. But I grinned. "Just couldn't help it, could you, old man?" I said.

It would take Pop a full day and seventy bucks to fix the geyser in his radiator. But at least he had given himself plenty of time to make Amarillo by Saturday.

Chapter 28

AMARILLO

As the team bus left Lubbock Friday morning, snow was blowing horizontally across Highway 87 and the dark clouds to the north spoke of trouble.

Rusty Russell had been up most the night diagramming pass plays on hotel stationery. The only hope for the Mighty Mites was to out-think and outmaneuver the giants from Amarillo. Now, as the snow began to pile up along the shoulder of the highway, Russell was becoming a worried man.

Snow had blanketed much of the Panhandle since Thanksgiving. Now, just five days until Christmas, the two-laner looked like a ski run. There was no telling what the weather might be in twenty-four hours, when the Mighty Mites and the Golden Sandstorm lined up against each other in the game that everyone had been waiting for.

The town of Amarillo had been to hell and back the past two weeks. On December 8, just twelve days earlier, a blizzard had struck with such intensity that it managed to shut down everything. At four o'clock that morning, sleet and snow began to freeze on the trees. In just a matter of hours, every tree in the county was groaning under the weight of the heavy ice. Telephone circuits went out and power lines were down all over the city by the next day. Western Union lost eight hundred poles, two thousand cross arms, and had a hundred thousand wire breaks. Telephone poles and radio towers were toppled. Thanks to a total electrical blackout, Amarillo's water supply went dry, as ten million gallons stored underground could not be pumped to the surface. Amarillo's fire department, answering calls all over town, had enough water for about fifteen minutes of fire-fighting.

Amarillo sank deeper and deeper beneath this crush of ice, to the point that it was cut off from the outside world. Wide, clean streets became tangles of wires, as the nerves of civilization quietly parted. Now and again, ham radio operators got through to the outside world, but it was impossible for rescuers to approach the city, as the highway arteries were like ice rinks.

For forty-eight hours nothing happened in Amarillo. A pilot flying over the city reported no signs of life—no cars on the streets, no lights, and no trains moving along the tracks. It was like a pre–Ice Age civilization, crumbling beneath tons of frozen blocks.

Finally, the front moved away and a slight warm wind began to thaw out the place. To the relief of all, temperatures rose above the freezing mark and everything began to thaw. Remarkably, there had been no major catastrophes—no fires of consequence and no deaths. But the damage to property was in the millions, and it would take four days before telephone and telegraph communications could resume.

Russell just prayed that nothing like that happened between now and the one o'clock kickoff on Saturday.

Without question, the Amarillo team would benefit greatly if the ice and snow returned. The Golden Sandies loved power football.

Power. The word rolled around in Russell's mind. He knew that his Mighty Mites could handle a team with power, because they had done so in the past. What burned a hole in his stomach was the size of the Amarillo players.

There were other concerns on the coach's mind. Russell knew something that few people outside of Doc Hall had noticed. The orphans were actually shrinking, thanks to the grind of the long season. All twelve players were several pounds lighter than their preseason weight. They would be outweighed by at least thirty pounds per man, possibly even more.

As Russell watched the farmland of West Texas go past, he thought to himself, *Why does it always have to be Amarillo?* Every time the Masonic Home got on track for the state championship, it seemed the big boys of Amarillo stood in the way. Granted, one of Russell's greatest teams had defeated the Golden Sandies in the 1932 state semifinals by the score of 7–6. But two years later the Mites lost a heartbreaker 3-0 in a blowing Amarillo snowstorm. That would be the start of three state championships for Amarillo. Now, most of the sportswriters from West Texas were of the opinion that this was the Sandies' greatest team ever. The reason was a six-two, 220-pound fullback and linebacker with a name that personified size, power and strength—Greathouse.

Yes, Myrle Greathouse was the same size as Bronko Nagurski, the most dominant NFL player of the 1930s. And, yes, the orphans had heard several scarey stories about Nagurski when they stopped in Sweetwater on Wednesday to see Sammy Baugh.

Every Texas high school team that played against Greathouse dreaded the moment they walked onto the field against him. Most wished that he had already taken off for college, where he probably belonged. Greathouse had already verbally committed to the University of Oklahoma, and no one doubted the Sooners were about to sign the greatest Texas high school player to suit up in the last several years.

"In about six months that Greathouse boy will be in the starting lineup for the Oklahoma Sooners," Doc Hall said to Russell. "Now we've got to face him with a bunch of little orphans."

A cold wind was blowing when the team bus pulled up to the curb at the Amarillo Hotel shortly before noon. The Shriners Drum-and-Bugle Corps, in spite of the snow and ice falling all over the city, had already arrived and was trying to whip the crowd into a frenzy with a song that sounded faintly like the "Battle Hymn of the Republic." Several hundred fans lined the sidewalk, and there was already plenty of action among the bettors.

As the Mighty Mites filed off the bus and began to work their way through the crowd, somebody yelled, "Do those little boys really think they got a shot against Golden Sandies? Hell no!"

Another Amarillo fan hollered, "Where is your real football team?"

Russell did recognize a few Fort Worthians in the crowd. Most were busy placing their bets for Saturday's game. The point spread had opened at fourteen points and was moving up by the minute. One look at the scrawny orphans and some of the Amarillo backers were willing to lay three touchdowns.

At two o'clock that afternoon, the boys were bused to Butler Stadium for a brief workout. Russell thought about his old friend Moses and how he had brought the Mighty Mites some luck through the years. But no one had heard from Moses in two years, since the loss to Lubbock High in December of 1938, and there was a rumor that he had passed away.

After practice, the boys were given a couple of hours to do some window shopping around downtown and check out the Christmas lights. Most grew tired of being gawked at and called "little orphans." So they headed back to the hotel long before the sun set over the wide plains.

HARDY BROWN HAD received a letter from his brother, Jeff, saying he might make it to Amarillo for the big game. Jeff had just finished his second season as a guard at the Rice Institute, where he had been selected all-Southwest Conference. No one at the Home was surprised that Jeff was already having so much success in college football.

Now Hardy's high school career was coming to an end and it was time for him to start thinking about college football. Deep in his heart, though, Hardy wished his days at the Masonic Home would never end. He had grown up there and excelled on the football team and made the greatest friends of his life. He was not sure what life outside the fence held for him and, at the moment, he was not ready to test the real world.

At the moment, Hardy was carrying around a heavy heart. This might have seemed odd to most people, since the Mighty Mites were just one victory away from reaching the state finals. But Hardy hated the fact that his mother or father had never seen him play. Kirkland was about eighty miles southeast of Amarillo, and the past few days Hardy had spent a lot of time thinking about his childhood home.

He also regretted that he had never told his friends about the true story concerning the murder of his father. Some still believed the rumor that his mother had pulled the trigger. It made sense to a degree.

Maggie Ann Brown had simply vanished into thin air within hours after the murder and no one had heard from her since.

Before the trip to Amarillo, Hardy had never felt like talking about the horrible act. Tonight, though, it was on his mind. Around ten o'clock, he went looking for his two best friends, Wheatie Sealy and Brownie Lewis. He could not think of any two boys he would rather share it with.

"Both of y'all have wanted to know exactly what happened to my daddy and mama," Hardy said. "I guess this is a good time to get if off my chest. I've never told anyone about it. Now I'm going to tell y'all"

It was a hot summer day in the small West Texas town of Kirkland, he told them, and the fish were biting. Father and son had spent the better part of the day yanking white bass and crappie out of the clear, blue creek water. Dinner time was approaching and they decided to call it a day. Now they were walking down one of the long dirt roads that split the cotton fields. Nothing seemed out of the ordinary. In the distance, a wheat field was being burned off, and they could see the smoke line rising up just over the Jeffers property. A freight train bound for Fort Worth rumbled past and they heard the lonesome whistle. A blue heron flew overhead.

A cluster of houses were ahead, but nothing seemed to be stirring. Not yet, anyway.

"The first thing I heard was the footsteps behind me," Hardy said. "I could hear them kicking up rocks. I turned around there was two men—the Gossett brothers—with shotguns. I thought they were going out hunting or something. But they raised up their shotguns and I told my daddy to look out. It was too late. The shells hit him in the back and the side. I knew he was dead before he even hit the ground."

His eyes widening, Wheatie said, "What did you do?"

"I dropped the fish in the dirt and took off running. I thought they were going to kill me. I never looked back. I never stopped until I got back to our farmhouse and that was miles away."

"Where was your mama?" Brownie said.

"She was standing on the front porch. I told her the Gossett brothers had killed my daddy. She looked like she'd seen a ghost."

"What did she do?"

"Well, it was kind of weird. She ran into the bedroom. She started pulling on her stockings and putting on her Sunday shoes. I couldn't figure out what she was doing. Then she ran out of the house like a scalded dog. She ran down the road toward the train station. Not one of us kids has ever seen her since."

"She ran for the train station? Where was she going?" Wheatie asked.

"You got me. Nobody was sure if she headed north or south."

"Where is she now?" Brownie said.

"The last I heard, she went to Tulsa. At least that's what Jeff told me. She married somebody else and she's been living up there for awhile."

"When was the last time you talked to her?" Brownie asked.

"I guess it was the day they killed my daddy."

Brownie and Wheatie looked at each other. For the last dozen or so years, Hardy had never breathed a word of this. God knows, the boys had tried to pry it out of him.

"That is the craziest damn story I ever heard in my life," Wheatie said. "I watched my daddy die of a heat stroke. Seeing your daddy getting shot in the back, well, that must have been something else."

Brownie said, "I watched my daddy die, too. But my mother didn't take off running for a train."

Hardy shook his head. "You have to know one thing about my mother. She was scared to death of the Gossetts. That's why she took off."

Wheatie leaned forward. "Do you think about your mother much?"

"Been thinking about her lately. I just wish she could be here for the big game tomorrow."

The three boys talked well into the night about life, death, and their years at the orphanage.

They knew that their time was growing short at the Masonic Home. They all agreed that they were not ready to become city guys.

Chapter 29

LAST DANCE

A thick frost lay on the ground when the sun rose over West Texas. Rusty Russell cracked the drapes in his hotel room to see that the snow clouds had moved on and the sky was scrubbed clean. The temperature was still subfreezing, and Russell felt certain the wind would be singing down from the northern prairies. But the Mighty Mites' passing game could certainly click in this kind of weather.

Russell had grown up in West Texas and made countless trips into the Panhandle. But he knew he would never get used to the sight of the endless Amarillo sky—especially at dawn. The land was so flat in Amarillo that it was like sitting on the ocean. The horizon appeared to be a million miles away and the vast, hard blue sky seemed to envelop an earth that, at the moment, did not seem all that round.

Amarillo had started in 1887 as a railroad town that hauled cattle from Fort Worth to Denver. Before that, Amarillo was known only for its freakish weather, its wheat, its oil fields, and the nauseating smells of the stockyards. The place was so flat, with landmarks so rare that the settlers in the 1800s had to plow furrows from settlement to settlement to guide the pioneers across the treeless expanse.

The countryside was so bleak that an army officer who explored it in 1849 reported, "This country is, and must remain, uninhabited forever." The winds of the Panhandle became so famous that another observer said, "There's nothing but a sagging barbed-wire fence between Amarillo and the North Star."

Until the Red River War of 1874, it seemed that only the Comanches wanted anything to do with the Panhandle, known as the *Llano Estacado,* or Staked Plain. After the Comanches were roundly defeated and the survivors sent off to reservations, the U.S. Army had serious doubts that the white settlers would ever move in.

The type of rugged individuals that did inhabit Amarillo quickly came to love the game of football and all of its physical demands. The men who built the town were roughnecks, tool-pushers, cattle-drovers, and range bosses.

The cattle industry laid the foundation blocks for Amarillo, but it was the oil that lured the hustlers and the dreamers. They were a hardened bunch, willing to roll up their sleeves and make great sacrifices. The oil boom of West Texas soon turned one-horse towns into thriving communities. Thanks to the oil strike of 1917, the tiny West Texas town of Ranger grew by almost thirty-thousand people in one year. Amarillo was not far behind and, by December of 1940, was up to fifty-two thousand people.

It was little wonder that Amarillo became an overnight power in Texas football. With only one "white" high school in town, Amarillo High was soon bursting at the seams. Sports became a way of life there in the early twenties, especially when a new mascot was born.

On a windy spring day in 1922, the Amarillo High baseball team was practicing in the wind-blown sand of a minor league baseball stadium, when coach Astyanax Saunders Douglas shouted encouragement to his players: "Come on you golden sandstormers," he yelled. "Come on now, bear down!"

In just a matter of days, the team changed its named from "Savages" to the "Golden Sandstorm."

Amarilloans flipped for football. Legendary coach Blair Cherry coached the Sandies to the state title for three straight years (1934–1936) before taking off for the University of Texas.

Now all that stood in the way of the Sandies and another trip to the state championship game were twelve skinny orphans. No wonder the betting point spread was already up to twenty points with just a few hours remaining until kickoff.

The total enrollment of Amarillo High approached two thousand students. The orphans? Less than a hundred and forty.

AT DAWN ON game day, the orphans rose from their hotel beds and, before even thinking about getting dressed, made up their beds. Faces were washed, teeth brushed, hair combed, and pressed shirts and slacks put on. They looked more like choirboys than football players. But anyone who had ever suited up against the Mighty Mites knew better.

Pop Boone had confirmed it in his morning column:

> Yep, the Amarillo Sandies really rate favorites today. But let's not feel sorry for the poor little Mighty Mites. They don't want any sympathy, and they don't ask for mercy. They'll be out there battling, and so far they've been able to take care of themselves very well, thank you. Let's not give up—the kids haven't.

A few paragraphs down in the same column, Boone wrote:

> This is no pep talk, because nobody to my knowledge has ever scared the Mighty Mites yet. You must remember that I've been watching the Home elevens since away back yonder when some of them played in hobnails, a few had tennis shoes, and one actually had a good pair of football shoes. One of the players back then told me that the Mighty Mites were so tough because they lived on beans and nothing more. Well, they are just as tough today as they ever were.

Now, it seemed the whole world wanted to see if they could pull off the biggest upset of the 1940 season.

Even Russell was surprised at the gathering outside of the hotel. The drum-and-bugle corps was playing and hundreds of fans decked out in orange shirts, jackets, and sweaters waved orange banners and yelled the names of the Mighty Mites as each one boarded the bus. Gamblers were everywhere, as the point spread had risen overnight to twenty-four points. Backers from Fort Worth—especially the Masons— were busy taking the points in bets all over town. Bookies worked the streets in dark fedoras and kept everything recorded in little black books.

Cars stretched for more than a mile behind the team bus en route to the stadium. As they pulled through the stadium gate, the Mighty Mites were surprised to see the Amarillo players waiting for them. Gladiators were supposed to remain separated until the opening kick-off. But the Golden Sandies looked like a welcoming party.

Standing front and center with a smile wider than West Texas was none other Myrle Greathouse.

He started shaking the hands with the visitors as they filed off the bus.

"I've been hearing about you guys," he said. "And I had to come by to see you. Believe it or not, you fellas are actually smaller than I thought. You don't even look like football players."

Hardy Brown walked up to big fullback and stuck his nose in his face. "My advice to you is 'get your ass back to your locker room, smart boy,'" he said. "Because you're going to need all the rest you can get."

Greathouse threw up his hands. "No offense," he said. "I just wanted to see what the little orphans looked like."

Hardy reared back to throw a punch but was grabbed from behind by Brownie Lewis. Greathouse and the others walked away slowly, but they were still smiling, as if to say, "you poor little orphans."

"It's the same everywhere we go," Hardy said. "We always have to show the bastards just how tough we are."

This pregame clash had occurred far from the eyes of the fans and the press. Up in the press box, WBAP play-by-play man Cy Leland was manufacturing his own pregame drama:

They say this is the greatest Amarillo team ever to suit up. And that's saying a lot, when you consider the Golden Sandies won the state championship back in 1934, '35 and '36. But I can tell you for a fact that the Masonic Home Mighty Mites will never lay down against these boys. This is probably the best team that Rusty Russell's ever had. And this might just be the last chance they will ever get to win a state championship. You better stay tuned, because there's going to be some fireworks this afternoon in Amarillo.

THE GOLDEN SANDIES were already on the field when the Mighty Mites came running out for pregame warm-ups. The forty-seven play-ers in gold jerseys, gold pants, and gold helmets were ready to have some fun with the little orphans. They formed a circle around the dozen orphan players. Then they started lunging at them and yelling, "Whooommpff! Whooompff!"

Soon the Mighty Mites started lunging back., "Whoooompff! Whoooompff!"

"We might be orphans," Hardy Brown yelled at the big Amarillo boys. "But y'all are a bunch of faggots."

Sealy walked over to Hardy and grabbed him by the arm. "Some of those boys've got full beards. They've got to be in their twenties. They are a bunch of grown men."

The Mites tried to ignore the Sandies as they warmed up. Russell steered his team to the locker room earlier than usual and asked Doc Hall to deliver the pregame pep talk.

The old doctor looked at the floor and cleared his throat.

"As you know, boys, I've been doctoring around the Home now for some forty years. And standing out there on that field is the biggest football team I've ever seen in my life. I just want y'all to know that if any of y'all get hurt, I'll patch you up."

Hardy stood up and looked around the room.

"With all due respect, Doc, ain't nobody getting hurt today. We can take this team. Seems like nobody has any confidence in us. But the best team in Texas—and that would be us—is going to win today."

Doc smiled and said, "In that case, I have something to read to you boys."

He pulled from his pants pocket a yellowed sheet of paper. He slowly smoothed it along his right thigh. Then he spoke:

Listen closely,
You twelve regulars mostly,
Don't fumble!
Hit 'em like hell!
Don't grumble,
Hold the ball,
And we'll take all!

Yours truly,
Doc Hall

So fired up were the boys that they did not wait for Russell's signal. They just took off. Twelve orphans led by Hardy Brown tore onto the field as the drum-and-bugle corps cranked up the school fight song. Most of the twelve thousand spectators were dressed in gold, but the orphans had their share of orange-clad supporters.

Upon reaching the bench area, Hardy did not stop running. He led the orphans on a lap around the field. The boys yelled and shook their fists. The message was clear: *We are not intimidated.*

Two Guns McCoy bolted from the stands and started doing hand-springs behind the boys. His cowboy hat never fell off.

In the press box, Cy Leland said, "I don't know what has gotten into the orphans. But they look like they're ready for a fight. And now the cops are chasing Two Guns McCoy across the field and I don't think they're going to catch him. He can run faster on his hands than they can on their feet."

Russell finally stopped the boys and tried to calm them down.

"This is going to be a defensive struggle, gentlemen," he said. "The team with the most stamina wins this game. We will win this game in the fourth quarter. Each of you will have to fight to the very end."

The first few plays of the game looked like a street fight. Snoggs Roach broke through the line and tackled Greathouse for a two-yard loss. The big fullback looked stunned.

"That's the littlest boy on our team," Hardy said, stealing a line from his brother. "Wait till *I* get ahold of you."

The Golden Sandstorm was going nowhere fast. Quarterback M. T. Johnson threw two straight incompletions and retreated into punt formation.

Russell's plan was to run the ball early in the game. But the Sandies front line would not budge. The Mighty Mites made two first downs and punted the ball back to Amarillo.

Neither offense could put together anything more than a twenty-yard drive, and the game might have been scoreless at halftime, if not for Johnson's interception of a Wheatie Sealy pass that he returned thirty-six yards to the Mites' four. On the next play, Johnson faked the pitch and swept left end for the touchdown. Clyde Clark made the PAT kick for a 7–0 lead.

The Mites, however, were still filled with hope at halftime and got a surprising pep talk from an unexpected source.

"We can win this game, guys," Crazy Moseley said. "We've just got to keep playing as hard as we have."

Wheatie Sealy looked around the room. "Did Crazy Moseley really say that? When was the last time any of you ever heard that boy talk?"

"He must mean it," Hardy said. "Because I haven't heard him say a word since the third grade."

That is when Hardy walked to the middle of the locker room and a hush fell over the place.

"Since we were in the first grade, Mr. Russell has been talking about how great it would be for a bunch of orphans to win a state championship," he said. "He fought for years to make sure the politicians down in Austin couldn't take the dream away from us. Boys, this is just about it for me. My high school career is coming to an end. Right now, we are so close to winning it all that I can almost taste it."

Hardy put on his leather helmet and buckled his chinstrap. He thought about growing up with these boys, going all the way back to age five. Hardly a moment had passed when they were not together. Crazy, Pig, Brownie, Wheaty, Snoggs, Basel, the Coulter boys—they were all brothers.

"I came to the orphanage over twelve years ago with nothing," he said. "But I plan to leave with *everything*."

It was fortuitous that Doc Hall decided to open the door. Otherwise, the orphans would have torn it down. They charged back onto the field like twelve little bulls. It did not matter that their uniforms and their helmets did not match. It did not matter that they rode around Fort Worth in a rattling, smoke-belching truck. It did not matter that they were orphans.

They were ready for a fight.

The second half began with Hardy Brown tearing through the line and throwing Greathouse for a three-yard loss. Then, 190-pound fullback Otto Payne lost two more yards. The Mighty Mites' defense was holding.

But the offense, in spite of Russell's tinkering, was still stagnant. Wheatie Sealy threw two more interceptions in the third quarter and the Mites were back on the ropes.

Early in the fourth quarter, an alert M. T. Johnson intercepted a pitch from Sealy that was intended for Snoggs Roach. Grabbing the ball at full stride, Johnson sprinted twenty yards to midfield, where Hardy caught him from behind.

Johnson masterfully mixed the plays, sending Payne and Greathouse into the line, then carried around right end for a twenty-yard gain to the sixteen. Johnson gained eight yards on the next play, and four more to the four-yard line. He then handed off to the bull-shouldered Payne and the big fullback broke four tackles before stumbling into the end zone. Clark again made the extra-point kick and the lead was 14–0, with ten minutes to play.

The Mites needed to work fast. Throwing quick passes into the flat, Sealy completed four straight, moving the ball to the Amarillo forty-five.

It was time for some Russell trickery. Snoggs Roach flanked wide to the right—very wide, in fact. He was standing next to the sideline when he stumbled and fell. Surprisingly, he just lay there.

Amarillo coach Howard Lynch was not fooled. He instantly knew it was the "hideout" play. The plan was for Snoggs at the snap of the ball to stand up and take off down the sideline. No one would be covering him. Lynch started yelling "Hideout! Hideout!" and the entire Amarillo secondary shifted to that side of the field.

Now the Mites had them. Teague Roberts took off down the opposite sideline and there was no one to cover him. Sealy lofted a floater that Roberts caught at the fifteen. He scrambled to the two-yard line before Johnson tackled him. On the next play, Hardy charged into the line and suddenly realized there was nowhere to run. So he angled around left end and found a wide opening. Ray Coulter's kick made it 14–7, with three minutes remaining.

Everyone in the stadium knew the Sandies would run the ball. But on the third play, Hardy Brown knifed between the guard and the tackle and stole the ball from Greathouse near midfield.

The Mites' offense huddled with less than two minutes to play.

"Give me the ball," Hardy said. "Big Dewitt is tearing up the man in front of him. We got enough time to run it down the field."

They had two time-outs remaining.

Running behind Coulter's pile-driving blocks, Hardy gained eight, thirteen, and six yards. The ball was at the twenty-three with a minute remaining. He carried twice more to the fifteen, and Russell called a time-out.

With fifty seconds on the clock, and one time-out remaining, everyone was on their feet. The tension was almost unbearable. But Russell told Sealy to remain calm and to keep the ball on the ground. The quarterback faked to Hardy and carried the ball around left end for three yards. On the next play, Hardy bulled his way off right tackle to the nine. That is when Russell used the final time-out.

On third-and-seven, Sealy flipped a quick pass to Ray Coulter, who broke three tackles down to the four-yard line. The last play for the Mites was coming up.

In the huddle, Hardy looked deeply into the eyes of Dewitt Coulter.

"Son, I can't tell you how much you've improved as a football player this year," he said. "Ain't nobody calling you a sissy any more.

Give me one more block and we can tie this thing up. We lead 'em on penetrations, and we'll win this damn game."

The crowd began the countdown: "Ten, nine, eight, seven, six . . ."

Dewitt drove the big Amarillo tackle backward and Hardy bucked into the line. The Sandies knew he was coming. He was met at the three by Greathouse and Payne. Johnson hit him at the knees, but Hardy kept powering forward. The pile moved all the way to the one, where a total of six defenders slammed into him.

When Hardy finally went down, half of the Amarillo defense was lying on top of him. His momentum died just two feet from the goal. The Mites had lost 14–7.

"It was a valiant effort," Cy Leland told his radio audience. "But there will be no state championship, once again, for the Masonic Home Mighty Mites."

A silence that seemed surreal fell over Butler Stadium. The Amarillo fans should have been cheering their hearts out for the best high school team in the state, possibly the greatest ever in Texas. Instead, twelve thousand fans remained silent in their seats.

When Hardy Brown stood up, pulled off his helmet, and walked slowly toward the sideline, it finally began. "Mighty Mites! Mighty Mites! Mighty Mites!" The chant would continue for several minutes. The orphans looked into the stands and could not believe their ears. For all of their lives, they had been degraded and called "Orphans!" Now they were being cheered and honored by a bunch of strangers.

On the sideline, the gamblers were waiting. This time, they were offering five- and ten-dollar bills.

"We don't want your money," Wheatie Sealy yelled. "We didn't win and we don't want your damn money."

Hardy Brown, tears rolling down his face, walked up to his coach.

"Mr. Russell, I let you down."

"Son, you never let me down in your whole life."

The orphans, their coach, and an old doctor all held hands as they walked in unison toward the locker room. Twelve thousand fans stood and cheered wildly, as if they had won the championship.

Hardy looked into the stands and saw his brother, Jeff. He was standing behind Doug Lord, who was wrapped in a blanket and sitting in a wheelchair. Doc Hall had managed to save the leg by inserting a screw in the ankle and another close to the knee. He managed to scrub away the gangrene each day with sulphur.

Also in the group were Mighty Mite greats from the past—Scott McCall, Allie White, Donkey Roberts, Gene Keel, Miller Moseley, and Norman Strange.

"Hey, Lord," Hardy Brown yelled. "I see you still got your leg."

"And I damn well plan to keep it," the boy yelled.

Standing in the bright Amarillo sunshine on a cold December afternoon, the end finally came. The era was over. The Mighty Mites had come so close—reaching the state semifinals three times and the finals once—yet they had never won the big one. It was their last chance and everyone knew it. What they had accomplished was to become Texas's second-greatest team of the decade, just behind Amarillo.

More important, the orphans became a symbol of inspiration for every man and woman during the Depression. They were the most popular team in Texas in the thirties, with a cult following that stretched from New York to the West Coast. They were a reason to live. They were Seabiscuit and Cinderella Man rolled into one fighting little football team. They were devotion, hope, and the belief that winning lives within the heart.

Teams would come and go. But no one would ever forget the Mighty Mites.

Chapter 30

LIFE AFTER THE HOME

Right after the game, several Amarillo players decided to pay another visit to the Mighty Mites.

Myrle Greathouse and the other Golden Sandies strolled into the Masonic Home dressing room and it appeared they might be looking for a fight. Greathouse approached Hardy Brown and the Masonic Home fullback felt the hair rising on the back of his neck.

Greathouse said, "I have a question for you, Hardy Brown."

"What is that?" Hardy said.

"I was just wondering about that blocking and tackling technique you boys use."

"Why is that?"

"Because you guys sure block and tackle funny."

That is when Greathouse smiled and pointed to his split upper lip. A trickle of blood was rolling down his chin.

"All of us boys have split lips," Greathouse said. Indeed, the other Amarillo players smiled and pointed to their bloody lips.

Hardy laughed. "It's a technique around here that we call the Humper. It's one of the reasons that we're so danged tough. We're sorry that we messed up your lips. But we sure did want to win the ball game today."

Greathouse smiled and then winced from the pain. "We're just glad that we never have to play you boys again," he said. "That was the toughest high school game that I've ever played in my life."

It was little consolation. The pain that the Mighty Mites were feeling could never be erased, in spite of the heartfelt praise they would receive in the coming days.

It all began with Frank Tolbert's story that appeared Sunday morning in the *Fort Worth Star-Telegram*:

> After slugging twelve straight opponents with off-hand ease, Amarillo's Golden Gallopers got a proper workout here Saturday. The agile kings of Panhandle football left Butler Field with torn shirttails and a hard-earned 14–7 decision over twelve Masonic Home Mighty Mites who fought the huge Sandies with hornet-like hate for all of the sun-splashed afternoon.

To those who were surprised by the courageous effort, Pop Boone wrote:

> I have been watching this bunch of orphans play since they were little boys. I remember when they took the field without shoes. I find it impossible to believe that anyone who had ever seen them in person would believe these kids would be trampled by the Amarillo giants. Just the opposite was true. I think it was the Sandies nursing the biggest bruises when the final gun sounded.

It was close to midnight, and well past curfew, when the Mighty Mites' chartered team bus returned from Amarillo and pulled through the front gate of the orphanage. Normally, the dorms would have been dark and most of the kids long asleep. But this night, the football team was surprised to find the lights shining brightly and all of the kids standing along the winding road that led back to the big boys dormitory. They were holding candles and yelling at the bus.

The players were even more than surprised when they stepped off the bus and into the arms of practically every female in the place. For one night—and one night alone—the rule against touching had been suspended by Superintendent Thomas Fletcher, and the girls were taking full advantage of the situation. They mobbed the Mighty Mites as they filed off the bus. So many girls wanted to kiss and hug Hardy Brown that he barely made it through the crowd.

With two girls clinging to him, Hardy said to Brownie Lewis, "I thought we lost the game."

His friend, holding two other girls, laughed. "I'd like to see what'd happen if we'd won."

The drum-and-bugle corps was making an attempt at the school song, and the sour notes were painful to the ears. This was a scene reminiscent of December 26, 1932, when the high school team departed the Home for the state championship game in Corsicana. For boys like Hardy Brown, Dewitt Coulter, C. D. Sealy, and Brownie Lewis, the moment would bring them full circle. Hardy and Dewitt could remember skipping down the redbrick road that day as little kids and putting their tiny imprints on the cold windows of the team bus. It was an experience that would forever inspire.

A week after defeating the Mighty Mites, Amarillo defeated Temple with relative ease by the score 20–7 to win the state championship. Coach Howard Lynch and most of the players were quoted after the game as saying that Masonic Home had actually been the toughest opponent of their entire season.

Rusty Russell was accustomed to huge sacks of telegrams that arrived from all parts of America. But he could not fathom the number of missives that arrived at his doorstep following the loss to Amarillo. Some were sympathetic. Most were written to encourage the coach to keep trying. Fans still believed that a state championship was just around the corner.

As the days passed, and life at the Home returned to a normal pace, the hurt of losing to Amarillo would begin to fade. If nothing else, the orphans were a resilient bunch of kids, and it was not long before their thoughts turned to yet another season.

The Mighty Mites had come so close. Losing at the final gun would always haunt them. But in time, they were ready to move on.

RUSTY RUSSELL TRIED to pick up the pieces of his little football team in the ensuing months and to get ready for the 1941 season. He knew there was still enough talent to make a run at the playoffs. Russell had rebuffed the efforts by Highland Park to hire him away—at least for now.

Like so many other seasons, 1941 began with great hope and

gathered steam with each passing week. The Mighty Mites defeated number-one-ranked Wichita Falls 13–6 in the season opener, and the only other close game was a 12–7 defeat over the North Side Steers. The Poly Parrots were humiliated in the final week of the season 41–0, as Luther Scarborough ranted and yelled at the officials.

The Mighty Mites were undefeated as they entered the playoffs. It was their eighth trip to the postseason in the last ten years. During the 1941 season they had defeated nine opponents by the aggregate score of 244–32. Again, Russell had high hopes for a state title.

Just before the playoffs began, the Home held a cookout for the players and invited a few local dignitaries and politicians.

A local judge overheard a conversation between the boys and made a few mental notes. His curiosity was piqued when he realized the orphans were calling backup quarterback Louis Burress "the old man." The next day, the judge reported what he had heard to his good friend, Luther Scarborough. Naturally, the Poly High coach became instantly suspicious and could not wait to contact the Texas Inter-scholastic League to demand they check Burress's birth certificate. It was revealed that the boy had suited up the entire season as a nineteen-year-old, making him an ineligible player.

The TIL moved swiftly to punish the Mighty Mites. Their district championship was revoked and they were kicked out of the state play-offs. Russell pleaded to the TIL that he was unaware of the boy's actual age, and he had evidence to back it up. When the boy enrolled at the Home five years earlier, his mother had not given her son's true age on the application. The cut-off age for entering the Home was thirteen, and Louis was actually fourteen at the time. His mother faced a horrible dilemma; her husband was dead, and with the Depression at full tilt, she feared she could not support the boy. So she was willing to lie to get him into the orphanage. As a result, he played his final season as a nineteen-year-old.

The TIL would not accept the excuse and made their ruling stick.

It should be noted that Burress contributed very little to the team during the '41 season, as he was injured most of the time. He mainly held for extra points and field goals. But this did not matter to the TIL.

Ironically, Wichita Falls, the team the Home defeated at the start of the season, went on to win the state championship. At the end of the year, the Coyotes players sent a telegram to the Mighty Mites that said, "You were the best team we played all season. By all rights, you should have been state champions."

This setback—especially with it coming at the hands of the TIL—merely served to feed Russell's frustration. As Pop Boone had predicted, Highland Park finally managed to hire Russell away from the orphanage halfway through the 1942 season. The Highland Park coach had been called into active duty, and the wealthy supporters wasted not a single day luring Russell away from the Home. Few people blamed the coach. He had fought the TIL for the past ten years, and any hope of a state championship was fading. Highland Park boasted one of the most robust football programs in the state, and it just so happened that two outstanding players were reaching high school age—Doak Walker and Bobby Layne.

Russell had an odd arrangement during the 1942 season. He was being paid by Highland Park, but refused to turn his back on the Mighty Mites. He spent most of the weekdays, along with Friday nights, with his new team. But Saturdays and Sundays were dedicated to the Mighty Mites. Because the teams played most of their games on different days, he was on the sideline for most of the Masonic Home games.

"My boys at the Home won't have a coach, and I feel that I owe it to them what assistance I can give them the rest of the season," he told Harold Ratliff of the Associated Press. "Of course, this will all be unofficial and it will be on my own time. I certainly hate leaving the Masonic Home and those fine kids, but the opportunity offered me at Highland Park was too much to pass up."

That season, Highland Park won District 8AA and, the Home finished in a three-way tie for the 7AA championship. If the Mites could win the coin flip, the two teams being coached by Russell would meet in the first round of the playoffs. It was a potential scenario that had the entire state talking. But Russell's luck with coin flips did not change. He lost the flip on behalf of the Home and the

Mighty Mites would not be going to the playoffs. Only one of his teams would be suiting up for the postseason.

The 1942 season would be the Mites' final season in big-time Texas high school football. With the war on, Thomas Fletcher decided to drop the program completely for the 1943 season, saying, "We just don't have the boys to put an eleven-man team on the field. There is only one course open: Withdraw from competition until we can 'grow' some more boys." The Mighty Mites would return to football competition after World War II, but would never again compete any higher than Class B or the Texas private school league. The glory years were over.

AS THE 1943 season began at Highland Park, Russell was torn. Seven of his former players at the Masonic Home, including Hardy Brown, had enlisted with the Marines. Many of his current Highland Park players were also going off to war. So, at the age of forty-four, believing that he should be with his boys, he tried to reenlist. He was rejected because of his age and his failing eyesight.

Nothing, however, was going to slow him down at Highland Park. In 1943, the Scots reached the state semifinals and finished with a 12–1 record. The following season, they compiled a 12–1 record and outscored their opponents 426–73. But they lost in the state finals in 1944 to San Angelo. Once again, it was "close, but no cigar" for Russell.

During the 1943 and 1944 seasons, Doak Walker and Bobby Layne were recognized as two of the best high school players in America. Layne accepted a scholarship to play quarterback at the University of Texas and Walker was on his way to SMU.

In 1945, Russell became the interim head coach at SMU, with the understanding that Matty Bell would get his job back when he returned from the service. Upon Bell's return that year, Russell was moved to offensive coordinator. He would become Walker's personal mentor.

Walker earned All-American honors at SMU for three straight seasons, beginning in 1947. The highlight, though, was winning the Heisman Trophy in 1948. On the day of the Heisman announcement,

Walker told the national media that he never could have won college football's most coveted individual prize without the tutoring of Russell, who had become like a second father to the star running back. Russell traveled with the Walker family to New York for the trophy presentation at the New York Downtown Athletic Club.

Years later, Walker would name his first son after his coach—Russell Doak Walker.

In 1949, the Mustangs played one of the most exciting games in the history of college football, in spite of the fact that Walker was on the sideline with a knee injury. SMU played top-ranked Notre Dame down to the wire, with Rusty Russell Jr. throwing two touchdown passes and Kyle Rote dazzling the crowd with his running. Notre Dame scored a late touchdown to win 27–20, and the sportswriters called it the "Game of the Half-Century."

In 1950, with the retirement of Matty Bell, Russell was promoted to head coach. He could not have scripted a better start for the Mustangs that season. They won their first six games with Russell's son, Rusty, and Fred Benners splitting time at quarterback. In one of the most remarkable games of the era, the Mustangs overcame a three-touchdown deficit against Ohio State before eighty-thousand fans at Columbus, to win 32–27. Russell was named National Coach of the Week.

By the seventh week of the season, the Mustangs were ranked number-one in both wire service polls. It seemed too good to be true. But their season collapsed in the final weeks, with a three-point loss to Texas, another three-point setback against Baylor, and a five-point defeat by Texas A&M.

In 1951, the Mustangs pulled off a stunning upset over Notre Dame in South Bend, by the score of 27–20. Again, Russell was named National Coach of the Week.

But the Mustangs did not win consistently with Russell's wide-open offense. They finished the 1951 season with a 3-6-1 record, and disenchanted fans dumped garbage on the coach's front lawn. They went 4-5-1 in 1952, and the alumni bought out his contract. Russell decided he'd had enough of big-time college football.

"There are just too many Monday-morning quarterbacks around SMU," he said. "I want to go somewhere that I can run the team again."

In 1953, the United States government sent Russell to Japan to hold football clinics for the Far East Command. He returned to the states in time to coach Schreiner College to a 5–3 record, and in 1954 took over at Victoria Junior College, where, in seven seasons, he compiled a 40-27-2 record.

Russell retired at the end of the 1961 season, but it was short-lived. Howard Payne, his alma mater, was in desperate need of direction, and Russell grudgingly agreed to become head football coach and athletic director. It was a move that he deeply regretted. The team won but four games in two seasons, and his career ended on a rare sour note.

In 1971, Russell was inducted into the Texas Sports Hall of Fame. During his induction speech, he was quick to let everyone know exactly where his heart lay: "There will never be another squad like the Mighty Mites," he said. "That was the team that I loved the most and I will never forget. I have never been around a bunch of players who were more dedicated to the game. Those are the kids that I will never forget."

Remembering his former coach, Dewitt Coulter said, "Whatever Rusty Russell said, we did. We never had many players, but we believed we could hold our own against the bigger schools. I was to run the trick plays that Rusty showed us and to play a lot of different positions. When you spend that much time together, as we did at the orphanage, you become brothers for life."

Russell died in November of 1983, and one of his former Mighty Mites, Abner McCall, gave the eulogy. McCall was a smiling, awkward, talkative kid that endeared himself to Russell with his personality, not his football skills. Russell had predicted back in 1928 that McCall would someday be a U.S. Senator. The boy, however, had greater aspirations. He wanted to be President. McCall did ascend to the office of the presidency—at Baylor University. This, in part, is what he had to say about Russell at his funeral:

"Everyone has heroes. At least everyone ought to have heroes in his life. They serve as models. They inspire us to be better than we would be otherwise. Mr. H. N. Russell was one of my heroes. Our team was just an ordinary group of boys, and only half of us weighed as much as 140 pounds. We were not bigger, stronger, or better than our opponents. What made the difference for us was Rusty Russell, a most extraordinary man. But the genius of Rusty Russell was in his ability to make every boy a giant in his own eyes. His memory will remain fresh and green with us. We acknowledge again our debt to you this day."

Russell's record at the Home was 127-30-12. He went to his grave believing that he had never won a state championship. But years later, the interpretation of the 1932 game would change. Initially, Corsicana was crowned the outright champ by virtue of having more twenty-yard-line penetrations. But the University Interscholastic League—formerly the Texas Interscholastic League—now regards the tie as a cochampionship.

More than winning or losing, though, Russell reveled in watching his former players become successful men in their years after the Home. Those success stories have come in huge numbers.

Near the end of his career, Russell was asked to evaluate some of his favorite players at the Home: "I would have to say that little Miller Moseley, from the 1938 team, was my favorite paperweight of all time. No doubt, Scott McCall, of 1932, was one of the best players to ever suit up. As he grew up, Dewitt Coulter became an absolutely terrific high school player. But the greatest player I ever coached was Hardy Brown. That boy could do it all."

DURING HIS EARLY years at the Home, Dewitt Coulter was chided by his fellow orphans for being a "sissy." But by the time he graduated, he was regarded as one of the toughest players in Texas high school football.

In 1983, *The Dallas Morning News* chose Coulter as the best high school player from North Texas in the first fifty years of high school football. This was especially gratifying in that he was chosen ahead of three Heisman Trophy winners—Earl Campbell, Doak Walker, and Davey O'Brien—as well as quarterback Bobby Layne.

After graduating from the Home in 1943, Coulter enlisted in the army, but it was not long before he got the call from West Point. Coach Red Blaik instantly knew that the 6-foot-4, 250-pound tackle was just what he needed. Coulter made all-America in 1945, on the team that Blaik considered his best of all time. It included Glenn Davis and Felix Blanchard—Mr. Inside and Mr. Outiside. Both would win the Heisman Trophy in back-to-back years (1945 and '46). The other All-Americans were end Hank Foldberg and guard Johnny Green.

Many members of the sporting press thought that Coulter, with his dogged style learned at the Home, was the team's best all-round player.

The New York Giants could not wait to get their hands on the big tackle. In the postwar era, it was not unusual for teams to draft players before their college eligibility was up. Coulter was drafted in the first round in 1946, and when he encountered academic problems at West Point, he accepted the offer to join the Giants. He made the all-pro team as a rookie in 1946, and quickly developed the reputation as the best left tackle in pro football.

Among the toughest defensive players in the league at the time was Pittsburgh tackle Ernie Stautner. The hard-nosed Stautner liked to club opposing players with his heavily fortified forearms. He once tried this tecnhique on Coulter, who said, "Okay, rookie, if that's the way you want it, that's the way you get it."

"That's it," Stautner said.

Stautner regretted what he said.

"On the next play, he knocked me on my rear end," Stautner said. "I was looking up at him from the ground and I thought he was going to kill me. In fact, he beat me up pretty good all day."

Coulter made the All-Pro Team in three of his first four seasons. But he had another calling in life that would not let go. He dropped out of football after the 1949 season to become a sports cartoonist for the *Dallas Times Herald.*

His love of drawing and art had developed during the Masonic Home years, and now he wanted to pursue it on a professional basis. He also wrote an occasional sports column for the newspaper. But it did not take the Giants long to lure him back into football. In 1950, the Giants played a game in Dallas against the fledgling Texans. Before the game, coach Steve Owens convinced Coulter to come back. He played the 1951 and 1952 seasons for the Giants, before moving on to the Montreal Alouettes of the CFL. It was in Montreal where his love of art was rekindled, and Coulter began to make a name for himself.

After making the All-CFL Team four straight years, he retired to pursue his new career. He progressed from charcoal to watercolors to oils, and eventually to acrylics. That is when he moved from sports cartoons to portraits, and the Canadian critics began to recognize him as a rising star.

He moved back to Fort Worth, continued to pursue his art career, and in 1970 joined the first class to be inducted into the Texas High School Sports Hall of Fame.

Later, he would discover that his work as a commercial artist could not provide financial stability. So, in 1978, he became a homebuilder in Austin. Ten years later, he became the activity director for a special education school. He still lives in Austin and suffers from Alzheimers.

Dewitt's brother, Ray Coulter, was one of Texas's most-recruited high school players after the 1940 season and accepted a scholarship. A badly damaged knee ended his football career two years later. But Ray Coulter, after working for Swift Packing for several years, was inducted into the Texas High Sports Hall of Fame in 1997, three years after his death from leukemia.

DOUG LORD AND Opal Worthington could not wait to get married. Opal was still two years short of graduation when they decided to elope. One afternoon, the young couple caught a bus out of Fort Worth to Weatherford, thirty miles to the west. They were able to take a blood test at a drugstore across the street from the courthouse and to obtain a marriage license.

In less than an hour, they were married by a justice of the peace at the county courthouse.

It was the same path taken by C. D. Sealy and Earlene Alderson when they decided to elope. On the day that Doug married Opal, C.D. and Earlene were still living in a small house in Weatherford. They were willing to give up their humble abode to the newlyweds on their wedding night.

The next day, Doug and Opal got a surprise when they returned to Fort Worth. Betty Worthington was not pleased that her daughter had run off and gotten married two years shy of her diploma. She sat the couple down and delivered a lecture.

"As a married woman, Opal will never be able to go back to high school," she said. "You two have made a big mistake."

The couple agreed that they should annul the marriage. Within a few days, Doug would enlist in the Navy and left almost immediately for submarine school.

Four years later though, Doug and Opal were remarried.

Given his love for fighting and boxing at the Home, it was not surprising that Lord entered the boxing business and became one of the most successful trainers and managers in the country, beginning in 1955. He trained Curtis Cokes to the World Welterweight Championship in 1966, and Cokes defended the belt six times. Cokes fought twice in France, twice in South Africa, and once in Mexico.

"What I am the most proud of is that Curtis and I did it on our own," Lord said. "We didn't have a promoter and we arranged our own fights. I hustled all of the fights and tried to make sure that Curtis got the right money."

Doug continues to have trouble with the leg so badly broken as a Mighty Mite, and he walks with the aid of a cane.

Doug, 79, and Opal, 77, live in the Lake Highlands area of Dallas and spend a lot of time with their six grandchildren and six great-grandchildren. They continue to celebrate two wedding anniversaries—in 2007, they reached the sixty-second on the first and the fifty-ninth for the second.

Asked for his recipe on a long and successful marriage, Doug did not hesitate.

"Just say 'yes ma'am' and 'no ma'am' to your wife," he said. "You will never have any problems."

MILLER MOSELEY, THE valedictorian of the class of 1938, also finished at the top of his class as an undergraduate student at TCU, and upon graduation received a fellowship to North Carolina.

In Chapel Hill, he would be mentored by Dr. Nathan Rosen, who was both a collaborator and the right hand man of Dr. Albert Einstein. The two had begun working together in 1935, when Rosen became Einstein's assistant at The Institute for Advanced Studies at Princeton University.

It was in 1939 when Einstein wrote the famous Nassau Point letter to President Franklin Roosevelt that encouraged him to develop the atomic bomb ahead of the Germans. The letter read in part:

It may become possible to set up a nuclear chain reaction in a large mass of uranium, by which vast amounts of power and large quantities of new radium-like elements would be generated. By which, my dear President, it might be possible to unleash an immense destructive force.

In 1942, Moseley was being directed in his dissertation by Rosen. Einsten contacted Rosen and asked him to join the effort to develop the atomic bomb. Rosen, in turn, decided to bring along his brightest student with him to Philadelphia. A little more than four years after graduating from the Home, Moseley found himself working on the Manhattan Project at the naval yard in Philadelphia.

Moseley's job was to help create the separation of the isotopes through thermal diffusion. His mathematical genius, developed at the Masonic Home, quickly emerged in Philadelphia. He was working with an all-star cast that included Einstein, Edward Teller, considered "The Father of the Hydrogen Bomb," and Robert Oppenheimer, "The Father of the Atomic Bomb."

Moseley would officially become an enlisted man with the U.S. Navy, even though he would never leave project headquarters in Philadelphia, where he was also Rosen's roommate.

"It was a great experience," Moseley said. "But I can't say I ever fit in with the caliber of people I was working with."

After "the Bomb" was drop on the Japanese cities of Hiroshima and Nagasaki, Moseley returned to Chapel Hill, where, through the guidance of Rosen, he completed his dissertation. Then it was back to Fort Worth, where he would spend thirty-nine years as a professor in the physics department. He took a one-year sabbatical in 1956, to perform experiments at the Oak Ridge National Laboratory, the place that had served as the site of the first nuclear reactor for the Manhattan Project, in 1943.

At Oak Ridge, Moseley designed a magnet for a proton accelerator that further helped to develop nuclear energy.

Moseley retired from the TCU physics department in 1990 and now lives with his wife, Deanie, in the southwest part of the city.

CECIL "CRAZY" MOSELEY lived a far less distinguished life than his older brother, but no one could say he traveled the road most taken.

Out of the Masonic Home, he enlisted in the Marine paratroopers along with six other Mighty Mites, and within a few weeks was dispatched to the South Pacific. He was on an aircraft carrier in Hawaii when an ammunition boat blew up about a hundred yards away that inflicted injuries to several men. Cecil, suffering from numerous injuries, was returned to the States, where he was given 50 percent disability.

After the war, suffering from boredom, Cecil decided to reenlist, this time with the Air Force. In doing so, he forfeited his 50 percent disability.

"He decided he wanted to see Europe," Miller Moseley said. "Boy, did he get a surprise."

Within weeks, the Korean conflict broke out and Cecil was shipped to Asia. It was just a matter of time before he suffered multiple injuries from a bomb blast and again was shipped back to the States. This time, he received only 10 percent disability.

But Cecil was not to be deterred. He enrolled in the El Paso School of Mines and graduated in four years, whereupon he took a job in South America, mining for copper. But he became disenchanted with the company's hierarchy—mostly Americans—and returned to Texas. He soon found that no one in the mining industry was willing to hire an engineer who had broken his contract. So he went to work in the oil-fields, mostly as a roughneck, making minimum wage much of his life.

It was not surprising to his friends or family that Cecil would die as a recluse, in December of 2000, in his hometown of Dundy. The kid who rarely opened his mouth around the orphanage had virtually no contact with any of the neighbors. He died one night in bed, and his body was not found for several days.

C. D. "Wheatie" Sealy, within weeks after graduating from the Masonic Home, enrolled at Coffeyville Junior College in Kansas. He started every game as a freshman, and the plan was to enroll the next fall at Tulsa University, where he would play for the legendary Henry Frnka. But with the bombing of Pearl Harbor on December 7, 1941, Sealy, like many of the other Mighty Mites, enlisted as a paratrooper and was dispatched to the South Pacific. He suffered a fractured skull in a jeep injury, which cost him any hope of playing more college foot-ball. He worked as a coach and teacher in Fort Worth until 1970, and then for ten years as a home-school coordinator. He retired in 1980 and still lives in Fort Worth with his wife of twenty-six years, Joella.

Leonard "Snoggs" Roach enlisted in the army after graduating from the Home and fought in Europe during World War II. Upon returning, he played football at North Texas Teachers College. Then he worked for more than twenty years as a detective with the Houston police department.

Clyde "Teague" Roberts served more than thirty years in the Marines as a lieutenant colonel and fought in World War II, the Korean War, and Vietnam. He did a stint in both Korea and Vietnam as a tank commander. Teague died from complications of Alzheimer's in the spring of 2007.

Basel Smith, after serving in the army during World War II, played football at North Texas Teachers College. He later opened a Humble gas station near the SMU campus.

Floyd "Brownie" Lewis, like six of his teammates, enlisted in the Marines out of the Home and fought in the South Pacific. He later became a cocaptain of the SMU football team and an All-Southwest Conference selection at guard. He briefly tried professional football, but was considered too small for the NFL. He owned and operated the Brownie Lewis Door Company for several years.

Jeff Brown became an All-Southwest Conference guard at the Rice Institute and spent most of his life in the Houston area. He worked for several years at a car dealership in Galveston. He still lives with his wife, Doris, in Galveston.

John Mayo, also known as "Arizona Pete," managed to recover from the severe beatings he suffered at the Home and later became a wealthy man in the oil business. He invented a valve that made it easier to control the flow of the oil.

Doc Hall lapsed into poor health in 1945 and was replaced by his son, Doc Hall Jr. Neither man ever asked the Masonic Home for a single nickel for their services. The elder Doc Hall died July 7, 1949.

William Henry Remmert retired from the Masonic Home in 1960, after working there for thirty-nine years. Three months later, he died of a massive heart attack. Remmert, in spite of being a strict dean, was so roundly loved by his former students that the church could not hold them all on the day of his funeral.

Leon Picket, at age ninety-five, is the oldest living former student of the Home. He resides in a retirement apartment in Fort Worth and continues to live an active life. He worked for Gulf Oil in West Texas as a leasing agent for over forty years.

AFTER HIS HIGH school career, Hardy Brown accepted a football scholarship to SMU, but with a war raging all over the world, he enlisted in the Marines. He was joined by six former Mighty Mites. He became a paratrooper assigned to the South Pacific. According to his brother, Jeff, he was on his way to Iwo Jima when a call came, of all places, from West Point. It seemed that Dewitt Coulter, a tackle for Army, had put in a good word for his old buddy. Legendary coach Earl "Red" Blaik was so impressed with Coulter that he asked him if there were any other ex-Mighty Mites of his caliber. Coulter knew of one. It was not long before Hardy Brown was being shipped from the South Pacific to the famous military academy along the Hudson River.

Brown was enrolled at a local prep school for the spring semester of 1945, and he was performing well academically until he found his way to a local all-girls school. On the night before a crucial math exam, he did a little too much partying. He flunked the test and never made it to West Point.

But the University of Tulsa was happy to have him. Coach Henry Frnka, formerly of Greenville High School in Texas, had seen Brown play at the Home, and instantly knew that Tulsa needed his aggressive style.

By now, Hardy's life had moved into the fast lane. He got drunk one night and returned to his dorm room with his future wife, Betty, and shot up the place with a .22 rifle. Brown was the roommate of Jim Finks, who would beat out John Unitas as the starting quarterback of the Pittsburgh Steelers, and, years later, rise to the position as general manager of both the Chicago Cubs and New Orleans Saints. Of Brown, Finks said, "He was one of the wildest boys I've ever seen. But his football made up for his other problems."

Tulsa, competing in the Missouri Valley Conference, finished with two unbeaten seasons, with Brown as a starting fullback and line-backer. He made the Little All-America team in 1948.

After college, Hardy went straight to the pros and played his first two seasons in the upstart All-America Football Conference, with the Brooklyn Dodgers and the Chicago Hornets. He entered the NFL as a free agent with the Washington Redskins in 1950, moved to the Baltimore Colts in 1951, and, when the Colts folded, was picked up in the expansion draft by the San Francisco 49ers, where he rose to stardom.

During two of his five seasons with the 49ers, Brown was selected all-pro. But his real notoriety came from the Humper.

Few NFL people around in the 1950s would argue that Brown was the meanest man in pro football. Just as he had done at the Home, he broke noses, jaws, and cheek bones with his vicious right shoulder. Y. A. Tittle, in his book *I Pass,* claimed that Brown knocked out twenty-one players during the 1951 season alone, including three-fourths of the Washington Redskin's starting backfield in one game. All three players were carried off the field on stretchers. Brown estimated to Steve Sabol of NFL films that he knocked out somewhere between seventy-five and eighty players during his career.

Tom Landry, who spent most of his playing career with the New York Giants back in the fifties, said that Brown was wicked with the Humper.

"Hardy had a technique with his shoulder that ruined a lot of players," Landry said. "Now, he was mean. They should have outlawed him. He would aim at the head with the shoulder pad and it was like a gun going off. He hit one of our guys in the face one time and it split him from the top to the bottom of his nose."

A bounty was placed on Brown's head almost every game. Former kicker Pat Summerall, one of his teammates at San Francisco, remembered that Brown approached him before a game against the Rams and requested an onside kick. "The coach has to make that decision," Summerall said as he proceeded to kick it deep. Summerall said he would never forget watching all eleven players on the Los Angeles Rams kicking team ignore the ball and charge after Brown with intentions of hurting him.

"Dangerous is the word I would use to describe him," Summerall said. "Everybody said to look out for number thirty-three, because he would put you out of the game. You learned pretty quickly to stay out of his way."

The promising pro career of Felix "Doc" Blanchard, the Heisman Trophy winner from Army, was ended by the Humper. Brown hit Blanchard so hard in the head that he managed to blow out two ligaments in his right knee. Said Blanchard, "Hardy wasn't interested in tackling you. He wanted to annihilate you."

Ironically, Brown would also knock Blanchard's famous teammate, Glenn Davis, out of a game between the Rams and 49ers in the early fifties. During their college days at Army, Blanchard and Davis were known as "Mr. Inside" and "Mr. Outside." Both won the Heisman Trophy in back-to-back years. But it did not take Hardy Brown long to derail their pro careers.

Davis, after catching a screen pass against the 49ers, was trying to cut back when Brown delivered the Humper to his head. Davis was rendered unconscious and carried off the field on a stretcher. The Rams star at the time was dating Elizabeth Taylor, and the famous actress was not too fond of Hardy Brown.

"She called me a beast," Hardy told NFL films. "But I told her that it's all in the ball . . . game."

Brown and Coulter would line up against each other several times as pro players.

"I looked across the line once at Hardy and was thinking about saying hello to him," Coulter said. "But he had this look in his eyes like a rabid dog."

Chicago Bears coach George Halas harbored suspicions about Brown of the same nature that had once infiltrated the head of Poly High coach Luther Scarborough. He stormed onto the field during a game between the Bears and the Colts and demanded that the officials check Brown's shoulder pads for steel plates. Again, he was escorted underneath the stands, and again they found nothing but plastic shells protecting his shoulders.

Hardy Brown did not invent the face mask, but he inspired a great need for it. It was not a coincidence that the face mask became a popular item about the time Brown entered pro football.

He also inspired a highlight film of himself that was outlawed by the National Football League. The 49ers coaches pieced together a reel of Brown's most vicious hits and showed it to the rookies. The message was clear: If you can hit like Hardy Brown, you can play in this league. League officials got wind of it and warned of a heavy fine if the 49ers did not dispose of the film. Apparently, they did not. It fell into the hands of a rookie named Ronnie Lott in 1981, and the hardhitting safety patterned his hitting style after Brown. Look closely at the old videos and you can see Lott delivering the Humper.

Back at the Home, Brown had been a smiling, friendly boy when he was not playing football or fighting. But that amiable personality faded as the years passed. Friends said he had become obsessed with his image as the meanest player in the game.

By the midfifties, Hardy Brown was not a happy man, either on or off the field. Like many of his peers of the decade, he was a hard drinker. In many ways, he was morphing into his late father, Hardy Brown Sr. Dewitt Coulter noticed during a trip to the Pro Bowl in 1955 that Hardy had gone from genial to surly. They were sitting beneath some palm trees one afternoon near Malibu, looking out upon the majestic Pacific Ocean, enjoying the cool breeze, when Hardy said, "I hate everybody in the world."

"Do you hate me?" Coulter said.

In a slow cadence, emphasizing each word, Brown said, "I-hate-everybody-in-the-whole-world."

Dewitt persisted.

"Hardy, surely you don't hate me."

"No, D.E.," he said. "Not you or Arizona Pete or Crazy Lewis or Brownie Lewis or Wheatie Sealy."

It was not long before Brown's life began to unravel. He was drinking more and more and was an angry man around the clock. Because he tackled with the Humper, and did not wrap up running backs, he was starting to miss a lot of tackles.

After the 1957 season, the San Francisco 49ers cut him loose. He never saw it coming. In fact, Brown thought he was certain to play pro football well into the 1960s. The news devastated him and he went on a drinking binge that lasted for weeks.

His wife, Betty, drove to the 49ers headquarters and begged coach Frankie Albert to take him back.

"He has to face it," Albert said. "He's over the hill."

Tittle, his roommate in the NFL for seven seasons, admitted that Hardy was missing too many tackles.

"He was a legend in his era as hitting and crippling people," Tittle said. "But he was *not* a great linebacker."

No other team in the NFL was interested in Brown. So he decided to take the Humper to Canada, where the Hamilton Tiger-Cats gave him a shot in 1958. But he was released at the end of the season and completely out of football in 1959. His final season was with the Denver Broncos in 1960, in the brand new American Football League.

Hardy Brown was hardly ready for the real world. He bounced from job to job, and Betty said the family "almost starved to death" in the early sixties, when he got fired from a job at a rock quarry. The two divorced in 1969 and Hardy started moving from state to state, picking up odd jobs where he could. He even worked as a bartender at the Stardust Casino in Las Vegas.

He returned to California and remarried Betty in the midseventies, but his drinking was really out of control. Betty knew that her husband had mental problems, but did not know where to turn.

"He would get up at two o'clock in the morning, put on his hat and coat, and take off," she said. "It was all I could do to keep him inside."

Betty had him institutionalized at Crestwood Manor in Stockton, California, where he was diagnosed with dementia. Doctors said his condition had been accelerated by his drinking, along with too many hits on the head. Hardy Brown spent the last seven years of his life not knowing who he was or where he lived.

"You have to remember that Hardy Brown's life was football, and he gave up his life for it," Dewitt Coulter said. "I knew that Hardy was starting to take on water during his final years in the game. But there was nothing that anyone could ever say to him. Hardy was all about the physical side of football. He was a psychic occurrence."

That Hardy managed to overcome the horrific murder of his father was a miracle in itself. What he found inside the orphanage was a warm blanket, and it saved him. Hardy was one of the kids who never wanted to live beyond the fence. He never wanted to be a City Guy. He never seemed to be able to get the Home off his mind. He was once asked if he had ever seen another player that could hit as hard as him. "No," he said. "Unless it was one of the boys at the Home."

Dr. Don Beck, the founder of the Center for Human Emergence in Denton, Texas, has been evaluating people in the sports arena for more than forty years. He said that Brown's demise could be traced far back into his childhood.

"No doubt, the early traumatic shocks that the young Hardy Brown experienced had a permanent impact on his future development and capacity to deal with the real world," Beck said. "The years with the Mighty Mites within the orphanage setting, a term that we seldom see in modern society, provided him with a safe and non-threatening enclave with which to develop. Certainly, the competitive, action-oriented game of football, as meshed with positive team experiences, added to the supportive culture.

"Once he left that environment, however, and apparently for the rest of his life, the internal chaos within his mind, coupled with uncertainty in life itself, resulted in a series of emotional roller coasters."

In pro football, Hardy found some fame and fortune. But he also found a lot of unhappiness. He never was able to cope, and it got worse when the 49ers cut him. Sadly, one of the most talented and intelligent boys ever produced by the Masonic Home cratered in his final years of life.

Hardy Brown died at a mental institution in 1991.

AUTHOR'S NOTES

I was watching one of my favorite shows, *NFL's Greatest Moments,* on ESPN, in the fall of 2005, when the face of a bedraggled man with helter-skelter hair and a missing tooth popped onto the screen. He was described as the "meanest man in football" in the 1950s, and from his appearance I gathered he had been knocked around a bit himself.

Here came reels upon reels of the man clubbing opposing players with his right shoulder. Some of his victims did not get up. The narrator kept talking about how this "warrior" had sent chills of fear through the NFL during the decade of the fifties, and how he would never be forgotten.

Funny, I had covered the Dallas Cowboys and the NFL as a newspaperman for more than fifteen years, yet I had never heard of the man. Then something clicked in my head. What I was actually watching, I told myself, was just another blatant attempt to promote one more washed-up hero for the Pro Football Hall of Fame. I had heard it all before—too many times, in fact. I was about to change the channel when this nutty looking man peered straight into the eyepiece of the camera said, "You've got to remember that I played football at the Home. And the Home boys were *tough.*"

I was stopped in my tracks. I put down the remote control and forgot about changing the channel. In about three seconds, I was standing squarely in front of the TV, serving up my own questions.

"What is the Home?" I yelled. "Where the hell is the *Home*? Is the Home an orphanage?"

It's got to be, I said to myself.

I picked up the remote and turned up the volume and waited for answers. Indeed, in a matter of seconds, the gap-toothed man told me that he had played high school football at an orphanage in Fort Worth called the Masonic Home. The scrawny players, known as the Mighty Mites, had reached the state semifinals in 1940, against the mighty Amarillo High Golden Sandstorm. They had played in some of the biggest games in the history of Texas high school football and gained a cult following from New York to Los Angeles.

There was more. This man had lived a traumatic life, beginning with his childhood. As a four-year-old, he had watched his father gunned down by two men. That is why he had grown up at the orphanage, along with two brothers and a sister.

Yes, it was Hardy Brown, and he looked like a transient that had been sleeping beneath a bridge.

Hardy Brown was in the final years of his life, and these were not the golden years. NFL Films president Steve Sabol had tracked him down at a mental institution near San Francisco to do the interview. No doubt, the drinking life had taken its toll on Hardy. But that was not the object of my curiosity. I wanted to know about the glory years of the Home.

The next day I was on my way to Fort Worth. I would discover that the Masonic Home, after 106 years of operation, had closed its doors just months earlier. Thankfully, I was able to find several people, including Dr. Diane Thornton, the superintendent of the Masonic Home schools, and Bruce Riddle, and they would guide me on my research.

First, I would like to thank Bruce for answering every question I could possibly come up with. An orphan who lived at the Masonic Home in the forties, Riddle is the unofficial historian for the orphanage and the keeper of the museum. He is one of the most resourceful people I have ever come upon, providing pictures, newspaper clips, thoughts, theories, and a vast memory of people, places, and events. I hope that Bruce writes his own book someday on the complete history of the Masonic Home—a subject he truly loves.

Diane Thornton opened doors that I never could have found. She is a great friend and one of the biggest reasons this book is being published. I should also mention that her father, Norman Strange, was one of the best Mighty Mites players of the thirties and a large part of this book. Whatever happened, America, to those kinds of family ties?

In researching and writing a book, there is nothing more valuable than a living memory. I managed to find several former Home students that lived the experience back in the thirties and early forties.

Leon Pickett is the only living player from the 1932 team. He recalls the 1932 championship game against Corsicana as if it had been played yesterday. I spent hours with him at a retirement apartment complex in Fort Worth and enjoyed every minute of it.

My first interview with Doug Lord lasted more than six hours. The next time we sat down, I was fortunate to meet Opal Worthington Lord, who, as it turns out, was as helpful as Doug. We would talk several more times over the next year, and I doubt I could have written this book without them.

C. D. Sealy and I met several times for breakfast in Fort Worth. He brought remarkable depth to the research. We also spent a lot of time on the phone, sorting through details. C.D. kept reminding me that Hardy Brown was the greatest player ever to suit up at the Home. I believe him.

Hardy died in 1991. But his brother Jeff, living in Galveston with his wife, Doris, was a powerful resource. He provided great insight into the life of Hardy Brown Sr., who was murdered in 1928. Jeff, two years older than Hardy, knew his brother better than anyone. The amount of information he provided was priceless.

Two of the first people I interviewed for this book were Norman Strange and Miller Moseley. Both played for the Mites in the thirties and had great recall.

My deepest regret was that I never got to interview Rusty Russell for this book. He died in 1983. But his family could not have been more accommodating. There is not a more loving and admiring grandson in the world than Russ Morton, who has risen to the position of director at Smith Barney Global in New York. He was named after his grandfather and, as a young boy, went fishing with him. The stories about the Mighty Mites were devoured by Russ, and years later passed down to me. Then he directed me to his mother, Betty Morton, living in Albuquerque, and we spent the better part of the day remembering the halcyon days. Betty was born at the Masonic Home in 1928. For a time, she lived in the makeshift apartment behind the dining hall. She spent many days and nights with her dad watching the Mighty Mites, and went on scouting trips with him. She came to know the game of football better than any of us. Pictures, clips, stories, mental images of the past—you name it. Some writers dislike research. Now you know why I love it.

Along the way, I lost count of the days I spent at the downtown Fort Worth Public Library. I practically wore out one of the microfiche machines. There, I met senior librarian Tom Kellam, who had a wonderful connection to the story. He is the nephew of Miller and Cecil "Crazy" Moseley, and his mother, Dot, was both a cheerleader and a member of the debate team. Dot shared her recollections with me for several hours one day. Tom filled in spaces and provided research that made the book complete.

When I arrived at the Masonic Home in October 2005 to begin my research, only a handful of people were still working there. The contributions of Delane Jackson and Sharon Fulcher-Tatum are immeasurable.

One day I simply walked into the Childress County Courthouse and started asking questions about the murder of Hardy Brown Sr. The clerks inside the records office dropped everything they were doing to help. From the basement of the courthouse, they lugged huge books filled with legal briefs all the way back to the 1920s. Special thanks to Nancy Garrison.

Greg Collins, my good friend in Las Vegas, provided great advice for the manuscript, and the best of luck to him on upcoming books. Again, Chris Willis of NFL Films came through with the goods when I needed them. This book would not have been possible if NFL Films president Steve Sabol had not done the aforementioned feature on Hardy Brown way back in 1983.

Last but not the least, the story would have never been published without my agent, Jim Donovan, and my editor at St. Martin's, Peter J. Wolverton. Good fellows, with a great understanding of the book biz. Pete, you worked your butt off for this book, and I will never forget that.

Now it will be up to Joe Rinaldi, the best book publicist in the world, to make sure the damn thing sells. Amen.

—Jim Dent, August 2007

INDEX